IRISH VOICE AND ORGANIZED LABOR IN AMERICA

Recent Titles in
Contributions in Labor Studies

The Social Dimension of 1992: Europe Faces a New EC
Beverly Springer

Farewell to the Self-Employed: Deconstructing a Socioeconomic and Legal
Solipsism
Marc Linder

Trade Unionism and Industrial Relations in the Commonwealth Caribbean:
History, Contemporary Practice and Prospect
Lawrence A. Nurse

Eastern's Armageddon
Martha Dunagin Saunders

A State Within a State: Industrial Relations in Israel, 1965–1987
Ran Chermesh

Culture, Gender, Race, and U.S. Labor History
Ronald C. Kent, Sara Markham, David R. Roediger, and Herbert Shapiro, editors

Infighting in the UAW: The 1946 Election and the Ascendancy of Walter Reuther
Bill Goode

American Labor in the Era of World War II
Sally M. Miller

The American Labor Movement, 1955–1995
Walter Galenson

The American Fund for Public Service: Charles Garland and Radical Philanthropy,
1922–1941
Gloria Garrett Samson

Black Unemployment: Part of Unskilled Unemployment
David Schwartzman

The Quest for a Living Wage: The History of the Federal Minimum Wage Program
Willis J. Nordlund

IRISH VOICE AND ORGANIZED LABOR IN AMERICA

A Biographical Study

L.A. O'DONNELL

Contributions in Labor Studies, Number 49

GREENWOOD PRESS
Westport, Connecticut • London

Library of Congress Cataloging-in-Publication Data

O'Donnell, L. A., 1925–
    Irish voice and organized labor in America : a biographical study
/ L. A. O'Donnell.
      p.   cm.—(Contributions in labor studies, ISSN 0886–8239 ;
no. 49)
    Includes bibliographical references and index.
    ISBN 0–313–29944–7 (alk. paper)
    1. Trade-unions—United States—Officials and employees—
Biography.   2. Trade-unions—United States—History.   3. Labor
leaders—United States—Biography.   4. Irish-Americans—Biography.
I. Title. II. Series.
HD6508.5.036   1997
331.88'089'9162073—dc20
  [B]   95–48358

British Library Cataloguing in Publication Data is available.

Library of Congress Catalog Card Number: 95–48358
ISBN: 0–313–29944–7
ISSN: 0886–8239

First published in 1997

Greenwood Press, 88 Post Road West, Westport, CT 06881
An imprint of Greenwood Publishing Group, Inc.

Printed in the United States of America

The paper used in this book complies with the
Permanent Paper Standard issued by the National
Information Standards Organization (Z39.48–1984).

10 9 8 7 6 5 4 3 2 1

Copyright Acknowledgements

The author and publisher gratefully acknowledge permission to use the following sources:

Jones, Mary Harris. *Autobiography of Mother Jones*. Chicago: C.H. Kerr, 1925. C.H. Kerr Publishing Company, 1740 West Greenleaf Ave., Ste. 7, Chicago, IL 60626.

Excerpts from Peter J. McGuire's diary and letters. Used with permission.

Excerpts from Patrick H. McCarthy's unpublished memoirs. Used with permission.

John Mitchell Papers, collection number 3, and Mary Harris Jones Papers, collection number 7, The Department of Archives and Manuscripts, The Catholic University of America, Washington, D.C.

1950 Proceedings of the Twelfth Constitutional Convention of the Congress of Industrial Organizations, Chicago, Illinois, November 20–24, 1950, p. 21. The George Meany Memorial Archives, Silver Spring, MD.

Levitas, Mollie. Interview by Elizabeth Balanoff, Roosevelt University, Chicago, Illinois, July 24, 1970.

John Fitzpatrick Papers, Chicago Historical Society.

O'Donnell, L.A. "The Greening of a Limerick Man," *Érie-Ireland* (Summer 1976): 119–128; "Joseph Patrick McDonnell: A Passion for Justice," *Érie-Ireland* (Winter 1987): 118–133; "John Fitzpatrick, 1871–1946: American Labor Leader," *Érie-Ireland* (Summer 1991): 42–61. Copyright © 1997: Irish American Cultural Institute, 1 Lackawanna Place, Morristown, NJ 07960. Reprinted by permission of the publisher.

O'Donnell, L.A. "From Limerick to the Golden Gate: Odyssey of an Irish Carpenter," *Studies* (Spring–Summer 1979): 76–91.

O'Donnell, L.A. "The Making of an American Communist: William Z. Foster," *International Journal of Social Economics* 20, nos. 5, 6, 7 (1993): 142–152.

Selected articles by L.A. O'Donnell from the following newspaper publications: *Irish Echo*, New York; *Irish American News*, Oak Park, IL; *The Irish Herald*, San Francisco; and *Irish Edition*, Wyndmoor, PA. Used by permission of the publishers.

To my wife, Romy, without whom
this book could not be a reality

"One thing that explains more than anything about me is the fact that I'm Irish."

Eugene O'Neill*

"But they that are learned shall shine as the brightness of the firmament: and they that instruct many to justice, as stars for all eternity."

Dan. 12:3

*Croswell Bowen, "The Black Irishman," reprinted in Oscar Cargill, N. Bryillon Fagin and William J. Fisher, eds. *O'Neill and His Plays*, New York: New York University Press, 1961, p. 65.

CONTENTS

ACKNOWLEDGEMENTS

This book is the culmination of two consuming interests of mine, the history of labor and my Irish heritage. Although my great grandparents O'Donnell were famine immigrants (1849), I grew up hardly aware of my Irish antecedents. My education from elementary school through college taught me almost nothing about Ireland or collective bargaining. This void aroused my curiosity about labor organizations and Irish history. My first encounter with a union occurred in a steel mill in Gary, Indiana, my home town. Firsthand experience told me that workers needed a collective voice when dealing with a corporate employer. In 1950, I left the steel mills for a journey through Europe, beginning with three weeks in Ireland, where I first heard of Jim Larkin and James Connolly, pioneers of the modern Irish labor movement.

My interest in labor relations matured in the course of the trip abroad. On returning, I enrolled in the Institute of Social and Industrial Relations at Loyola University in Chicago. There, my understanding of labor relations and social justice benefited from inspiring mentors, specifically, James O'Gara (later a long-time editor of *Commonwealth*), and Karl Anrod, a refugee from Nazi Germany, who had served as a judge in a court of labor arbitration in that country. There followed a two-year instructorship at Loyola where a course in the history of labor was one of my responsibilities. The experience made me conscious of innumerable Irish names among leaders of American unions. It also led me to consider an academic vocation.

Pursuit of that possibility took me to the University of Wisconsin where it was my good fortune to study under Selig Perlman whose *Theory of the Labor Movement* remains a classic non-Marxist analysis. Another of my memorable teachers there was Edwin Witte, President Roosevelt's choice to draft what became the Social Security Act of 1935.

Jack Barbash, formerly associated with the Congress of Industrial

Organizations (CIO), and its successor, the AFL-CIO, joined the economics faculty at Wisconsin just prior to Professor Perlman's retirement and my departure. He became my thesis director and proved to be a highly supportive one. Later, he endorsed my proposal to undertake this book-length study.

The road to completion of this book is strewn with debts of gratitude owed to individuals and institutions. Sean Wilentz of Princeton counseled me early on and supported my application for a sabbatical and for financial assistance. Dennis Clark, historian of the Irish in Philadelphia, read the entire manuscript and recommended important ways of improving it. He also gave encouragement when it was needed most. Thomas Green, my colleague from Villanova's history department, applied his editing skills to polishing several chapters. David Brody, eminent historian of labor, read two chapters in the early stages and responded favorably. Two labor priests, Monsignor Charles O. Rice and Monsignor George G. Higgins, both close friends of Philip Murray, reviewed the chapter on the CIO at my request. My understanding of Philip Murray benefited from conversations with Monsignor Rice. He also arranged for me to interview Murray's son, Joseph, in Pittsburgh.

Villanova University approved two sabbaticals to support my research on this manuscript. The Irish American Cultural Institute of Morristown, New Jersey, through the Friendly Sons of St. Patrick of Philadelphia, awarded financial assistance to complete the project.

The reference desk at Villanova's Falvey Library competently and expeditiously answered my numerous requests. Equally helpful were Curator Archie Motley at the Chicago Historical Society and Dr. Anthony Zito (now retired), Archivist at Catholic University of America. The staff of the Wisconsin State Historical Society in Madison and that of the Historical and Labor Archives of Pennsylvania State University in University Park, courteously supplied valuable materials for this study. At University Park, Denise Conklin was particularly helpful.

I owe special thanks to Iris Rossell for lending to me documents and photos of her grandfather, Peter J. McGuire. Gratitude is in order, as well, to Eileen Bradley White, of Suffolk, England, for clarifying the family background of her granduncle, John Fitzpatrick.

For the essential job of word processing the entire manuscript I am indebted to Kathleen Brown, Nancy Carpenter and Angela McCollum, all of Villanova University.

For any and all errors and omissions remaining in the book, the burden of responsibility is mine alone.

INTRODUCTION

A substantial gap in our understanding of the Irish experience in America arises from overlooking the Irish influence on American trade unions. Studies of the Irish in American politics abound, but assumption of leadership in trade unions by the Irish has been given little scholarly attention as an ethnic phenomenon. Irish labor figures have almost always been treated as part of the mainstream of labor history and not as leaders emerging from a distinctive ethnic background. Other than labeling them as Irish and making passing references to general social factors conditioning their rise, there has been little analysis of their subcultural orientation and development. Yet, these labor stalwarts were strongly influenced by Irish attitudes, group experience, leadership networks and an Irish rhetorical style, influences that greatly affected their concerns and the American labor movement.

A cursory look at any labor history text will reveal innumerable Irish figures in the forefront of labor leadership from Terence Powderly to George Meany. This phenomenon has been pointed out by students of American labor in a number of instances. Jack Barbash, for example, noted, that "The leaders of most important unions (historically and currently) are predominantly of Irish extraction" and that "the beginnings of permanent unions in many trades and industries are inextricably associated with the pressing needs of immigrant Irish workers for economic protection."[1]

David Montgomery tabulated entries in the first (1975) edition of the *Biographical Dictionary of American Labor Leaders* and found that only two countries, the Russian empire and Great Britain, surpassed Ireland's contribution to the dictionary's listings. But "neither of them," he commented, "equaled the mark left on American unions by the children, grandchildren and great-grandchildren of immigrants from Ireland." He estimated that "between one-fifth and one-fourth of the

notables in this list were Irish-Americans." These observations were
included in one of the rare pieces interpreting Irish influence on the
American labor movement.[2]

In his doctoral study of the San Francisco building trades, Michael
Kazin, recognizing the ubiquity of union officials of Irish descent in the
industry, felt obliged to append a section entitled "The Limits of Irish
Domination." Drawing on David Montgomery's observations, he
explained the advantages of Irish immigrants for rising to leadership in
terms of the earlier arrival "of the famine generation, their knowledge
of the English language and political system and lack of concentration
in any one industry." Their importance intensified as they became
"leaders and power brokers for old and new immigrants alike." He also
noted that they benefitted from the lack of a nativist movement in the
Bay Area. Partly because only about 1 percent had come to San
Francisco directly from Ireland and partly due to their close association
with workers of other ethnic groups, their Irish nationalism was more
of a ceremonial one than a deeply engaged one, at least until the Easter
Rising of 1916.[3]

In a review essay of a series of book-length studies of the Irish in
America (none of which was devoted specifically to their labor movement involvement), historian Sean Wilentz observed that "by the 1870s
Irish immigrants and their sons were a most conspicuous power among
local and national trade union leaders." One of his conclusions was "An
American Labor History minus a thorough account of the Irish cannot
even pretend to the name."[4]

Historical treatment of other ethnic groups and American unions
does indeed exist. Clifton Yearley examined the impact on American
labor of immigrants from the United Kingdom. His study embraced
both British and Irish immigrants, but although a few of Irish origin,
such as miners' organizer John Siney, appear in his story, Yearley
offered little if any insight into what influence was uniquely Irish.[5]

Two works by Melech Epstein, one of them running to two volumes,
describe the Jewish labor movement. Additionally, there is a book by
Abraham Rogof, a pictorial history by Jacob Hertz and a number of articles on Jewish Labor.[6] Blacks and unions have been the subject of books
by Ray Marshall, Milton Cantor, Philip Foner and others.[7] The history of
Italians and organized labor is the focus of a book by Edwin Fenton.[8]
Comparable scholarship on unions and the Irish has yet to be published.

This research on one aspect of America is undertaken in recognition
of the contributions to our society made by the numerous and diverse
ethnic groups which comprise it. The traditional view of our republic as
a melting pot has lost favor. The persistence of ethnicity is acknowledged
and—more often than not—welcomed as a source of richness in our land.
The challenge of our society is to achieve harmony in the midst of diversity, a challenge only imperfectly realized. It is, therefore, the object of
this investigation to shed some light on the influence of one ethnic
group, the Irish, on one of our culture's less-honored, but nevertheless
important institutions—the labor movement. Bona fide trade unions, that

is organizations of workers enjoying economic and political power independent of government, are found only in democratic societies. If they permit them at all, totalitarian regimes turn unions into mere instruments of the state. The right of employees to organize and bargain for economic protection and advancement is one of the marks of a truly democratic system. Needless to say, American trade unions are neither an invention of the Irish; nor have they been a monopoly of the Irish; that they have been influenced by the Irish is undeniable.

Other than Montgomery's chapter in *America and Ireland, 1776–1976*, there are few articles and no book-length studies dedicated to the analysis of this topic. In one of the few articles, "Class, Ethnicity and Radicalism in the Gilded Age: The Land League and Irish America," Eric Foner explores 1870s Land League agitation. He explains that it mobilized support from all elements of the Irish-American community. Terence Powderly was deeply involved, and the Knights of Labor, which he headed, incorporated land reform in its program. However, Foner also notes that conflicts surfaced between a conservative coalition (consisting of the Democratic party, the small Irish-American middle class and the Catholic Church) and the organized social radicalism of the Knights of Labor along with radical branches of the Land League. The conservative alliance, while enthusiastic about land reform, could not endorse labor reform and trade union building. These latter concerns opened channels of communication and mutual aid with labor reformers of Protestant persuasion. Such objectives ran counter to the individualism of middle-class Irishmen as well as the cautious social reform advocated by the Democratic party and the Catholic Church in the 1880s—in Foner's reading of that period.[9]

In its second (1984) edition, *Biographical Dictionary of American Labor Leaders* created fictional labor leaders to illustrate the dominant characteristics of trade union officials in different eras. The method was to design a composite that typified the leaders of each stage in the development of the labor movement. In this way, the cold statistical data analyzed could be humanized. For the turn of the century, a mythical Gordon Mahoney, vice president of the National Union of Molders, was chosen. By implication, this choice acknowledges the importance of Irish-American leadership at that time. His father, presumably an immigrant from Ireland, was also a molder. Mahoney, born in 1859 of Roman Catholic parents and raised in a small Midwestern community, was obliged to leave school after eighth grade in order to help support the family due to the severe depression of the 1870s.

The world that Gordon Mahoney witnessed as a young man was one of manic swings of the business cycle, bitter labor-management struggles and the ultimate emergence of craft unionism characteristic of the American Federation of Labor (AFL) which he embraced. At twenty-five he married Mary Sullivan, who subsequently bore him a son and daughter. Loyalty to the union cause was a legacy passed to Mahoney by his parents, but he aspired to a middle-class existence for his family, especially his children for whom he insisted upon better opportunities. For his son, an education better than his own was essential. For his daughter, marriage out of the working class was his goal. At middle age, Gordon Mahoney surveys possibilities beyond the confines of trade union activity and those of employment as a skilled craftsman. His commitment to the cause has its limits.[10]

The benign image which emerges from the above composite portrait of Irish-American labor leaders contrasts sharply with the view of them which, according to Dennis Clark, actually prevailed during the nineteenth and much of the twentieth century. A prolific historian of the Irish in America, Clark sketched what he believes to be the reality of it in a letter to the author. His description is as follows:

A factor in the psychology of labor militancy was the image of the Irish, partly attributed, partly cultivated within the group. It was an image of combativeness, of protest, of frequently restless challenge. It was partly stereotype and partly actual response to the harshness of the Irish history. In the United States this combative elan was portrayed on the stage, in cartoons, popularized in cults of athletic prowess and military valor. It attended perceptions of the Irish as members of what was for generations a working class feared by socially conservative Anglo-American leaders and a middle class intent upon its own status. The image of the hard-jawed Irish antagonist surrounded the careers of these labor advocates.[11]

Clearly, understandings of Irish-American experience differ sharply. The quote from Clark's letter reflects both the reality of discrimination faced by the Irish and their militant response to it. The image presented in the dictionary conveys no sense of this aspect of the world of Irish unionists. Gordon Mahoney looks to the future optimistically and considers opportunities outside trade unions. A study of this kind should shed further light on what it felt like to be Irish and to champion organized labor in America.

METHOD OF INVESTIGATION

The research undertaken here is essentially an exploratory study. As indicated above, no one has attempted an extended study of this topic before. As an exploratory study it is extensive in the geographic sense in that it is not limited to a single region or community in the country— the East and West Coasts are represented, as is the Midwest. It is also extensive in the chronological sense in that it is not limited to Irish figures from a single historical period, but considers some born prior to the American Civil War, one born in the twentieth century, and others born in the interim period. The exploratory nature of this effort is also reflected in the eclectic approach to choosing sources. As described below, they include published and unpublished ones; those authored by labor historians, specialists in immigration history, Irish history, Irish-American studies, economic historians and others. A variety of ideological viewpoints is represented. As an exploratory study, its conclusions must be considered tentative and subject to additional research before a definitive understanding is realized.

The method of this study is a biographical one, rather than a statistical one. Since analysis of, as well as writing about, the Irish and the labor movement is distinctly limited, the approach used here was to select a group of significant leaders of Irish extraction who were important national figures in American unionism. This method was suggested by Professor Moses Rischin, a scholar of American immigration, who recommended that, if one hoped to contribute some observations about Irish-American labor leaders, it would be necessary to study a number of them, "conservatives and radicals alike."[12] A dozen have been chosen with that in mind.

Biography has an appeal which is almost universal. It relies on the stories of flesh and blood human beings rather than abstractions. Furthermore, it appears to be most fruitful for a study of this kind. The effort is to discover what connection there is between what emerges in the careers of these leaders, and what is distinctive in the experience in Ireland—of themselves or their parents—and what is distinctive in their experience as Irish-Americans in the New World. What characteristics as labor leaders may reasonably be related to that background? In short, what did they have in common attributable to their Irishness?

The reader will note that the comparative leadership method is employed herein. It is utilized specifically in four of the six chapters which make up the body of the book but, also, is integral to the concluding chapter. This is done because, in the writer's experience, it is an effective means of identifying similarities as well as differences between those examined. It is useful in an effort to isolate what all twelve of those considered here had in common.

In recounting the lives of these figures and their immediate forebears, the political, religious and social baggage the Irish carried with them emerges. These elements affected the manner in which they adapted to the work climate of nineteenth-century America. The environment, one of a rapidly industrializing nation, forced them (and Irish ethnics generally) to take whatever opportunities it offered and go wherever it led them. Their often hostile reception in an evermore individualistic society conditioned their reaction to it. There was no alternative but to make the best of it while relying on family, neighborhood and religious associations to ease the pain and provide support. Their stories illustrate how the need to cushion the pain gradually led to entrance into labor organizations and eventually to leadership of them.

The following individuals were chosen for this study. As recommended by Professor Rischin, the list includes both moderates and radicals. Their names appear in chronological order of their birth along with their principal, but by no means only, affiliation.

Name	Principal Affiliation
Mary Harris "Mother" Jones	United Mine Workers
Frank Roney	Molders Union

Joseph Patrick McDonnell	*Labor Standard* (Editor)
Terence Vincent Powderly	Knights of Labor
Peter James McGuire	Carpenters' Union
Patrick Henry McCarthy	San Francisco Building Trades Council
John Fitzpatrick	Chicago Federation of Labor
William Zebulon Foster	Communist party
John Brophy	United Mine Workers
Philip Murray	Congress of Industrial Organizations
Elizabeth Gurley Flynn	Industrial Workers of the World
Michael Quill	Transport Workers Union

This is a very modest sample of the scores of Irish-American labor leaders who led aggregations of thousands and thousands of Irish and others in the American work force. Together, Irish-American trade union leaders were a crucial group of immigrant background who shaped the American labor movement.

Those in this study were chosen to represent the variety of Irish people in leadership positions from historical periods ranging from the 1870s to the post–World War II period. These twelve individuals were not selected on the basis of ideological sameness. They vary in this regard. Furthermore, the outlook of all of them changed over their lifetimes. Thus, the sample is not biased in favor of some preconceived conclusion for the study. It was chosen with the idea of testing hypotheses outlined herein. There are craft unionists of the AFL stripe and industrial unionists of the Congress of Industrial Organization (CIO) era, as well as Wobblies (Industrial Workers of the World functionaries) and one from the Knights of Labor. The careers of a number of them embody several of these categories.

There was, of course, no dearth of racketeers (nor excess) among Irish labor figures; however, no one on the list was chosen as an exemplar of the type. In the body of the study, however, a few practitioners of the rackets, such as "Skinny" Madden and "Umbrella Mike" Boyle of the Chicago building trades appear briefly.[13] Also, corruption of a different sort is evident in the story of William Z. Foster after he secretly entered the Communist party (see Chapter 6).

While this is an exploratory study, a number of hypotheses are available to give direction to this research. Many of them are drawn from studies of the Irish in American politics, including those by Nathan Glazer and Daniel Patrick Moynihan, William Shannon, Edward Levine, Steven Erie, James Walsh and Andrew Greeley.[14] Leadership in trade unions appears to have engaged the same traits and skills that came to be considered characteristic of Irish politicians. The similarity of roles between politicians and labor leaders is striking. Both are "politicians" in the sense that they typically seek power in a complex environment, represent a constituency, must command a following and periodically stand for election. They differ in the greater breadth of constituency of the politician and in the fact that union officials rarely are confronted within their organization by anything resembling a permanent two-party system.

Command of the English language and institutions (especially government ones) gave the Irish an advantage over other immigrant groups in politics, enabling them to assume the role of broker or mediator between diverse nationality groups. Irish ethnic politicians became adept at arranging the balanced ticket providing representation for minority groups according to their relative strength in the electorate, and working out compromises that could command the widest possible acceptance. Presumably, Irish labor leaders enjoyed a like advantage and fell naturally into the job of harmonizing the interests of the variety of nationality groups in the labor force and welding them into a unity for the sake of economic protection and advantage. The comment of Michael Kazin on Irish unionists in San Francisco lends validity to this hypothesis. Does it also have a nationwide validity?

As the Irish became a key group in the electorate, providing a substantial constituency for Irish politicians to call upon for support in their rise to political office, so too were the Irish a substantial part of the work force and could provide a nucleus of backers for those of their countrymen who aspired to leadership in organizations for economic protection of working people.

The motive for supporting labor organizations was surely there in view of the exploitation of immigrant workers, which characterized nineteenth-century America and visited the Irish especially. Their low status in the work force caused them to be subject to all manner of economic injustice.

An additional aspect of their experience fostered a tendency toward Irish influence in trade unions. It is generally understood that they avoided American agriculture and gravitated toward urban environments. American agriculture, dominated by (usually isolated) family farms, was a most unfavorable venue for unionization; while industrial communities, where working people lived and worked together in relatively large groups in close proximity, were far more promising as sites for organization. The typical American farm was run as a small business with most labor provided by family members. Large employers with impersonal employment relations were to be found primarily in urban environments.

One of Daniel P. Moynihan's observations about Irish politicians was that, after finally rising to power, they failed to use that power to promote social reform. In a word—they were conservative. Was this also true of Irish-American labor leaders? It is possible to distinguish between right and left in the realm of trade unionism. In which direction did the Irish tend when they arrived in positions of leadership—in spite of what they may have espoused as youthful aspirants to power? Needless to say, Moynihan's conclusions about Irish politicians is not universally accepted, but it does provide a useful focus for this study.

An additional reason for expecting that the Irish would inevitably rise to the top in American trade unions is that their role as manual workers in the labor force lasted for more than a century. While their influx burgeoned just prior to the mid-nineteenth century, they did not emerge in large numbers in high-status occupations until after World War II. For a very substantial cohort of them, mostly third or fourth-generation immigrants, it was the GI Bill that opened the door to occupations above manual work. Within the blue-collar category, one of the few avenues out of the shop was to become a union official. It is to be expected that those with ambition would choose this route.

Another hypothesis suggested by reading about the history of Ireland is that periodic risings against British rule in Ireland, and the injustice of that system of governing which caused them, conditioned Irish Americans to embrace organizations (trade unions) that ran counter to establishment institutions in the United States. As conceived by immigrants and their children, Irish nationalism was a matter of seeking deliverance for their native land from an oppressive foreign power. Irish-American culture reflects this preoccupation. Did it also attract them, from the vantage of low rungs in the work force, to organizations that sought relief from grievances against industrial employers? Some of those, such as Frank Roney, J.P. McDonnell, and Mike Quill, who were directly involved in nationalist movements in Ireland, became involved in organizing unions in America. Others, specifically Mother Jones, Elizabeth Gurley Flynn, Philip Murray and William Z. Foster, had parents or grandparents who were involved in nationalist movements in Ireland.

In general, was labor leadership associated with Irish nationalism? Lawrence McCaffrey asserts that, in the case of Irish-American politicians "in most cities, and Chicago was a good example, there were close associations between Irish politics and Irish nationalism."[15] Assuming this generalization to be accurate, was there an analogy in the relation between Irish-American unionists and Irish nationalism? The relationship is explored in the lives of the subjects of this investigation.

The study, therefore, involves close attention to the Irish antecedents of the subjects. Three of those examined (William Z. Foster, P.J. McGuire and Terence Powderly) were born in the United States of parents who were immigrants, all of whom were Irish except for Foster's mother, who was Scottish and English. Six of them (John Fitzpatrick, Mother Jones, P.H. McCarthy, J.P. McDonnell, Michael Quill and Frank Roney) emigrated from Ireland themselves, and all of them had relatives in the United States, except Roney. McDonnell had lived in London for over three years and married there before coming to America with his wife. John Brophy and Philip Murray emigrated in the company of parents (Brophy) or male parent (Murray). The parents of both men were born in the United Kingdom outside of Ireland. Grandparents of Brophy and Murray emigrated from Ireland to Britain and Scotland, respectively. Elizabeth Gurley Flynn's grandparents on her father's side came directly to America from Ireland; however, her mother was born in Galway.

Predictably, as immigrants or second-generation immigrants, most of those in the study came from lower income families, but a few were from middle-income levels. At least two came from rather prosperous upbringings. Their educations varied accordingly; most of them had quite limited formal schooling, but in one case some college training (or more realistically preparatory school training) was achieved and more than two spent some time in private schools. Intelligent, curious individuals, typically impatient with the status quo in America, for nearly all of them learning was a lifetime avocation.

Occupations of the fathers of these twelve union activists varied from manual worker, farmer, and white-collar worker, to businessman. J.P. McDonnell's father conducted a business in Dublin. Frank Roney's father was a carpenter who made the transition to prosperous contractor in Belfast. Elizabeth Gurley Flynn's father worked at laying out tracks for urban trolley lines, a semiprofessional civil engineering occupation for which he had prepared at Dartmouth (without graduating). Semiprofessional work of the father, however, did not enable the Flynn family to rise out of poverty. Fathers of two of those studied were farmers (McCarthy and Quill) in Ireland. Of the others, two were sons of manual workers. One was the son of a retired veteran of the British army (Fitzpatrick). Three—Brophy, Murray and Powderly—were miner's sons. Although Powderly's father was, for a time, operator of a small mine, he later became a teamster. McGuire's father was a porter for a department store, Foster's a stableman. Railroad laborer was the calling of Mother Jones's parent.

Unionists examined here all married at least once, seven only once. Elizabeth G. Flynn had, in addition, a long-term common-law relationship with Italian anarchist Carlo Tresca. Powderly, McCarthy, McGuire and Quill all outlived their first wives and subsequently married again. Frank Roney married three times, the second time after becoming widowed, but circumstances concerning the third marriage are unknown. The remaining activists each had but one marriage, which lasted a lifetime, except for Mother Jones whose family was wiped out by an epidemic while she was still a relatively young woman.

All twelve of those examined had a Catholic upbringing, except Elizabeth Gurley Flynn whose parents subscribed to no religion. Of the other eleven, four remained faithful to the Church throughout their lives. They were Fitzpatrick, McCarthy, Murray and Brophy, of whom the last two were particularly devout adherents. McGuire, Quill and Mother Jones wandered from their commitment only to return late in life. Foster, Roney and Powderly left the Church permanently, but for different reasons. Foster became disenchanted as a teenager after reading revolutionary and anticlerical literature. Roney became disillusioned with Church leadership while a young man in Ireland; Powderly, late in life—at which time he joined the Free Masons. J.P. McDonnell did not remain in the faith, but whether he eventually returned is unknown.

Resources for a study of this kind include biographies and autobiographies of the individuals involved, where they exist, and several unpublished doctoral theses. Four of the subjects left personal papers. Others, such as William Z. Foster, were prolific writers and some, such as P.J. McGuire and J.P. McDonnell, edited labor papers and wrote much of the material published in them. Histories of American unions in which these Irish leaders played important roles and which deal with them at some length are also available. The definitive history of American unions by John R. Commons and Associates as well as less definitive ones, which bring the story along to a more recent period, have not been neglected. There are in addition oral histories given by associates of leaders represented in this investigation. In a few cases, living relatives of the subjects of this study have been interviewed, and in a few cases they made useful material available for examination. All such sources have been grist for this research.

NOTES

1. Jack Barbash, "Ethnic Factors in the Development of labor Movement," in *Interpreting the Labor Movement*, George W. Brooks et al. eds., (Madison, Wisc.: Industrial Relations Research Association, 1952), 73.

2. David Montgomery, "The Irish and the American Labor Movement," in *America and Ireland, 1776–1976*, David N. Doyle and Owen D. Edwards eds., (Westport, Conn.: Greenwood Press, 1980), 205–18. Of the 503 entries Montgomery counted, 20 were "born in Ireland, another 93 can be clearly identified as being of Irish Catholic descent, and at least a dozen others probably were."

3. Michael Kazin, "Barons of Labor: The San Francisco Building Trades, 1896–1922," (Ph.D. dissertation, Stanford University, 1983), 573–78.

4. Sean Wilentz, "Industrializing America and the Irish: Toward the New Departure," *Labor History* (Fall 1979): 585–86.

5. Clifton K. Yearley, Jr., *Britains in American Labor* (Westport, Conn.: Greenwood Press, 1974).

6. Mellech Epstein, *Jewish Labor in the USA., 1914–1952*, 2 vols. (New York: Trade Union Sponsoring Committee, 1953); M. Epstein, *Jewish Labor in the USA: An Industrial, Political and Cultural History of the Jewish Labor Movement* (New York: KTAV Publishing House, 1969); Jacob S. Hertz, *The Jewish Labor Bund: A Pictorial History, 1897–1957* (New York: Farlag Unser TSAIT, 1958); Abraham M. Rogoff, *Formative Years of the Jewish Labor Movement in the United States, 1890–1900* (New York: Columbia University Press, 1945). See especially Will Herberg, "Jewish Labor Movement in the United States: Early Years to World War I," *Industrial and Labor Relations Review* (July 1952): 501–23; Will Herberg, "Jewish Labor Movement in the United States: World War I to Present," *Industrial and Labor Relations Review* (October 1952): 45–65; Selig Perlman, "Jewish-American Unionism, Its Birth Pangs and Contributions to the General American Labor Movement," *Publication of the American Jewish Historical Society*, (June 1952): 297–337.

7. Ray Marshall, *The Negro and Organized Labor* (New York: Wiley, 1965); Milton Cantor, ed., *Black Labor in America* (Westport, Conn.: Negro Universities Press, 1969); Philip Foner, *Organized Labor and the Black Worker, 1619–1973*, (New York: Praeger, 1974).

8. Edwin Fenton, *Immigrants and Unions, A Case Study: Italians and Americans Labor, 1870–1920* (New York: Arno Press, 1975).

9. Eric Foner, "Class, Ethnicity and Radicalism in the Gilded Age: The Land League and Irish America," *Marxist Perspectives* (Summer 1978): 6–47.

10. Gary M. Fink, ed., *Biographical Dictionary of American Labor Leaders* (Westport, Conn.: Greenwood Press, 1984), 10–13.

11. Dennis Clark, letter to the author, December 22, 1991.

12. Moses Rischin, letter to the author, December 23, 1980.

13. For a condemnatory treatment of corrupt Irish labor leaders in construction, including "Skinny" Madden, Simon O'Donnell, "Umbrella Mike" Boyle and Timothy Murphy, see William Z. Foster, *Misleaders of Labor*, (Trade Union Educational League, 1927), Chap. 5 "Organized Graft in the Building Trades," 163–81; for an examination of the criminal activities of Joe Fay of the Operating Engineers Union and Joe Ryan of the International Longshoremen's Association, see Malcom Johnson, *Crime on the Labor Front* (New York: McGraw-Hill, 1950), Chap. 4 (Fay), Chap. 11 (Ryan).

14. Nathan Glazer and Daniel Patrick Moynihan, *Beyond the Melting Pot* (Cambridge, Mass.: MIT Press, 1963), espec. 223–26; Andrew M. Greeley, *That Most Distressful Nation* (Chicago: Quadrangle Books, 1972), Chap. 11; Edward M. Levine, *The Irish and the Irish Politicians* (South Bend: University of Notre Dame Press, 1966); William V. Shannon, *The American Irish* (New York: Macmillan, 1963), Chap. 4; Steven P. Erie, *Rainbows End: Irish Americans and the Dilemma of Urban Machine Politics, 1840–1985* (Berkeley: University of California Press, 1988); James B. Walsh, ed., *The Irish: America's Political Class* (New York: Arno Press, 1976).

15. Lawrence J. McCaffrey, "The Irish-American Dimension," in *The Irish in Chicago*, L.J. McCaffrey, Ellen Skerrett, Michael F. Funchion and Charles Fanning (Urbana: University of Illinois Press, 1987), 10.

1

ORIGINS AND ENCOUNTERS

One of the developments that make history is the migration of peoples. The human drama of movement of massive numbers from one geographical area to another, and their encounter with other economic and social environments is a major source of change in the human condition. The causes of these movements are no less important for our understanding of human history. It is from this vantage that a study of the Irish and organized labor in America begins. This chapter commences with a concise treatment of the causes and magnitude of the Irish immigration, analyzes the entry of the Irish into the work force and finally deals with their first encounters with, and early participation in, organized labor.

IRISH IMMIGRATION

Hibernian migration to America took place in the context of an outflow of humanity from Europe in the nineteenth century. This outflow was the result of a doubling of the population of Europe in the century from 1750 to 1850 and the modernization of European economies in the eighteenth and nineteenth centuries. It was a complex process involving different regions at different times, but our purpose is to concentrate on the emigration from Ireland to the United States by way of providing background for understanding the emergence of Irish in trade unions.

Emigration from Ireland to America (and elsewhere) took place in a period when the conquering British were consolidating their control of the island. It occurred when landlords, both British absentee owners and Anglo-Irish Protestants, were transforming agriculture in Ireland from a backward, small-scale, primarily subsistence activity to a modern, larger scale, market-oriented one. This development, beginning roughly in the second half of the eighteenth century and continuing through the nineteenth, involved enclosing lands, gradually moving from a tillage or cultivation enterprise to greater and greater emphasis on pasturage. As they took control of nearly all the really productive acreage on the island, landlords sought to maximize their financial returns from the land and pushed farming into the modern age. Accordingly, Ireland became an integral part of the British and, to a degree, the world market. Its fortunes were thus dependent on prices over which its tenant farmers had no control. The famine of the 1840s greatly accelerated this restructuring of Irish agriculture and Irish society.[1]

This change dramatically reduced the number of farm laborers required for a given plot. It was due to the larger scale and advanced methods in agriculture as well as increasing emphasis on pasturage. The interaction of these forces and the rising rural population up to the period of the great famine (in the second half of the 1840s) foreclosed opportunities for Irish farm laborers, small leaseholders cultivating an acre or two and their families. With the authority of English law and government behind them, landlords pursued the goal of maximizing rents with all the vigor of nineteenth-century capitalism. Inspired as they were by the new dispensation of laissez faire individualism with its emphasis on the rights of private property (regardless of how obtained) and little on its responsibilities, they were, with few exceptions, unconcerned about its effect on landless Irishmen.

While tenants were dependent on the market to meet the rent, they largely nourished themselves with potatoes, porridge (oats) and, when they could afford it, milk. Even before the great famine this method of sustenance suffered from natural causes. Partial failure of the potato crop occurred in 1829–1830, 1832–1834, 1836, 1839 and 1841–1843. In each case emigration from Ireland increased sharply.[2]

By the 1840s emigration as an alternative to the grim conditions at home in a conquered land was well understood. It became an accepted, if painful, necessity. Life as a tenant raising potatoes to nourish the family and cultivating nearly all else for the market in order to pay the rent and escape eviction was a frustrating and most insecure kind of life. For the grown children of such (typically large) families, the prospect of inheriting the lease was itself not very attractive. It was generally available only to the oldest son, in any case, leaving little hope for his siblings. Another force adding to emigration was the conscious "clearance" of lands by the eviction of laborers and tenants in the tens of thousands. Little wonder, therefore, that Ireland became a major source of recruits for the work force of America as well as those of other countries. Not surprisingly, there were periodical risings against British authority and Anglo-Irish rule: in 1798 (United Irishmen), 1840s (Young Ireland), 1860s (Fenians) and 1870s (Land League).

The Irish wave of new entrants came from a politically aroused atmosphere. One of their early mentors in political organization was Wolf Tone, leader of the United Irishmen of 1798, who, though a

Dublin Protestant, captured the imagination and hearts of the people with his vision of a nonsectarian Irish democratic republic, free at last from John Bull. This free-spirited, witty and fatalistic man became the classic Irish rebel, the more so when he chose self-destruction rather than execution by the British at the end of his failed revolt.

More fruitful, if less violent, was the career of Daniel O'Connell, "The Great Liberator," who mobilized peasants for a successful campaign of Catholic emancipation in the 1820s. His genius was to use British political institutions to create and organize a demand for democratic reform. Through marches, mass rallies, petitions and election campaigns, he demonstrated what might be accomplished with a peaceful and pragmatic approach. His work made nationalism a permanent feature of Irish life. It cultivated a political consciousness in the sons of Erin whether at home or abroad, which manifested itself in a desire for democracy in the workplace as well as political democracy.[3]

Howard Harris chronicled this characteristic tendency in the early textile manufacturing town of Paterson, New Jersey, during the 1820s and 1830s, where Irish people, both Catholic and Protestant, were highly visible in both Jacksonian democratic politics and in strikes against employers when their work was threatened by technological developments and instability. Harris discovered that, in 1828, an association called the Friends of Ireland and Religious Liberty in Paterson was dedicated to ending English tyranny and raising funds for O'Connell's campaign. He found it a testament to their understanding of republicanism, as it applied to both political and economic affairs—but notes that the level may have been somewhat lower among refugees from the great famine (who arrived later.)[4]

From Ireland to the United States, the pattern of immigration was cyclical in response to economic conditions in both countries. Recessions in America were the cause of substantial declines in immigration, ordinarily a year after downturns in business. Return of prosperity marked a significant rise in the inflow of Irish born. Wars involving the United States also deterred Irishmen from coming to this country. Depressed economic conditions in Ireland, most catastrophically during the great famine—but also at other times of partial crop failures, exerted a strong push to Irish emigration. Good economic times in America during the nineteenth century often were concurrent with surges in railroad building, which created work laying track, and producing iron and lumber for the railroads; as well as other products demanded in new markets opened by the rails. Immigration responded to these opportunities accordingly.[5]

The composition of Irish immigration changed during the period before the famine. Early in the nineteenth century it consisted, in the majority, of those who left not of necessity, but out of choice. They tended to be from Ulster Protestant stock and in the main skilled artisans, shopkeepers and professionals, but also from hard-pressed farm families. Not always impoverished, they often came with a certain amount of money in their pockets, normally enough to get them through the initial adjustment to a new environment. Poor farm girls and young men were in the minority at this time.

By the late 1830s, and early 1840s, the complexion of immigration had shifted to a majority of young adult Catholics from poorer families of tenants. They were unskilled farm workers or servant girls. Moving out of necessity, they came from counties in the province of Connaught and from western Ulster (Donegal and Tyrone). They had little if any wherewithal upon arriving in the New World. Other rural areas chiefly in the western counties of Munster (Limerick, Kerry and Cork) also became important sources as time went on. The great famine not only ignited an explosion in the magnitude of emigration, but also dramatically intensified the changes in its composition described above.[6]

Migrants from elsewhere in Europe consisted of a high percentage of males, but those from Ireland were, to a large extent, equally divided between men and women. Single young adults of both sexes accounted for roughly one half of the Irish migration to America; the remainder were migrating families. This was the pattern until the famine, at which time the proportion traveling in families increased substantially. Thereafter, single young adults under thirty-five became a substantial majority of the Irish migrants.

The outflow from Ireland has been categorized as a chain migration. That is, earlier leavers, once adjusted to the new nation and having accumulated sufficient savings, would then pay the passage for other members of the family—normally of the same generation, rarely parents. This method was facilitated by emergence of passenger brokers who marketed prepaid passage tickets, financed by remittances from relatives, who had migrated earlier. Probably more than a third of the remittances were in the form of prepaid passage tickets. In any case, financial assistance overwhelmingly came from family sources, although aid from government and some landlords played a minor role. Between 1848 and 1887, thirty-four million pounds were sent to the British Isles by emigrants in North America, "the bulk of it going to Ireland."[7]

Of the five million immigrants entering the United States from 1815 to 1860, two million, or about 40 percent, were Irish. From 1860 to 1915, twenty-five million arrived, about 10 percent of whom were from Ireland. Emigration from Ireland prior to the famine (1815–1845) was significantly over one million, and of this entire group, one third, or in the order of four hundred thousand, came to the United States. During the famine period (1846–1855), approximately two and a half million left Ireland, more than had departed in the prior two and a half centuries. Of these, 52 percent, or about 1.3 million, came to this country. From 1856 to 1914, four million Irish people emigrated and approximately two-thirds, or 2.6 million, came into the United States.[8]

In the period from 1847 through 1854, as a result of the famine, Irish immigration to the United States exceeded one hundred thousand annually—surpassing one hundred fifty thousand in five of those years (1849–1853).[9] It was slightly over two hundred and twenty thousand in

1851.[10] This tidal wave of humanity, destitute and in poor health largely, was not exactly welcome in the republic of mid-century America.

Passage to America was a traumatic and dangerous experience for the typical Irish immigrant of the famine period. The length of the voyage—from one to three months—and, the primitive conditions of accommodation, sanitation, privacy, and food and water provision combined to produce misery for passengers. The casualty toll to typhus, dysentery and other diseases was epidemic on the "coffin ships." Only the prospect of starvation at home made departure an acceptable alternative.[11]

ENTERING THE WORK FORCE

Thus a rising tide of humanity washed on to American shores—rural people, minimally educated, unprepared for life in an industrializing nation, faced with a daunting adjustment to unfamiliar employments in a new land, weak, vulnerable to diseases rare in their homeland and with prospects, therefore, of limited life expectancy. They were destined for the humblest reaches of the work force, and even there greeted with a jaundiced eye by earlier arrivals of Anglo origin, who would be their overseers or the skilled tradesmen they would serve as carriers of hod, drawers of water or shovelmen. That it was a dispiriting encounter is not surprising. What was exceptional was the large number whose spirit was not broken and who thrived, if not in their own lives, then, in those of their children and grandchildren.

Immigrants flooding into America in flight from the famine had hard times in store for them. Typically devoid of funds, they had nothing to cushion the adjustment to a new land of strange climate, alien culture and commercialized living. Although helped to some extent by Irish societies and relatives in the large cities, they were greeted with hostility by a large segment of native Americans. In addition to health problems resulting from a long and painful voyage, homesickness and poverty, they lacked skills needed to command a decent livelihood.

Hostility to Irish immigrants and their "papist" religion did not begin with the famine immigrants. At Charlestown, Massachusetts, near Boston, in August of 1834, a crowd of nativists burned a convent conducted by Ursuline nuns. A more violent outbreak occurred in May of 1844 at Kensington, a textile mill center in Philadelphia, and a neighborhood where Irish immigrants had settled. Skilled weavers from Ulster had formed the anti-Catholic Orange Society in the 1830s, angered by the influx of low-paid Irish laborers into the mills. It was revived by renewed nativist activity in the city. The upshot was three days of rioting in which mobs burned down two Catholic churches, a convent and thirty Irish houses. Another attack on a Catholic church occurred on July 5th of that year in the Southwark section of Philadelphia.

Similarly inspired incidents occurred in other East and Gulf Coast cities. New York was spared by the aggressive posture of Archbishop John Hughes, who informed the city's mayor of his intention to protect

Catholic property and warned him that churches other than Catholic should beware if any events like those in Kensington threatened.[12]

Therefore, to a work force already divided and in contention was added religious conflict and social alienation. This complex of disabilities tended to relegate Irish working people to a most unenviable position in or barely above the lowest rung of the economic scale.

This massive infusion of new arrivals seeking a livelihood came at a time when the young American nation could readily (if somewhat grudgingly) absorb them. Mid-century found the economy well along the path of continuing growth, though one interrupted by periodic recessions of varying intensity. An ongoing transportation revolution in the United States required manual labor for building canals and railroads, as well as hands for its river, Great Lakes and coastal shipping. These opportunities drew Irishmen to a variety of locations within, but also far beyond, the cities.

This developing infrastructure consumed much from extractive industries—of coal, metal mining, quarrying and lumbering where immigrants also found work in places far afield. Urban communities grew apace. They commanded much output from these same extractive industries for their commercial and residential building. Expanding cities created demand for construction laborers, not a few of whom were unskilled greenhorns from Ireland. Growing ports on seacoasts, rivers and lakes offered jobs in increasing numbers for longshoremen and team drivers.

Cities and their nearby communities afforded a living for innumerable young Irish women in domestic service for middle- and upper-class American families. The Irish serving girl symbolized inferior status in the nation's social structure, just as did the Irish hod carrier in the building of its cities.

As it replaced household production, factory work steadily advanced. By the 1850s textiles furnished immigrants (men, women and children) with wage-earning prospects, as did its outgrowth industry—clothing manufacture. Jobs in iron making and foundries were rising in response to the needs for such things as nails for construction, axles for transportation equipment and plows for the farm implement industry. Steel was a mere infant by the Civil War. However, driven by demand for steel rails, it would later absorb a multitude of Irish as well as other workers.[13]

Paradoxically, Catholic Irish, coming from a rural agricultural background in the overwhelming majority of cases, did not gravitate toward farming in the United States. This is the more curious when the land hunger of the Irish peasant could be satisfied so cheaply in America—for a mere registration fee after the Homestead Act of 1862. Furthermore, agriculture grew vigorously throughout the nineteenth century and outstripped manufacturing in numbers of persons engaged until 1920.[14]

Unlike their Protestant fellow emigrants, to a great extent, the Irish tended to become urban dwellers in the New World. According to the 1860 census, of the Irish born, almost "two thirds were to be found in

New York, Pennsylvania, New Jersey, and New England, though there were large numbers in practically every city of any size from San Francisco to Boston, and from New Orleans to Chicago."[15]

Social historians have ascribed the absence of Irish people in American agriculture to, first of all, their gregarious nature which was ill-suited to the isolation common to farms in the United States, but more congenial to life in city ghettos teeming with displaced country-men. The scale of farming here was not suited to people accustomed to the spade cultivation practiced on much smaller plots in Ireland. Another deterrent was lack of capital to start a farm.

In addition there was opposition of some Catholic prelates, notably Archbishop John Hughes of New York, who feared that loss of religious faith would occur if Irish Catholics moved to the no-priest lands of the Midwest and the Great Plains. The Irish reluctance to live in rural America was confirmed by the failure of Bishop Mathias Loras of Dubuque and later Bishops John Ireland of Saint Paul and John Spalding of Peoria, as well as others, in their attempts to promote colonization of rural areas by Irish Catholics.[16] The avowed goal of these colonization movements was to attract Catholics away from the corrupting influences found in large cities. Presumably, there was also a wish to populate sparsely settled dioceses.

The preference for urban life, long considered characteristic of Catholic Irish, has been challenged by Canadian historian D.H. Akenson. Despairing of the adequacy of United States census data to identify ethnic and especially religious origins, he relied upon those from Canada, New Zealand and Australia. He also denied any difference in patterns of settlement between Catholics and Protestants existed. His conclusions have not been accepted by scholars of Irish-American history. However, traditional views have been clarified by pointing out that Irish not found in large cities were not necessarily to be found in farming. To a large extent, they were to be found in smaller industrial communities—towns and villages located along rivers, canals and railroads to benefit from waterpower or cheap transportation. Often they were enclaves outside of sizable communities or in mining regions and contained both transient individuals and more permanent residents. Indeed traditionalists agree that some Catholic immigrants did go into agriculture but only a minority and to a much lesser extent than was true of Protestant immigrants from Ireland.[17] The assertion that Irish immigrants were land locked in the large cities of the East has been overstated. Almost surely they were more mobile than this assertion implies. The fact is that they were, in the main, single young people and thus rather footloose. Additionally, they were anxious to accumulate funds, in order not merely to survive, but to finance passage of other family members to America—which they succeeded in doing in truly impressive proportions. This concern made them responsive to opportunities for higher earnings in different regions and different cities. High saving rates alone cannot account for the enormous amounts returned to Ireland to facilitate this "chain migration."

Work digging canals and laying railroad track took Irishmen far into the hinterlands. Anecdotal evidence tells us that they did not hesitate to leave their current employer when higher paying work was available elsewhere. Anthracite and bituminous coal mining also drew them away from large communities. Hard rock mining in the Far West had pecuniary appeal as well. The Irish were well represented in the "floating body of prospectors, perhaps 100,000 strong, ready to fan up the coast and back to the East at the slightest rumor of gold" which had been created by the California gold rush of 1848–1850.[18] Study of American folk music also reveals geographical mobility of the Irish. The Irish musical imprint is evident in the North, Midwest and Far West, where Irishmen labored on railroads, on canals, and in lumbering, fishing, shipping and cattle industries. From Maine to Wisconsin, in the logging business, according to folklorist William H.A. Williams, the Irish "virtually dominated the singing."[19]

This raises doubts concerning the view of Oscar Handlin and others about Irish immigrants immobilized in urban ghettos.[20] Discrimination in employment plagued Irish people most severely with the coming of famine immigrants. It was a daunting experience to face the ubiquitous "No Irish Need to Apply" placards, but generalizing from studies of Boston and a few other Eastern cities, which describe an Irish underclass that required generations to break out of the ghetto and ghetto mentality, may not be valid. While data on regional differences in such discrimination are lacking, it is reasonable to speculate that such banners appeared less frequently the farther west one journeyed. In San Francisco, where the Irish influx arrived in time for the creation of that "instant city," there was little or none. The Irish had come to the Golden Gate well prepared to contend for economic and social advantage seasoned through experience in other American cities. On the West Coast no WASP elite yet existed to inhibit their advance or give them a sense of inferiority associated with life in an urban ghetto.[21]

Statistical evidence confirming mobility of the Irish comes from a 1972 study of British and Irish immigrants by Vedder and Gallaway. Using data from the U.S. Census and elsewhere, the research concluded that the Irish (and English, Scots and Welsh as well) were quite mobile in moves westward after initially settling in ports of entry on the East Coast for a few years. After acquiring "a minimum competence, only then could they move on both geographically and economically." The investigators found that "the Irish, in particular, seem to be extraordinarily responsive to income differentials and the Scots and English only slightly less so." Furthermore, the Irish preference for cities over rural communities was evident. Of the four groups, the "Irish seemed to settle in states with relatively high population density during the latter half of the nineteenth century" verifying that "the Irish were indeed attached to urban areas more than other groups."[22]

While the tide of Celtic immigration peaked in the famine years, it did not disappear thereafter. In fact, it averaged forty thousand per year through 1921, with the usual cyclical variation described above.[23]

According to historian Emmet Larkin, postfamine immigrants were subject to less hostility from native Americans because of a devotional revolution that occurred in Ireland from 1850 to 1875. Its driving force was Paul Cardinal Cullen, primate of Ireland from 1849 to 1878. Under his leadership, numerous churches, convents and rectories were built, financed by Irish and Irish-American laity. As a result of this movement, Irish people became far more regular in their church attendance, sacramental life and general behavior. Preaching against the hazards of alcohol, Larkin believes, also had a salutary effect. Thus Irish newcomers were accepted more readily by middle-class Americans than their predecessors.[24]

Other factors undoubtedly contributed to this new acceptability, which, of course, should not be exaggerated. Among them would be that these later arrivals tended to be better educated due to the system of national schools in Ireland conducted in English, which had become widespread by the second half of the nineteenth century.[25] The fact is, therefore, that a smaller proportion was Gaelic speaking and that their poverty was not as desperate as that of their precursors. Needless to say, beginning in the 1880s and rising mightily, came a new immigrant horde from Eastern and Southern Europe speaking alien tongues. To a considerable degree, it displaced the Irish as a target for nativist prejudice and disdain.

INTRODUCTION TO UNIONISM

Arrival of immigrants unfamiliar with labor organizations, as the vast majority were, has always posed problems for the labor movement in America. It is not surprising that the American Federation of Labor from its very beginning championed restricted immigration. Put most simply, increases in the supply of workers means a wage lower than what otherwise would exist. Coming from diverse nations and cultures, usually very poor, they were ordinarily willing, at least initially, to take jobs regardless of pay levels and conditions, thereby threatening existing levels for earlier Americans. Not infrequently they were lured to work as strikebreakers, thus earning the jeers and hatred of those on strike. They entered, unwittingly, no doubt, into the employers' game of playing one ethnic group off against another.

A case in point is a dispute which occurred at Amesbury and Salisbury, Massachusetts, in 1851. When employees of a textile mill there went on strike they were replaced by newcomers from Ireland who were provided with accommodations in the dance hall of a hotel because no boardinghouse would accept them. The floor of the dance hall was supplied with mattresses and blankets, and the Irish remained to defeat the strike. The entire affair was witnessed by George McNeil, who at the time was a boy employed in the mill. Partly as a result, he became a champion of labor reform.[26]

Irish refugees not only were no exception, they were the classic example. When they came in increasing numbers late in the first half of the nineteenth century, desperate and "papist," they were despised by the heavily Protestant community. To the craft unions in American cities, whose members themselves had nativist leanings, they appeared more of a menace than material for building labor organizations. These reasons prompted more than one historian to assert that "the heavy Irish immigration probably retarded unionization in the United States."[27]

An early adaptation of the Irish to the bewildering commerce of wage earning was to band together on the basis of neighborhood, or parish, or even of county of origin in Ireland and attempt control the most accessible areas of the job market in the vicinity. The docks in East Coast cities (such as Boston, New York, Philadelphia and others) were a favored job site. An example from the ten-hour movement of the 1830s was the coal heavers along wharves of the Schuykill River in Philadelphia. Their work was to unload coal from boats coming down the Schuykill Canal from the anthracite region. In August of 1835, they struck for a wage increase and for a ten-hour day. Though not a formally organized union, the men militantly patrolled the wharves frightening off anyone who might wish to take their jobs. The coal unloaders lived in an Irish enclave along the Schuylkill, a section somewhat remote from the main part of the city, which came to be known as "Ramcat." Their dispute, nevertheless, spread to organized workers throughout the city who struck for a ten hour day, considered essential for intelligent citizenship in the young republic.[28]

The plight of unskilled Irish immigrants and their efforts to overcome it in the New World is also dramatized in the story of the Chesapeake and Ohio (C&O) Canal.[29] Planned to penetrate the Appalachian barrier, as were a number of the early canals, the C&O, a case of mixed private and public enterprise, was begun in 1828. The C&O Canal Company sought 10,000 workers from foreign countries. It obtained capital through bonds marketed domestically and overseas. Contractors to the canal company were directly responsible for the work and, having little credit of their own, relied upon monthly advances from the C&O Company for capital. The C&O Company itself was chronically underfinanced. Unfortunately, contractors typically estimated costs (this being a relatively new type of undertaking in the United States) far below what they actually proved to be, and were, therefore, almost continually in financial straits—often unable to meet payrolls scheduled monthly. For unskilled Irishmen earning from ten to twelve dollars a month plus board, failure to receive their pay was a catastrophic event. Payment was essential for their physical survival. Digging a canal through mud and rocks alongside the Potomac River west from Georgetown, using only shovels and black powder, was both dangerous and backbreaking. To burden workers with financial risks of the enterprise through periodic nonpayment of wages was unconscionable. Add to this the risk of malaria in the warmest months and suspension of all work (and wages) in the coldest months of winter and you have almost unendurable labor conditions. But this was not all—there was competition in the canal workers' labor market from immigrants of different ethnic backgrounds especially when, under these circumstances, Irishmen became less than tractable and even unruly.

The response of Irish workers to these conditions was reminiscent of rural uprisings back in their native land. Associations of workers formed spontaneously and attempted to protect their members from these hazards. When contractors failed to pay on time they received threats, and when demands were not satisfied violence resulted—on more than a few occasions. Militant reactions also occurred when other workers were brought in to replace the Irish. More than once, Irish societies took control of sections of the canal and refused to work until pay was forthcoming. Contemporary accounts referred to these occurrences as riots, although they more closely resembled strikes or sit-down strikes. Normally they were resolved by calling out the Maryland State Militia.

Dismal conditions for Irish laborers on the C&O canal dig were repeated again and again in the canal building era (1815–1860). Capital was scarce. Almost everywhere financing was a severe problem. Casualty rates were high for this dangerous work, carried out in health-threatening environments where medical care was almost completely lacking. Initially driven by competition of seacoast cities to become the prime thoroughfare of commerce with the trans-Appalachian region, it was interrupted by periodic financial failures—which meant layoffs for the heavily Irish work force.

New York governor DeWitt Clinton's "Big Ditch," completed from Albany to Buffalo in 1825, was the making of New York's commercial preeminence. Philadelphia merchants hoped to contest it by promoting the Mainline Canal from the city of brotherly love to Pittsburgh, as did Baltimore merchants in financially supporting the C&O canal. Baltimoreans also craved a waterway across the narrow neck of land between Chesapeake Bay and the Delaware river—and got it.

Next, young states of the Midwest—Ohio, Indiana, Illinois—undertook to connect the Great Lakes with the Ohio and Mississippi river systems. In all, over four thousand miles of canals were constructed, in most cases by Irishmen supplied with picks, shovels, wheelbarrows and blasting powder. Those who survived the exhausting work, frequent cave-ins, floods, cholera, malaria, and miserable shanty quarters—very many did not—often became boatmen on the canals or rivers. For their important contribution to establishing a market-expanding, growth- stimulating transport system they were rewarded with poverty wages and the disdain that middle- and upper-class Americans typically reserve for common laborers of immigrant origin.

Documenting labor experience of the entire canal era for both Canada and the United States, Peter Way's *Common Labour* describes an evolution from small-scale, paternalistic, personal labor relations in the early stages—to a large-scale, impersonal, highly commercialized, depressed relationship by the 1840s. Slaves, indentured servants, German immigrants and native farm labor utilized initially were, by the 1830s, largely replaced by Irish immigrants. Never satisfactory, economic conditions for canallers seriously deteriorated in the long run. Provided early on with victuals, liquor, shelter in crude shanties and wages at subsistence levels irregularly to begin with, workers' conditions worsened with the financial panic of 1837 and continued to decline thereafter. States, financially insolvent, suspended canal projects, causing labor surplus, intensified competition for jobs, substantial wage reductions, hiring by day instead of by month and an end to board and bed by contractors unless purchased out of wages.

Strike data offers a rough index of this decline, quadrupling from the 1820s decade to that of the 1840s. Strikes were orchestrated by primitive labor organizations modelled on Irish secret societies. Their premise was the right to subsistence. Unemployment fostered interethnic as well as intraethnic (Irish) conflict—Corkonians versus Longfordians, for example. This grim passage was ameliorated, to a degree, by high turnover rates due to those fleeing in search of a more humane, less unstable, less migratory work. The canal story forecasts the full-throated, corporate capitalism that was to characterize the railroad era.[30]

Railroad building, begun in 1830—expanded rapidly, if cyclically, through the nineteenth century—was no more of a picnic for Erin's emigrés than the canal works. In 1832, for example, a group of Irish workmen who contracted cholera while excavating a roadbed for tracks leading to a junction with the Philadelphia and Columbia Railroad (which connected with Pennsylvania's Mainline Canal at Columbia on the Susquehanna River) were refused care of any kind by everyone except the Catholic Sisters of Charity, who came all the way from Philadelphia. A mass grave containing the bones of fifty-seven of them near the Amtrak line twenty-five miles west of Philadelphia is today marked only by a low rectangle of stone, now overgrown, whose existence is almost unknown in the community.[31]

The tendency to band together for protection, evident in the C&O story described above, was also present in construction of the Baltimore and Ohio (B&O) railroad (along much the same route). Bitter conflict developed between Irish laborers and contractors over failure to pay wages on time. At one point, accumulated back pay amounted to $9,000. Irish militants insisted that B&O agents go to Baltimore and come back with the money. When B&O agents returned, they brought soldiers to suppress the uprising, but no money. Similar conflicts over wages and working conditions occurred on the Erie, New York Central, Reading and other railroads—usually with similar methods of resolving them.

Railroads, furthermore, employed substantially more men than the canals. Controlled by bold and unscrupulous capitalists, railroad labor policies were no less scandalous than were their notorious financial practices. As the first authentic models of giant enterprise, they cast a villainous image for workers, farmers and small businesses. They became skilled at deploying strikebreakers, using blacklists and obtaining troops to put down work stoppages.

Bitterness toward railroad barons exploded with spontaneous

strikes and violence in 1877 when they announced wage cuts. At rail centers across the country rolling stock and round houses were torched. Regiments of troops mustered to quell the rampage.[32] The reactions of Irish workers to their grim circumstances reflected their own experiences in Ireland and forecast their continued inclination toward informal societies, customary militancy and, later, emergence as a force to be reckoned with in organized labor.

One of the few institutions that welcomed the Irish to the New World was the Democratic party. Seeing the greenhorns as a potential source of strength for the party in the large cities, it assisted them in obtaining citizenship—often through extralegal methods—and recruited them to vote for party candidates. Help in finding employment and offering assistance in other ways tended to bind the Irish to big city Democratic machines. This was especially true of Tammany Hall in New York (Philadelphia, however, was a conspicuous exception to this tendency). The Democratic party's opposition to the Union cause in the Civil War and the disposition of its leaders to vilify President Lincoln, exerted a significant influence on many Irishmen toward the war between the states.[33]

Another illustration of the Irish impulse toward neighborhood organization to protect limited work opportunities occurred in the prelude to the 1863 draft riots in New York City. In the 1850s, they had formed the Longshoremen's Benevolent Society. By then Irish workmen had secured most of the longshore work in the city, having succeeded in their contests with black workers who had previously done it. In June of 1863, dock workers went on strike for higher wages in response to inflation brought on by the Civil War. Black workers, recruited as strikebreakers, came under the protection of city police. Racial disturbances broke out along the waterfront.

In early July, violence fanned out across the city and led to the worst street riots in any American city up to that time. The rioters were not all Irishmen, but very many of them were. Sparked by racial antagonism, the violence fed on resentment against enforcement of the recently enacted draft of men to fight in a war to free blacks from slavery. Its intensity grew from a sense that emancipated blacks would come north to compete for work in enterprises owned by white Anglo-Saxon Protestant Americans who despised Irish Catholic immigrants. It demonstrated the rage of tenement dwellers toward their wealthy landlords, who could depend on government authority to preserve their privileged position—most immediately, for example, to pay a $300 penalty or hire a substitute to serve in their place if their own names should turn up in the list of draftees.

The Longshoremen's Society was dedicated to keeping work and neighborhood exclusively for "whites," meaning primarily Irish people, though some German Americans also worked on the docks. But the term emphatically excluded blacks and any new immigrants employers might attempt to bring in (called "contrabands") during the war. The object was to protect jobs, waterfront wages and maintain stability for the neighborhood, friendship and kinship network. Outsiders whose coming threatened to upset this social arrangement ran the risk of physical injury or worse.

Blacksmiths, boilermakers and iron molders in the metalworking shops around the uptown waterfront, most of whom were from adjacent, heavily Irish neighborhoods, felt a pervasive sense of economic insecurity. Deeply suspicious of the Republican party, they feared it planned to draft fellow artisans who had not volunteered for military service and replace them with so-called contrabands, black freedmen, or foreign labor imported for that purpose. They fought to defend their neighborhood from Republican conscription agents.

Union craftsmen in the reawakening construction unions, where Irishmen were few in number, participated in the first day of the week-long riots, but desisted thereafter at the behest of their leaders. The five-day outburst, begun Monday, July 13th, took a toll of over one hundred dead, conspicuously among them black people, but also policemen and conscription agents. Another part of the toll consisted of rioters felled by regiments of federal troops brought in to quell the troubles on Thursday. Arson also visited homes of some wealthy Republicans, draft offices and certain business establishments.

By no means alone among the rioters, the Irish, nevertheless, suffered reinforcement of prevailing nativist prejudice against them as wild, simian-like creatures of questionable humanity, as portrayed by cartoons in the popular press. Though moderated somewhat by their visible presence in the Union Army at Gettysburg and elsewhere, on balance the public image of the Irish worsened.[34]

Resistance to the draft was also a reality in the anthracite region of Pennsylvania and for reasons similar to those in New York. Wartime demand for anthracite coal promised operators a rare opportunity for substantial profits in a highly competitive, low-wage industry. Mine workers, beset by wartime inflation, sought to obtain significant wage increases through labor organization. Not a few strikes resulted. In 1863 federally appointed provost marshals responsible for enrolling conscripts tended to view strikes and draft resistance in the same light—interference with the war effort verging on treason. This view was vigorously cultivated by mine owners, who denounced Irish militants and unions in general. Agents appointed by the Republican administration were seen as allies of the operators, where, in fact, their sympathies leaned heavily. Irish miners there, loyal to the Democratic party, resented the bigotry of the operators, who were nearly all native American, English, or Welsh. Immigrants from an island almost totally devoid of coal mines, they lacked any experience in the pits and were forced to start at the bottom doing the heaviest physical work as laborers attending skilled Welsh and British miners. This in the most hazardous and unhealthy of industries, where employers refused liability for occupational accidents and chronic lung disease. Ethnic antagonism with their Protestant fellow workers contributed to the low estate of Irish Catholics in the mining communities.

Under the circumstances, convinced (with good reason) that they could not obtain justice from the courts or local or state government, the Irish resorted to direct reprisal for injustices meted out to them by mine operators or others.[35]

These actions by a secret association, dubbed the "Molly Maguires," resembled similar ones in Ireland perpetrated by groups known as the Whiteboys, Ribbonmen, or in some cases Molly Maguires. A careful study by Wayne Broehl discovered no direct connections between those in Ireland and those in eastern Pennsylvania; instead, he found strong similarities in the economic distress of the Irish in both countries and in the British Protestant character of their adversaries, be they landlords, mine operators, or local officials.[36] The sense of having traded the oppressive environment of Ireland for another almost equally repressive in anthracite country (and elsewhere in America) explains much about Irish protest movements and the drastic methods they sometimes employed.

Into the troubled anthracite region came one John Siney, a native of Queens County in Leinster, who, subsequent to his father's eviction, had lived and worked in Lancashire where he had imbibed ideas of Chartist reform and trades unionism. He had helped organize, and later served as president of, the local bricklayers association in Wigan (Lancashire). After arriving in Saint Clair, Schuylkill County in 1863, he went into the mines, and in 1868, with others, he formed the Workingmen's Benevolent Association and later headed a countywide miners' union as its full-time president. From 1868 to 1875, this organization eased the frustrations and calmed the bitterness that were the cause of the secret societies. Miners' grievances were handled through negotiations. Hazards were reduced by lobbying successfully for a mine safety law. Ethnic friction was minimized by spreading a sense of solidarity. Schuylkill enjoyed a season of relative peace.[37] It was an important lesson in trade unionism for Irishmen.

Siney's nemesis proved to be Franklin Gowen, who rose from Pottsville attorney to president of the Reading Railroad and to control the anthracite fields of Schuykill County.[38] Under his leadership, the firm quietly invested heavily in mining properties and looked upon the union as an impediment to anticipated profits. His strategy was to identify the union with the Molly Maguires, infiltrate both with Pinkerton spies, and ultimately eliminate both organizations. Gowen's remarkable instinct for public relations enabled him to sensationalize and exaggerate the crimes of the secret association, convince the public that it was part and parcel of the union, and finally destroy the miners' organization in the long strike of 1875.

With the union's demise, resolving grievances reverted to a more violent form. Gowen took personal charge of prosecuting Irishmen accused of crimes attributed to the Molly Maguires. With oratory, theatrical skill and the testimony of his star Pinkerton spy, James McParlan, he won convictions. Twenty of those convicted were hanged in 1877 and 1878. Sufficient residue of ambiguity remained to perpetuate controversy and embarrassment up to the present. It was only intensified by Gowen's suicide in 1888.

This episode demonstrated what might be accomplished by a militant organization of workers if ethnic rivalries were replaced with solidarity. It also revealed how such efforts could be thwarted by a ruthless, resourceful and determined business leader aided by allies in the community establishment in late nineteenth- century America.

A quality of the Irish temperament is evident in this story. It is a conviction, nurtured over generations under the yoke of a foreign power, that when authority is the source of grave injustice, then its laws have no claim on your compliance. In its extreme form, it has caused many Irishmen to confuse lawlessness with heroism. It is a conviction not unknown in independence movements in the Third World.

During the 1860s, a corporal's guard of Irishmen emerged as trade union leaders. In the words of David Montgomery, "By the 1880s the majority of American labor unions would be headed by Catholics of Irish descent, but in the sixties this role was new to them. Furthermore, the new role subjected the traditional role of Catholic Democrats to severe stress." In Montgomery's view, Irish workers needed to learn the lessons of solidarity with other ethnic groups in the work force as the price of admission to the trade union movement. That is they had to move beyond ethnic neighborhood and parish loyalties in order to identify with existing trade unions, which were usually led by Native Americans, British, Welsh, Scottish, or Ulster-born individuals.[39]

On the other side, it required suspension of Know Nothing and nativist attitudes toward Irish Catholics to embrace their membership in, let alone leadership of, existing or emerging unions of skilled craftsmen. In the pragmatic manner of American thinking, however, it was the only way to conduct successful labor organization amid a work force as diverse as that in America. It was not easy, however, nor did it happen without innumerable lapses and setbacks.

While Irish workers had to transcend parochial loyalties, that is not to say that such associations were not helpful in organizing and especially in strikes. The networks of parish, nationalist, social and political connections were much in evidence in support of trade union activity in Troy and Cohoes, New York, in the study by Daniel Walkowitz covering the period from the 1850s to the 1880s.[40] When their livelihoods were threatened by wage cuts and technological innovation, unions, especially the molders of Troy, would resist and they could count on individuals having multiple membership in the union, Clan na Gael, Fenians and Labor and Land Leagues, as well as Irish-dominated political machines for support.

When employers imported strikebreakers, the entire worker community (in which Irish people were the largest ethnic group) ostracized them and not infrequently attacked them in order to preserve what had been gained through trade unionism.

In Troy and Cohoes there were important examples of ethnic collaboration in the face of threats to their employment and working conditions. Original organizers of the molders union were skilled artisans who were native American, Scottish or English Protestants; but by the 1870s, leadership was largely Irish Catholic. "By then," in Walkowitz's account, "such workers were overwhelmingly Irish, and associational traditions of resistance which had carried over from Ireland also shaped their militancy." The depression of the 1870s in Troy produced a "reign of terror" and allegations of Molly Maguireism were heard in the town.[41] The crisis in Troy and Cohoes was comparable to that in Schuylkill County during this same period and, as far as trade unions were concerned, results were much the same. Capitalist owners overcame the protest of workers' organizations.

During the prosperity of the 1860s, induced by the Civil War, trade unions revived and, with railroads expanding the market, a number of national unions appeared (though very few endured through the severe depression of the 1870s). There was even a premature attempt at centralization in the labor movement in the form of the National Labor Union. A modest Irish representation emerged among the leadership of these organizations. Some individuals of Celtic origin had sufficiently paid their dues through toil in the vineyards of organized labor to be recognized and accepted into the fledgling fraternity of American labor leaders.

This was also a time in America when movements such as the eight-hour leagues, the Greenbackers and a revival of land reform got under way—largely in the political arena. To a considerable degree they sprang from the Protestant, abolitionist traditions in New England. Champions of the eight-hour day, Ira Steward, George McNeil and George Gunton drew much of their inspiration from William Lloyd Garrison of Massachusetts. As pointed out by Eric Foner and David Montgomery, it was at this point that Irish labor activists (immigrants or their sons) began to make common cause with these other forces for labor reform.[42] It was not unusual for them to step from trade union officialdom to candidacy in such organizations as the Greenback Labor party or either of the two major parties.

A further current which, according to David Montgomery, favorably disposed Protestant reformers and trade unionists toward Irish activists was the temperance movement sponsored by Fr. Theobald Mathew, who urged the total abstinence pledge.[43] The extent of its impact, however, may have been exaggerated.

In the mining industry, the forementioned John Siney's pioneer work in Schuylkill County led to his becoming a founder in 1873 and three-term president of the Miners National Association, which effected a short-lived combination of local mining unions stretching as far west as Illinois, until it was wiped out by the depression of the 1870s. In 1869 he had turned down the opportunity to become first vice president of the National Labor Union (NLU). But he did involve himself in the Labor Reform party, which grew out of the NLU, serving as president of this party's Schuylkill branch. When the Greenback Labor party succeeded this earlier party, Siney became its chairman in Schuykill County.[44] Kate Mullaney, a pioneering leader and president of the Collar Laundresses' union in Troy, New York, became a vice-president of the National Labor Union.[45]

Along with Mother Jones (see Chapter 5) Kate Mullaney was one of the earliest female Irish activists, but others began to appear in the 1890s. "Rebel Cork" was represented in the person of Leonora Barry (a widow with two children) who found work in a hosiery mill exploitive, joined the Knights of Labor, and eventually became a full-time organizer and troubleshooter for that noble institution. Leonora O'Reilly learned about unionism from her mother, an active member of the Knights of Labor. Leonora O'Reilly became a highly visible figure in the labor movement serving as an organizer for the United Garment Workers Union and a leading figure in the Women's Trade Union League.

Elizabeth Flynn Rogers officiated as master workman of Chicago Area District 24 of the Knights of Labor. In Chicago, Irish immigrant Agnes Nestor emerged as a glove industry unionist and went on to become international president of the Glove Workers Union. The first woman organizer to be employed by the American Federation of Labor was Mary Kenney O'Sullivan, a trade unionist in the craft of bookbinding. She was a founder of the Women's Trade Union League in 1903.

Leaders in organizing public schoolteachers around the turn of the century were Margaret Haley in Chicago and Kate Kennedy in San Francisco.[46]

Another vice president of the politically oriented NLU was Thomas M. Dolan from Detroit, who was active in cigar-making unionism. Also from the cigar-makers trade was John Heenan, Catholic, Irish-born and a vice president of the Cigar Makers International Union by 1872.[47]

Martin Foran was the son of an immigrant family from pre-famine Ireland which settled in northeastern Pennsylvania near the New York line. His mother was Catherine O'Donnell, and his father, James Foran, untypically for an Irishman, operated a farm and conducted a cooperage. After Civil War service in the cavalry, Martin Foran completed an apprenticeship in cooperage, worked as a journeyman in Cleveland reviving a local union of coopers there, and became its president. His participation in forming the International Union of Coopers led to his election as its president for three years. Better educated than most of those cited in this early group of Irish activists, he studied law and embarked on a political career in the Democratic party, which saw him rise from prosecuting attorney in Cleveland, United States congressman, and finally a Court of Common Pleas judge in Cleveland. While in Congress, he was instrumental in passage of legislation prohibiting import of contract labor. All the while he retained close associations with unionists.[48]

A career resembling that of Foran was mounted by Patrick Collins, a child of the famine, whose mother emigrated with him to Boston when he was four. As a boy, he was subjected to nativist prejudice in public school and in unsuccessful attempts to enter apprenticeship. Later, working in a furniture factory, he became acquainted with a member of the Fenian Brotherhood who enabled young Collins to join the Fenians and eventually to become an organizer for it. Meanwhile Collins collaborated with others to form the Upholsterers Union of Boston of which he became president. His union commitment involved serving as a delegate to the Boston Trades Assembly, a body composed of representatives of local unions in the city. Comfortable with leadership, he entered Democratic party politics in 1867 and ran successfully for the Massachusetts legislature (first in the House, later in its Senate). Studying law along the way, he proceeded, after passing the bar, to election to the federal Congress and finally to become the first Irish mayor of Boston. In politics he was known as a champion of civil rights for Catholic citizens.[49]

Hugh McLaughlin was an important figure in the springing up of Irish immigrants (and their sons) in the labor movement. It is known that he was born in Donegal, of Catholic parents in 1831 and, after several years of schooling, worked in a variety of jobs until coming to America in 1853. Moving about the country with remarkable frequency, he finally chose, after trying numerous other jobs, work in the iron industry. On the strength of organizing a local lodge of the Sons of Vulcan in Chicago, he eventually won election, twice as the president of that national union of iron puddlers, before launching a long and successful career in politics. During his entire political career, he kept a foot in labor's camp as a delegate to the Industrial Congresses which grew from the ashes of the National Labor Union. His political calling extended from service in the Illinois legislature to the Democratic machine in New York City.[50] He, as well as Patrick Collins and Martin Foran, demonstrated the ease with which one could embrace politics from a base in trade unionism. Whether this tendency worked to the advantage of permanency in the union movement or not remains an open question.

In any case, these early union officials of Irish descent (especially those who were not sidetracked into politics) opened a road for their successor Irish ethnics to achieve eminence in organized labor, one of the three preferred avenues of opportunity for a displaced peasant people—the others being religious life and politics. Of their cohorts, some chose ministries in the Roman Catholic Church, and in time numbers of them—John Spalding, John Hughes and James Gibbons to mention a few—became a highly visible cadre in that Church's hierarchy (to the consternation of some of their German and French coreligionists). Still others made a profession of politics and gravitated to big city Democratic machines in New York, Boston, Chicago and elsewhere, where Irishmen frequently emerged as party chieftains. Our focus, however, is on a dozen individuals who chose the organization of workers as their vocation. Their stories constitute the body of this study.

NOTES

1. Victor A. Walsh, "The Great Famine and Its Consequences," *Eire-Ireland* (Winter 1988): 6.

2. David Fitzpatrick, *Irish Emigration*, 1801–1921. (Dundalgan Press, 1984), 27.

3. Sean O'Faolain, *The Story of the Irish People* (New York: Avenel Books, 1949), 119–27.

4. Howard Harris, "The Eagle to Watch and the Harp to Tune: Irish

Immigrants, Politics and Early Industrialization in Paterson, New Jersey, 1824-1836," *Journal of Social History* (Spring 1990): 575-97.

5. Stanley Lebergott, *The Americans: An Economic Record* (New York: Norton, 1984), 187.

6. Fitzpatrick, *Irish Emigration*, 9; Kerby A. Miller, *Emigrants and Exiles* (New York: Oxford University Press, 1985), 295; Walsh, "The Great Famine and Its Consequences," 19.

7. Fitzpatrick, *Irish Emigration*, 7-8, 20-21.

8. Ibid., 3; Maldwyn A. Jones, *American Immigration* (Chicago: University of Chicago Press, 1960), 94; U.S. Bureau of Census, *Historical Statistics of the United States: Colonial Times to 1970* Series c89 119 (Washington, D.C.: U.S. Government Printing Office, 1975), 105-6; Miller, *Emigrants and Exiles,* 291.

9. U.S. Bureau of Census, *Historical Statistics of U.S.* 106.

10. Data here presented are based on recorded emigration, but Cormac O'Grada, a student of the subject, believes much of it went unrecorded. He therefore offers a rough estimate of total emigration from Ireland from 1815 to 1921 of eight million and believes at least two thirds of it was destined for the United States. See Cormac O'Grada, "Irish Emigration to the United States in the Nineteenth Century," in *America and Ireland 1776-1976,* David N. Doyle and Owen D. Edwards eds. (Westport, Conn.: Greenwood Press, 1980), 93-94.

11. Fitzpatrick, *Irish Emigration,* 25; Terry Coleman, *Going to America* (Garden City, N.Y.: Doubleday, 1973), Chap. 9.

12. John Cogley, *Catholic America* (Garden City, N.Y.: Doubleday, 1973), 37-40; Andrew Greeley, *The Catholic Experience* (New York: Doubleday, 1967), 122-23; Elizabeth M. Geffen, "Industrial Development and Social Crisis, 1841-1854," in: *Philadelphia: A 300-Year History*, Russell F. Weighley, ed. (New York: Norton, 1982), 356-57.

13. For an overview of growth in the American economy in the nineteenth century, see: D.C. North, T.L. Anderson and P.J. Hill, *Growth and Welfare in the American Past* (Englewood Cliffs, N.J.: Prentice Hall, 1983), 27-38. For employment growth by major industry group, see, Stanley Lebergott, *Manpower in Economic Growth* (New York: McGraw Hill, 1964), 510. For Irish participation see Dennis Clark, "The Irish in the American Economy," in *The Irish in America*, P.J. Drudy, ed. (Cambridge, England: Cambridge University Press, 1985), 234-38.

14. Lebergott, *Manpower In Economic Growth*, 510.

15. Jones, *American Immigration*, 118.

16. Ibid., 121-23; Miller, *Emigrants and Exiles*, 321; Greeley, *The Catholic Experience*, 154, 170.

17. See Donald H. Akenson, *Being Had: Historians, Evidence and The Irish in North America* (Port Credit, Ont.: P.D. Meany, 1985), especially Chap.3 ,"The Historiography of the Irish Americans;" Donald H. Akenson, *Small Differences: Irish Catholics and Irish Protestants, 1815-1922* (Kingston, Ont.: McGill-Queens University Press, 1988); David N. Doyle, "The Irish As Urban Pioneers In The United States, 1850-1870," *Journal of American Ethnic History* (Fall 1990-Winter 1991): 36-57; Lawrence J. McCaffrey, *Textures of Irish America* (Syracuse, N.Y.: Syracuse University Press, 1992), 183n. See also Review of *Small Differences* by David W. Miller in *Labour/Travailleur*, 23 (Spring 1989), 366-67.

18. Lebergott, *Manpower in Economic Growth*, 232; Lance E. Davis, Richard A. Easterlin, et al., *American Economic Growth* (New York: Harper and Row, 1972), 98; Roger D. McGrath, "Two Silver Kings," in *American Irish Newsletter* (August–September 1987), 1,4.

19. W.H.A. Williams, "Irish Traditional Music in the United States," in Doyle and Edwards, *America and Ireland, 1776–1976*, 283–84.

20. Oscar Handlin, *Boston's Immigrants* (New York: Atheneum, 1977); Robert Ernst, *Immigrant Life in New York City* (Port Washington, N.Y.: Ira J. Friedman, Inc., 1949).

21. James P. Walsh, "The Irish in Early San Francisco," in *The San Francisco Irish*, James P. Walsh, ed. (San Francisco: Irish Literary and Historical Society, 1978), 21. Dynamic mobility is evident in David M. Emmons's account of Irish people converging on Butte, Montana in the last quarter of the nineteenth century. They came to work in the copper mines of Butte from a wide variety of other areas—Michigan's upper peninsula, Pennsylvania's anthracite region, silver and gold mines in California, Colorado, Utah and Nevada. A number came directly from West Cork, one of the few locations of mining in Ireland. Experienced miners in large part, they sought better wages, stable employment and a town understood to be a substantially Irish community. See David M. Emmons, *The Butte Irish* (Urbana: University of Illinois Press, 1989), 13–19.

22. Richard K. Vedder and Lowell E. Gallaway, "The Geographical Distribution of British and Irish Emigrants to the United States after 1800," *Scottish Journal of Political Economy* 19 (1972): 29–31.

23. U.S. Bureau of Census, *Historical Statistics of the U.S.*, 105–6.

24. Emmet Larkin, "The Devotional Revolution in Ireland, 1850–75," *American Historical Review* (June 1971): 651-52.

25. Irish nationalists opposed them as a form of linguistic imperialism designed to root out Gaelic language and culture since they were conducted in English, but the Catholic Church dropped its opposition after winning the right to teach religion in these tax-supported schools. See Lawrence J. McCaffrey, *Ireland from Colony to Nation State* (Englewood Cliffs, N.J.: Prentice Hall, 1979), 52.

26. George McNeil, ed., *The Labor Movement: The Problem of Today* (Boston: A.M. Bridgeman, 1887), 118–20.

27. Carl Wittke, *The Irish in America* (Baton Rouge: Louisiana State University Press, 1956), 216. The same view is expressed in George Rogers Taylor, *The Transportation Revolution* (New York: Holt, Rhinehart and Winston, 1951), 287.

28. *Pennsylvanian*, June 5, 1835; Dennis Clark, *The Irish in Philadelphia* (Philadelphia: Temple University Press, 1973), 18.

29. For an excellent account on which this section is based see Peter Way, "Shovel and Shamrock: Irish Workers and Labor Violence in Digging of the Chesapeake and Ohio Canal," *Labor History* (Winter 1989): 489–519.

30 Peter Way, *Common Labour* (Cambridge, England: Cambridge University Press, 1993), Chaps. 7, 8, 9; Dennis Clark, *Hibernia America* (Westport, Conn.: Greenwood Press, 1986), Chap. 2 "Diggers;" Taylor, *The Transportation Revolution*, 289.

31. Marianne Schmitt, "Early Irish Workers Shunned in Sickness," *Suburban Advertiser*, March 14, 1985, 1; John M. Nugent, "Cholera Killed 57 Gandy Dancers at Malvern," *Main Line Times*, March 14, 1957,1–2; *Village Record*, November 7, 1832 (from the archives of Chester County Historical Society, West Chester, PA).

32. Clark, *Hibernia America*, Chap. 3, "Steel Rail Men."

33. Although there were numerous Irish enlistments in the Union Army, encouraged by Fenians to gain experience for future risings in Ireland, and the highly visible example of the all-Irish 69th Regiment (known in WWI as the "Fighting 69th"), nevertheless, according to J.H. McPherson, Irishmen "were

the most under-represented group in proportion to population, followed by German Catholics." He argues that the data, inexact though it is, proves that position. See James M. McPherson, *Battle Cry of Freedom* (New York: Ballantine Books, 1989), 606. See also exchange of letters on this issue in *Irish Edition* (Philadelphia), October 1991, 9 (Frank Boyle), November 1991, 9 (James McPherson).

34. David Montgomery, "The Irish and the American Labor Movement," in *American and Ireland 1776–1976*, 209; McPherson, *Battle Cry of Freedom*, 609–11; Iver Berstein, *The New York Draft Riots* (New York: Oxford University Press, 1990), 41, 100–24; David R. Roediger, *The Wages of Whiteness* (New York: Verso, 1991), 133–34; Dennis Clark, "Images and Indignation: How Cartoons Shape Our Views" (A teaching kit with thirty-seven cartoons dealing with the Irish, drawn from newspapers and magazines, including commentary) unpublished, no date.

35. Anthony F. C. Wallace, *St. Clair* (New York: Knopf, 1987), 358–60; Grace Palladino, *Another Civil War* (Urbana: University of Illinois Press, 1990), 104–17.

36. Wayne G. Broehl, Jr., *The Molly Maguires*, (Cambridge, Mass.: Harvard University Press, 1964), 321.

37. Wallace, *St. Clair*, 388–403.

38. Gowen was the son of an Irish Protestant family whose father, James Gowen, had migrated to Philadelphia in penury but became a wealthy merchant in that city. See Broehl, *The Molly Maguires*, 104.

39. David Montgomery, *Beyond Equality* (New York: Knopf, 1967), 126–27.

40. Daniel J. Walkowitz, *Worker City, Company Town* (Urbana: University of Illinois Press, 1981).

41. Ibid., 251–52.

42. Eric Foner, "Class, Ethnicity, and Radicalism in the Gilded Age," *Marxist Perspectives* (Summer 1978), 6; Montgomery, *Beyond Equality*, 126.

43. Montgomery, *Beyond Equality*, 204.

44. Wallace, *St. Clair*, 401–2.

45. Walkowitz, *Worker City, Company Town*, 174.

46. Hasia R. Diner, *Erins Daughters in America* (Baltimore: Johns Hopkins Press, 1983), 100–102; *Biographical Dictionary of American Labor Leaders*, 1984 (contains biographies of all but Kate Mullaney and Elizabeth Flynn Rogers).

47. Montgomery, *Beyond Equality*, 126, 204, 464, 465.

48. Ibid., 205, 214–15; *Biographical Dictionary of American Labor Leaders*, 1984, 229.

49. Montgomery, *Beyond Equality*, 212–13.

50. *Biographical Dictionary of American Labor Leaders*, 1984, 381-82.

2

PATHFINDERS: McGUIRE AND POWDERLY

On a winter evening in 1906, a grizzled, worn-out veteran of the labor wars sat at the kitchen table of a small house on Byron Street in Camden, New Jersey. He suffered from an illness of several years duration, but on that evening was, abstractedly, playing a game of hands with his eighteen-year-old daughter, Kathryn, who helped support the family with work in Hunts Pen Factory. His hair was white and he looked very tired. The house was unheated for lack of money to pay for coal. Abruptly, he began to shake and, shortly, collapsed. Lingering semicomatose for three days mumbling barely audibly about carpenters' unions needing his help, he died on the eighteenth of February. He was fifty-three. Thus ended the worldly tenure of Peter James McGuire. Recognized in his prime as the outstanding American labor leader, he was in demand all over the nation for organizing and counseling labor groups.[1] The impoverished condition of his last years typified treatment accorded pioneers of the trade union cause.

Some eighteen years later, in a comfortable home on Fifth Street NW, in Washington, D.C., not far from the campus of the Catholic University of America, a contemporary of McGuire, Terence Vincent Powderly, drew his final breath at age seventy-five. The contrast was dramatic, for he had concluded his leadership in the labor movement thirty years earlier and had subsequently pursued a career in law and government service which, while not actually lucrative, enabled him to avoid, in his last years, the poverty endured by McGuire. Indeed, he had not sacrificed himself (for reasons of health and otherwise) in the cause of labor to the extent that McGuire had. Although his dedication was less than total, his contribution to the movement was of comparable significance.

Of the three most important labor leaders active in the last three decades of the nineteenth century, two—Peter J. McGuire and Terence

V. Powderly—were of Irish descent. They rank in significance with Samuel Gompers in their contribution to the movement of organized labor in America. Sons of Irish immigrants, they both had a deep sense of social justice due in considerable measure to their ancestry in a land oppressed by a great colonial power. It is not extravagant to argue that the American Federation of Labor (AFL) could not have succeeded without the building block of the carpenters' union, an organization crafted almost single-handedly by P.J. McGuire. Neither is it unreasonable to attribute the AFL's growth and durability in large measure to the organizational leadership and counsel of McGuire, its secretary from 1886 to 1889. Indeed, it is not excessive to credit Terence Powderly with making peace between the Catholic Church and workers' organizations, essential in an immigrant work force substantially Catholic in its affiliation. This Powderly acomplished during his tenure of fourteen years as leader of the Knights of Labor, in its prime the largest labor organization in nineteenth-century America.

It was McGuire whose creative energies have bequeathed a holiday to remind thoughtful citizens of the nobility of work and the dignity of those engaged in it. It was he who conceived the idea of celebrating labor just as we celebrate Independence Day, Thanksgiving and religious occasions important in our heritage. Exerting his splendid capacity for persuasion and exhortation in speeches and in personal contacts, he was the prime mover of the initial parade held in New York in 1882. He lobbied for and propagandized for institutionalizing the holiday through editorials in *The Carpenter*, a monthly paper he founded in 1881 and edited until 1902. This achievement was possible due to McGuire's widespread associations and the high regard he enjoyed in labor circles across the country.[2]

These two men, born little more than three years apart, were raised in large immigrant families, Powderly in a small northeastern Pennsylvania community only recently emerged from the frontier stage, and McGuire in a ghetto on the lower east side of Manhattan. By occupation each was a skilled craftsman who had undergone a thorough apprenticeship. Powderly enjoyed a few more years of grammar school, but both men were devoted to learning well beyond their experience of formal schooling. Remarkably accomplished with words, they wrote effectively and prolifically, but used words even more persuasively to exhort their audiences. Their careers embodied the various ideologies circulating in the American republic of the post–Civil War era. Personally affected by the intense depression of the 1870s, their attitudes were profoundly influenced by it. They shared a deep sense of need for an economy that would treat workers fairly.

In both cases, their ideas evolved. Although McGuire, heavily influenced by German-speaking socialists, began well to the left of Powderly, the views of both men gravitated toward the center. In their mature years, they veered away from the politics of their youth.

On the other hand, they differed greatly in physical appearance and behavioral style. Although about equal in height (McGuire was five feet eight and a half inches, Powderly five feet nine), with his shock of strawberry blond hair, strong gray eyes and florid complexion, McGuire was emotionally tough, physically robust and dedicated to almost continuous tours of exhausting organizing—in the tradition of William Sylvis, fabled organizer of the molders' union. McGuire found solace through indulgence in strong drink (and was later confounded by it).

Powderly, a teetotaler, was more fragile physically and suffered life-long respiratory problems and intestinal difficulties. Never burdened with excess weight, he was myopic, wore thick lenses and avoided demanding trips where possible. He was foppish, inordinately sensitive to criticism, inclined to be vindictive. While McGuire was a classic case of burnout by age fifty and finally succumbed to alcoholic excess, Powderly was more careful about his health and lived five years beyond the biblical three score and ten. He even departed from total abstinence in later years for an occasional cocktail as a concession to better health on advice of his doctor. Both men married again after the death of the first wife and were survived by the second spouse.

Each of these two men found inspiration for his career in the heritage of oppressive conditions experienced by their parents in Ireland and as greenhorn immigrants struggling to find their way in the industrializing society of nineteenth-century America. With this background, the language of protest came easily to their lips.

MCGUIRE'S PARENTS

McGuire's parents came to America as refugees from the potato famine in the latter half of the 1840s decade. His mother, Catharine Hand O'Riley, was a typical victim of the potato blight which reduced the population of Ireland from over eight million to six million through starvation, famine-related disease and emigration. She came to America at age twenty-one, with two surviving children of the eight she bore from her first marriage at fifteen.

Her first husband, Matthew O'Riley, did not survive Ireland's disaster as a colonial people of the British empire, an empire whose leaders, Prime Minister John Russell and Charles Trevelyan of Treasury in particular, who, blaming the tragedy on the people themselves, made pitifully inadequate efforts to relieve the suffering of their conquered subjects. Their refusal to do more arose out of contempt for the Irish and rigid adherence to a laissez faire ideology. Regular reports of thousands of dead bodies rotting unburied along the roads of Ireland were of no avail. In their minds, the market had to be the essential mechanism for solving the problem and severe limits had to be maintained on any debt incurred by British government to relieve the plight of a starving people.[3]

In 1847 John James McGuire emigrated from Ireland. On board ship, according to family tradition, he met Catharine Hand O'Riley, a widow with daughters Mary and Catharine, age five and three, respectively. A bachelor, he began his search for a livelihood in New York and married the widow O'Riley there in 1850. The fact that they settled in New York suggests that their poverty was such that they were unable to seek beyond the immigrant ghettos of their port of entry.

The emigré couple and their two children became tenement dwellers in the seventeenth ward of the lower east side of Manhattan, an area chiefly composed of German immigrants, but dotted with Irish enclaves. The couple produced five children, of whom the first, born July 6, 1852, was Peter James. He saw three sisters, Susan, Theresa (Tessy), and Kathryn, and one brother, John James, Jr., added to the family. John J. Senior supported his growing family with wages earned as a porter at Lord & Taylor's department store.

During inflation—brought on by government issues of greenbacks to finance the Civil War—real wages fell. The McGuire family's plight, reasonably desperate for a porter with seven children to feed in 1863, was enough to induce John J. McGuire to serve in the Union Army for two years under an assumed name. At the time, affluent draftees found it possible to hire someone else to serve in their place for a consideration of from three hundred to five hundred dollars. Authorities were preoccupied with filling quotas, rather than verifying the identity of draftees. John J. McGuire, therefore, could find financial relief by reporting for service in the place of a draftee of means sufficient to hire a stand-in—and did so.[4]

P.J. McGuire never had time to write his autobiography and, less introspective than Powderly, it is doubtful that he would have chosen to do so. Nevertheless, he vividly described life in the seventeenth ward for a congressional committee in 1885:

Look at this city, with its long rows of tenement barracks, with its working people shrinking back into alleys and back lanes and huddled together into deep cellars and basements. In the 17th ward of this city the average space of land occupied by each inhabitant is 9 1/2 feet square—but little more than a living grave—filth, foul air abounding, the sunshine of heaven denied them, crowded and packed together; such conditions have been more destructive to human life than even war itself and all its horrors. In these tenements of the city, 28,000 children are born every year, 10,000 die annually, and thousands are sent to prison, and yet the majority of these people have paid by way of rent enough to purchase for themselves, not only one house but several, and still after all this outlay they are at the cruel mercy of landlords, who on failure to pay the month's rent, will cast them out into the streets homeless and houseless.

By Mr. George: [Senator from Mississippi]

Q. Have you made any personal inspection?—A. Oh, yes. I was born in this city and I know the city thoroughly.

Q. I mean an inspection of what you have just described.—A. I speak from personal knowledge. I speak of the ward in which I was born and in which I have resided, except when I have been traveling.

By the Chairman:

Q. Which ward is that?—A. The seventeenth.[5]

Social historians confirm McGuire's version of these conditions. The typical immigrant family lived in a tenement of four or five stories, divided in such a way as to contain four families on each floor. For each family, cooking, eating, sleeping, washing and fighting was carried on in an eight-by-ten foot room and a bedroom six feet by ten. It was not unusual for such a family to take in another family to board. A court-yard in the rear hung with the day's wash, and on its muddy floor stood an outhouse for the accommodation of all families in the building. The crowded surroundings tunneled with dark hallways, "oozing with pollution," stinking of filth and crawling with roaches were spawning grounds for disease. Cholera was a constant hazard and periodically ravaged immigrant hovels. The Irish in particular had an abnormally high mortality rate.

Families moved frequently, renting by the week or the month. They were free to look for more economical lodging or could be evicted for failure to pay rent, normally due in advance. It was a transient town, where those who believed they could do better elsewhere inside or outside the area did not hesitate to change. Social life revolved around the neighborhood grogshop, and each block had several. Saloon keepers were usually involved in ward politics and could serve customers in many ways, in addition to offering them whiskey at three cents a glass. Irish people relied heavily on parish, pub and politics to see them through the depressions of 1855 and 1857.[6]

Another aspect of the immigrant experience in New York was the vivid contrast between their abysmal poverty and the prodigious wealth in evidence only a few blocks away. The seventeenth ward, where the McGuires lived, was contiguous to Stuyvesant Square with its ambience of elegant residences. For a perceptive youth like Peter McGuire, this environment had its impact. His feelings about it must have deepened with the departure of his father for the Union Army in 1863. In March of 1864, he was obliged to leave Saint John's Parish School and, at age eleven, begin contributing to the support of the family, by now grown to seven children. Nevertheless, he must have been well schooled in the English language, "To judge from his subsequent literary output," observed labor historian Walter Galenson.

Further testament to his journalistic ability appeared in a review of *The Carpenter* (which McGuire edited and for which he did most of the writing for twenty years). Full of praise, it was published in *The New York Sun* on March 30, 1887. Among other favorable comments it observed:

Next in the editorial page, an aggregation of pertinent, sensible, practical para-graphs and articles calling forth by occurrences in the country or the Brotherhood. It is a peculiarity of this little journal that every line that is writ-ten for it is distinguished for the simplicity, directness and good taste of the language used. In this respect the Carpenter could be read with profit in the offices of some of the most prosperous newspapers even in New York.

A reading of monthly issues of *The Carpenter* leaves no doubt of the validity of these comments about McGuire's talent as a wordsmith.[7]

The eleven-year-old McGuire occupied himself with the usual boyish jobs of hawking newspapers, stable boy, shining shoes and errand boy for the Lord & Taylor department store. For one of his intelligence and appetite for learning, his father's departure for army service undoubtedly moved him to reflect upon the justice of so much poverty in the presence of equally visible wealth.

Relations between John James McGuire and his son Peter were complex and are difficult to comprehend. A famine refugee, the elder McGuire found it a heavy burden to support his growing family. Yet he was literate and, in fact, taught Gaelic at Peter Cooper's Institute—indeed, this may have led to his son's subsequent close associations with that school. Furthermore, he undoubtedly taught his son the native language of Ireland, as well as its culture. One of P.J. McGuire's talents was language. He is said to have studied several foreign languages and used them effectively in organizing campaigns.[8] Not only his original mentor in language, the father would have been obliged to sponsor his son's successful application for apprenticeship.

Genuine affection existed between father and son, but serious differences arose. The elder McGuire, an immigrant, sought acceptance in his adopted country, which usually connotes conformity and uncritical patriotism—the antithesis of radical ideas. However, it is not unusual for a son, especially the son of immigrant parents, to turn to an outlook opposite to that of his father, a kind of rebellion. The milieu in New York fostered this attitude, especially for an intelligent and impressionable young man as McGuire was in the early 1870s.

In the midst of P.J. McGuire's agitation for the unemployed in the winter of 1873–1874, conflict with his father erupted. Whether out of exasperation or from a desire to protect his son by currying favor with authorities, John James McGuire denounced his son before the church of Saint John the Evangelist on Sunday, January 11, 1874. He blasted his son for idleness, atheism, radicalism and socialist associations. It was done with the connivance of police commissioner Oliver Gardner, who found John McGuire vulnerable to manipulation when the elder McGuire came to speak to the commissioner about the danger to his son. When P.J. McGuire and the fellow militants sat in at the police station to press for a parade permit on January 13th, Commissioner Gardner confronted him with his father's words. The young man was affected to the extent that he wept. Yet the twenty-one-year-old agitator was not dissuaded from his campaign. He persisted.[9]

The stark reality of abysmal poverty and prolonged jobless spells for breadwinners so characteristic of the 1870s inspired a lifelong commitment by Peter J. McGuire to restore the balance, to establish economic justice, to eliminate the contradiction of great wealth side by side with abysmal poverty. This impulse, it appears, was not comprehensible to his father.

Nevertheless, the estrangement, if there was one at all, was momentary. Evidence of this appears in a letter to Gabriel Edmonston, fellow carpenter official and longtime friend, shortly after the elder McGuire's death on March 17, 1884. McGuire wrote: "This sad occurrence has been hard upon one as my father was very much attached to me. He was sick since the 13th inst. And I was nursing him and he was apparently convalescent when I went away."[10] In spite of long and frequent absences from home and family on labor matters, McGuire does seem to have clung to a remarkably warm and affectionate relationship with his kin.

POWDERLY'S ORIGINS

In *The Path I Trod*, his autobiography, published posthumously, Powderly traces his origins to a French Huguenot (Protestant), Hugo Powderly, who emigrated to Ireland by way of England in 1685 to escape persecution at the hands of the Dragonnades after Louis XIV revoked the edict of Nantes—a fact which may have foreshadowed the Scrantonian's own difficulty with some members of the American hierarchy. Born in Carbondale, Pennsylvania, on January 22, 1849, Powderly was the eleventh of twelve children and last of eight sons born to Terence Powderly and Margaret Walsh, both of whom emigrated from Ireland in 1827, a year after their marriage. They left an Ireland where, although most of the abominable Penal Laws had been repealed, the laws had done their work well. They had secured ownership of the land for Protestants, and had frustrated Catholic hopes.

Beginning earlier, but proceeding vigorously under James I, land in Ireland was systematically transferred to English Protestants through a process of plantation. By 1695 nearly all the good land in the island was in the hands of British landlords.

Penal Laws originated with the English Reformation in Elizabethan times, but late in the seventeenth century the Irish Parliament (peopled with Protestant landlords) undertook to codify them in a far more severe form. The laws were designed to strengthen and perpetuate control of land in Ireland by English Protestants. Their method was to suppress Catholicism through economic and political sanctions. Provisions of the laws prohibited Catholics from voting, entering the legal profession, or running for office. The laws forbade Catholics to own arms, purchase property, establish schools, or educate children abroad. If an eldest son turned Protestant, he could, under the laws, purchase for himself the family estate regardless of the wishes of his parents.

The laws were designed to humble and demoralize the masses of Catholics, thereby entrenching the power of the Protestant minority. The conquered Irish were thus reduced to serving their masters in a system only one notch above slavery. It was ironic that descendants of French Protestant refugees from persecution by French Catholics, now generations later as converts to Catholicism, faced treatment of this kind. Furthermore, the Irish population was growing rapidly due to early marriage, and tenant farmers' small plots were being subdivided to make room for the additional humanity.[11] But levels of subsistence were dwindling. It was in this atmosphere that Powderly's parents found prospects bleak enough to consider the option of migrating.

Terence Powderly senior, a tall, sturdy and strong-willed individual of independent mind, found restrictions on the rights of Catholics intolerable. Caught shooting a rabbit on the estate of Lord Cunningham, he was jailed for three weeks at Trim, County Meath. His crimes, which violated laws laid down by British authority, consisted of "carrying a firearm without warrant of law, trespassing on a gentleman's estate and willfully taking the life of a hare." On release from gaol he announced to his wife, "Let us leave this damn country and go to America where a man may own himself and a gun, too, if he wants to."[12]

An ocean voyage of eight weeks on the Royal George brought the young couple (by now expecting their first born momentarily) to Montreal. At this site where, twenty years hence, thousands of their countrymen fleeing the famine would perish from typhoid fever on the "coffin ships," the Powderlys were more fortunate. A baby girl arrived on July 26, shortly after the couple embarked on a Saint Lawrence riverboat bound for Ogdensburg, New York. One of their shipmates on the Royal George was Thomas Mullen who later crafted some of the first coal-carrying cars for the anthracite mines.[13]

In 1827 the American republic was young, John Quincy Adams was in the White House, and the future looked bright to Irishmen of an enterprising turn of mind. Down to their last shilling at this point, the venturing young family, with its breadwinner earning wages as a farmhand around Ogdensburg, managed to survive and even save something over two years. There followed a journey of 260 miles on foot and, where possible, by stage and haywagon to a frontier community on the Lackawanna River, fifteen miles northeast of Scranton. This settlement eventually became known as Carbondale.

In Carbondale, Powderly's father found work in what would become one of Pennsylvania's major industries, anthracite mining. For fifteen years, he labored in the pits and then, characteristically enterprising, opened his own small mine. In the meantime, the family grew at the rate of one child every two years. In spite of the Powderly mine's failure in 1858, the brood was well provided for. Unlike the stereotype of immigrant Irish forced to settle into flimsy miners' cabins or crowded into tenements in the big cities, like the McGuires, the Powderlys occupied a six-room frame house.

The children remained in school until their early teens, and their father, undaunted by the demise of his business venture, took a position in another of Carbondale's essential enterprises, transportation of coal. He joined the Delaware and Hudson Canal Company, which served the New York market. As an early settler, he earned respect, was elected to the first town council and honored by having one of Carbondale's thoroughfares named after him. His standing in the community enabled him to open doors to desirable jobs for his sons. The Powderlys had twelve children—eight sons and four daughters, three of whom (two daughters and one son) did not survive beyond infancy. Terence Vincent was the youngest son; Sister Margery was the last born.[14] In 1862 son Terence Vincent hired on as a switch attendant with the Delaware and Hudson Railway Company (successor firm to D&H Canal Company).

On the first day of August 1866, after a succession of other jobs on the coal-carrying line, Terence Powderly was, with his father's help, apprenticed to James Dickson, master mechanic in the Delaware and Hudson Railroad shops. It was an association in which the young man took pride. He held his mentor in high esteem, found satisfaction in the work and succeeded admirably in learning the craft. He became a full-fledged journeyman on August 1 of 1869.

IRISH NATIONALISM

Two months into his first year as an apprentice, Powderly made a down payment on his lifelong commitment to Ireland's cause. He bought a five dollar bond of the Irish Republic after listening to a lecture in Scranton by Civil War Colonel John O'Neill about the Fenians and their plan for Ireland's liberation. The speaker had only recently led Irish veterans of the American Civil War on an unsuccessful invasion of Canada, designed to bring pressure on the British. The movement appealed to the teenaged apprentice after listening to tales of that oppressed land from his parents. Thereafter, his talents were often invested in the cause during a lengthy career.

When, in 1867, a British policeman was accidentally killed in Manchester, England, during a successful attempt to free Fenian prisoners being transported in a prison van, three members of the rescue party were later captured, convicted of the killing without conclusive evidence and executed. They became known as the Manchester martyrs. Others imprisoned for alleged involvement included a certain Captain E. Condon, an Irish-American veteran of the American Civil War, who remained in prison. Terence Powderly actively participated in a committee which obtained 21,000 signatures on a petition for Condon's release in 1875. Condon was released in 1878.[15]

Terence Powderly was active in Clan na Gael, originally a secret organization, formed for the purpose of providing financial support for the Fenian Brotherhood in its declining years. Powderly chaired the financial committee of that organization at its convention in Wilkes Barre, Pennsylvania, in 1878. Among his circle of acquaintances was journalist Patrick Ford, an ardent Irish nationalist.[16]

While engaged as a journeyman machinist, Powderly regularly read Patrick Ford's *Irish World*, the leading Irish newspaper in the United States, and his interest in the land question deepened. A friend in Scranton, William Synott, whose relations in Ireland had been evicted by their British landlord, apprised him of the movement of Michael Davitt, founder of the Land League in Ireland. In December of 1878 Powderly was introduced to Davitt in Boston in the company of Irish journalist, John Boyle O'Reilly.

Davitt, a released Fenian prisoner, had capitalized on rural frustration (brought on by an agrarian crisis in the 1870s, caused by poor crops and heavy grain imports from America) to organize Irish farmers. The Land League aimed for a transfer of land from British and Anglo-Irish landlords to Irish tenants. It struck a responsive chord and spread rapidly.

It extended to America through a visit in 1880 by Charles Stewart Parnell, Irish nationalist and member of Parliament, who assumed leadership of the movement with Davitt's blessings. Parnell's fund-raising tour was well received in the United States by the Irish community, and others as well, even to the extent of being invited to address the U.S. House of Representatives. The entire Irish-American community, including the middle class and clergy, who disapproved of the Fenians, enthusiastically supported the Land League.

Early in the tour, Parnell came to Scranton where he was introduced to a large audience by Terence V. Powderly, who had been elected mayor of the town in 1878. According to Powderly, no less than $3,500 were raised for the cause at that time. In August of 1880 a Scranton branch of the Land League was established with Powderly as its elected president. Subsequently, Mayor Powderly was selected as a member of the Central Council of the Land League, and one year after Parnell's visit to Scranton, Powderly attended a national convention in Buffalo which chose him as second vice president of the organization.[17] *The Irish World* of Patrick Ford was full of news about the Land League, and much of the money raised for that cause was funneled through this newspaper. The *World* published figures in 1881 that showed that industrial communities large and small were the largest contributors, and among states, Pennsylvania led them all. Within the Keystone State, the anthracite region was the single biggest source of funds. In that region, where mine workers had struggled to deal with harsh working conditions by forming a union under John Siney and had resorted to more direct means through the Molly Maguires, antilandlordism had a magnetic appeal.[18]

An additional reason was the fact that Terence Powderly travelled extensively in the area speaking on behalf of the Land League. While the Land League had wide appeal and publicity, the Knights of Labor, of which Powderly had become grand master workman in 1879, was still a secret organization of limited scope.

Powderly used these occasions not only to promote the Land League, but also to organize local assemblies of the Knights of Labor. In this way, labor unionism and land reform coalesced. Powderly's advocacy of land reform in Ireland, an issue popular with the Roman Catholic hierarchy, also enhanced his chances of overcoming their disapproval of the Knights of Labor.

Indeed, there was no dearth of critics of land speculators and land monopolists in America in the late nineteenth century. Witness the reception of Henry George's *Progress and Poverty* in 1879 and the single-tax movement which grew from it. His assault on the inequality of incomes, particularly unearned incomes, fitted very well into the ideals of the original American republic which predominated in industrial towns such as Carbondale and Scranton when Powderly was growing up.

For skilled workmen and small entrepreneurs in this milieu, God's earth and human labor were to be used for the benefit of all—for the commonwealth. Work ennobled the individual. It enabled him to realize his talents, his humanity. It amounted to participation in God's creation for it produced goods for society's happiness and progress. The worker-citizen must have a voice in making rules for the shop, as well as for the governance of society. To be a productive member of both, one must be free of tyranny from his employer and his government. An orderly republican form of democracy would make this possible if its members exercised the responsibilities of informed, intelligent citizenship.

Active citizens could ensure that human and civil rights were protected. It is essential that citizens exhibit virtue in the form of restraint of individual indulgence or aggrandizement in favor of the common good. The just society need not be classless, but required equality of opportunity and fair reward for thrift and hard work. Such was the nature of what historians have begun to call artisanal republicanism, an ideal to which Terence Powderly was exposed as a youth.[19]

This background and his embrace of the Land League movement explain Powderly's career-long advocacy of a cooperative commonwealth in which space for producers' cooperative enterprises, family farms and small businesses would be available. It also offers insight to his oft-proclaimed desire to see an end to the "wage system," which, under the advance of large corporations, he believed, reduced the once-proud citizen-craftsman to a mere day laborer, denying him satisfaction in his craft, a voice in the enterprise and little chance for meaningful participation in governance of society.

MCGUIRE'S SOCIALISM

The life of P.J. McGuire was one long adventure in agitation and organizing. It began in earnest when his apprenticeship in carpentry was completed, shortly before the panic of 1873. Ignited by the bankruptcy of Jay Cooke and his Northern Pacific Railroad venture, the economy's severe and long-lasting reversal caused young McGuire to be out of work for eight months and brought far greater distress to large numbers of unskilled immigrants with families. The young journeyman was at the center of controversy over unemployment during his jobless spell.

Peter J. McGuire was initiated into the world of radical ideas after his apprenticeship at the Haines Piano Company on 21st Street and 2nd Avenue in Manhattan. His tutors were German carpenters, who were socialists. At the same time, he also learned to speak German. His grasp of unorthodoxy was enhanced in evening classes at Cooper's Union

Free School, where his budding talent for oral combat was cultivated in the Rising Sun Debating Society. Here he met a youthful Samuel Gompers, who years later recalled him as "Peter McGuire, then an alert attractive young Irish American hungry for information and opportunities to discuss current problems."[20]

In the economic upheaval of the 1870s, over a century ago, Manhattan harbored an infinite variety of reformers, socialists, anarchists and other critics of "the system," numbers of them were refugees from the 1871 commune in Paris. A focal point for arguing such conceptions was the International Workingmen's Association (or First "Internationale"), an organization dominated from their base in London by Karl Marx and Friedrich Engels. These two had moved their headquarters to New York to put it beyond the reach of followers of Russian anarchist Mikhail Bakunin, who had threatened their control of it. Association with it was important to McGuire's radical education. He met regularly at the Tenth Ward Hotel with an inner circle of ten men who debated endlessly notions of how to uplift the condition of workers.[21]

The ideas of Ferdinand LaSalle, carried to America by emigré German socialists, were most persuasive for young McGuire. LaSalle, son of a wealthy German Jewish merchant family in Breslau, accepted Karl Marx's dictum that social revolution was inevitable, but he was convinced that it could be accomplished without violence and that politics could be a catalyst. He is credited with initiating the first independent labor party on the Continent. An advocate of manhood suffrage, he believed it could greatly enhance the power of such a party, enabling it to obtain from the state a series of reforms that would substantially reduce labor exploitation. But the more important goal was to secure from the state capital for enterprises owned and controlled by workers—producers cooperatives, which would attain command over the means of production, eliminate capitalist enterprise and do away with the wage system. LaSalle's concept of using the bourgeois state for assistance to establish a socialist society was, needless to say, anathema to Marx, who saw government exclusively as an instrument of the ruling class.[22]

By the onset of the panic, McGuire was twenty-one and well schooled for rhetorical assault on the establishment. On December 11, 1873, six days after he lost his job at Haines Piano Company, a formidably large group assembled at Coopers Union out of concern for unemployment. From its ranks it formed a Committee of Public Safety modeled after the committee by that name functioning during the French Revolution. McGuire was elected a member of the committee. His campaign as a street corner orator began immediately. He called for the city government to provide jobs for the unemployed on public works and to declare a moratorium on payment of rent. Not long thereafter New York papers began to report concerns about "the dangerous young rebel."

The culmination of his agitation for unemployment relief occurred in January 1874 at Tompkins Square Park, which is bounded by Seventh and Tenth streets and Avenues A and C in the city. By then McGuire had become chairman of the Committee of Public Safety. He called for a rally on January 13th in the square. After bringing pressure on the mayor's office, a permit was issued for the outdoor meeting, but at the eleventh hour, unbeknownst to McGuire, the permit was rescinded. Nevertheless, on the morning of the appointed day from seven to ten thousand people assembled in the park. They were milling about. McGuire was on hand distributing copies of *The Toiler*, a radical paper newly published by him and a socialist comrade, Lucien Saniel. Suddenly, at about ten thirty, before speeches could begin, police on horseback and on foot waded in, using nightsticks to disperse the crowd. Samuel Gompers, present on a street just outside the park, narrowly avoided the attack by "jumping down a cellarway." He described the scene as "an orgy of brutality" in his autobiography.[23]

For Gompers, the Tompkins Square debacle was convincing proof that radicalism was not only ineffective but seriously impeded efforts to improve the lot of workers in the capitalist society of America.[24] McGuire, on the other hand, saw it as a reason to redouble efforts to effect changes in the system, and embarked on a seven-year period of campaigning for socialism of the LaSallean or politically oriented variety. He became the only English-speaking organizer for the Social Democratic party of North America, founded in New York by German-speaking socialists in May of 1874. Moving to New Haven in the fall of 1875, he stumped all of New England for the cause of reform through political action. Earning his livelihood as a journeyman joiner, he established sections of the party in industrial communities.

The character and intensity of McGuire's activities is illustrated by an account of them recorded in his diary for the year of 1877. From February 22 to March 18, he "went on an extended tour of New England." On March 23 he became "engaged in behalf of Wamsutta strikers in New Bedford, Mass. for four weeks and a half." On June 6 he "went to work in New Haven Folding Chair Company." On September 2, he "went to Cincinnati and engaged 6 weeks in local pol. campaign" in which he "got 9,067 votes for Workingmen's Party." On October 23 he was "nominated in New Haven for legislature on Workingmen's Ticket" but declined. In November he was nominated "for town clerk on Workingmen's ticket" and also for assessor, but declined in both cases. From December 26 to 31, he was a "delegate to the Newark Congress of Social Democrats from New Haven."[25]

In the Newark convention, McGuire played a crucial role in the party's decision in favor of deeper political involvement. This move alienated members who objected to immediate political engagement and who insisted on thorough trade union organization as a prerequisite for such an undertaking. The movement also changed its name to the Socialist Labor party, a second mutation for the original Social Democratic party of North America, which in an earlier one in 1876 had become the Workingmen's party. McGuire was a highly visible and vocal participant in the 1876 convention (in Philadelphia) as well.[26]

In August of 1878, McGuire's travels took him as far west as Chicago and Saint Louis, with frequent stops en route and returning, to spread the gospel of LaSallean solidarity.

During the 1870s, a vital and attractive young man, he met and courted a number of young women, among them a Nettie Shoemaker, whom he had met in New Haven in 1877 and again in Cincinnati, the same year he broke off with her according to his diary. Another was Maggie Richardson from upstate New York, a young woman two and a half years his elder, down on her luck and, according to family tradition, suffering from a problem with alcohol. The warmhearted young journeyman was moved by her plight, doubly so because of her five-year-old daughter, Sadie, an engaging child. Subsequently McGuire married the woman on October 3, 1878, and left for Saint Louis with his new-found family almost immediately.[27]

McGuire's three years in Saint Louis were filled with the same intense activity as his days in New Haven, but they saw a gradual shift in emphasis toward trade unionism. Supporting his newly established family through carpentry, he, nevertheless, found time to successfully lobby legislators in Jefferson City for passage of a series of LaSallean labor reform bills. His first breakthrough was a law creating the Missouri Bureau of Labor Statistics in April of 1879. Two years later, his efforts led to laws restricting child labor, protecting workers from competition of prison labor and one requiring ventilation of mines.

He lobbied as the representative of the Saint Louis Trade and Labor Assembly, a central labor body in the city, where he had been quickly recognized for his leadership qualities. Not the least of his advantages was a fluent command of German, developed among his German-speaking comrades in New York and welcomed here where it was commonly spoken.

Successful promotion of the Bureau of Labor Statistics led to McGuire's appointment as the bureau's deputy commissioner. He accepted, but constrictions of a career as a public official did not suit his activist personality, and late in March 1880 after six months in the job, he resigned. The Greenback movement (inspired by a desire of farmers and some labor groups to counteract persistent price deflation in post–Civil War America), which attracted Powderly in Pennsylvania (and on whose ticket he was elected mayor of Scranton in 1878), held a national party convention in Chicago in June of 1880. McGuire was on hand as the delegate of Saint Louis socialists. He held no brief for currency reform and in fact considered it meaningless, but lacking any faith in the major parties he became involved with this third party hoping to invest it with socialist principles. At the Chicago convention, which nominated General James B. Weaver for president, McGuire served on the platform committee with Adolph Douai, the German-American, socialist editor and author, and Denis Kearney, the San Francisco anti-oriental demagogue, who enjoyed a considerable following at this time.

Indeed, in spite of his reservations, McGuire jumped in with both feet and became involved in the Missouri State Convention of the party as a member of its platform committee and secretary of the convention—even to the point of being nominated as Greenback candidate for secretary of state before declining the honor. That summer and fall, his diary records that he campaigned for the party through towns in Missouri, Indiana, Kansas and in Cincinnati and Louisville.

In October of 1880, perhaps out of funds to support his ailing wife and small daughter, he resumed carpentry at a place called Filley's Foundry and began to concentrate on trade union activity. By the spring of 1881, he was the secretary of a strike committee for a new carpenters' local union that was successful in raising wages to three dollars a day. It was his first successful experience with trade union leadership.[28]

BUILDING A BROTHERHOOD

By the spring of 1881, Peter J. McGuire, at age twenty-nine, was ready to undertake a venture for which he will always be remembered—organizing a national union of carpenters. He began by forming a preliminary committee with socialist comrade Gustav Luebkert to establish a nationwide brotherhood of carpenters. They invited delegates from sixty-two local carpenters' unions for a convention in Chicago on August 8, 1881. Moderately successful, it drew thirty-five delegates from fifteen cities representing approximately 4,800 carpenters.[29] It elected McGuire the full-time secretary of the union at a salary of fifteen dollars a week and provided a focus for his impressive creative energies for the next twenty years. On May Day 1881, three months before the convention, McGuire published the first issue of *The Carpenter*, a monthly consisting of both English and German columns—the latter written by August Overbeck—to propagandize benefits of the brotherhood and publicize its successes. In October of 1886 McGuire reported circulation had grown to over 22,000 for *The Carpenter*.[30]

The goal of building a brotherhood now absorbed him. It was a noble and selfless work from which he reaped nothing of material rewards. All of the charisma, skill, continuous journeying and sacrifice he had devoted to socialism were now committed to trade unionism.

Historians do not concur on the question of whether he gradually gave up his ideal of a cooperative commonwealth or worker-controlled economy. Traditional chroniclers John R. Commons and Selig Perlman were convinced that he did, but Mark Erlich, of more recent vintage, is confident that McGuire held tenaciously to the idea, while establishing a strong democratic union as a preliminary to achieving the broader goals of eliminating the wage system and overcoming the grip of capitalism on society. He believed, according to Erlich, that to realize these ultimate ends would require a long, hard struggle, and in the meantime trade union institutions could foster class consciousness among workers while advancing their pay and job conditions so that they would, one day, be prepared to establish a society based on progressive principles.

It was in this sense that, says Erlich, he never became a "business unionist," a term denoting those without any long-range plan, lacking any sense of worker solidarity and with no idea of society's reform. According to Erlich, the pure and simple approach of incremental improvement in wages and hours was for McGuire only a concession to immediate realities. It was feasible for the present, but in time more basic restructuring of institutions was, in McGuire's mind, essential.[31] It is clear, however, that circumstances prevented his realizing the long-range goals which, Erlich believes, he continued to envision.

In the midst of his struggle to establish a national organization of carpenters, McGuire faced personal tragedy. His wife Maggie died on January 26, 1884, after several years of serious illness and hospitalization.[32] Tempted to give up the struggle, McGuire, nevertheless, carried on with typical tenacity. In less than a year, he married again. On October 16, 1884, in New York's Church of the Nativity, he married Christina Iris Wolff, a woman thirteen years his junior.

"Teenie" Wolff, a Lutheran from Stapleton, Staten Island, bore him three daughters (Lillian, Kathryn, and Myrtle) and one son, P.J., Jr. She also raised Sadie, his stepdaughter by his first marriage, then twelve. Christina Wolff patiently suffered the tribulations of McGuire's irregular income, his illnesses, treachery at the hand of fellow union officials and widowhood for thirteen years after his death in 1906.[33]

In the course of developing the carpenters' union, McGuire often had occasion to review its progress as well as the principles he professed for it. One revealing piece, entitled "A Chapter in Our History," appeared in *The Carpenter* in the fall of 1886. After proudly noting the expanding circulation of his paper, McGuire recounted:

The growth of the organization has been none the less marvelous! From 12 local unions in 1881, the Brotherhood has increased to 214 local unions at the present writing, and from a membership of 2,042 it has grown to 42,521 members—a gain of 18,481 members the past two years. Its jurisdiction stretches from Union No. 83, of Halifax, Nova Scotia, to San Francisco, Los Angeles and British Columbia, with 11 local unions in Canada, and more than a score of unions in the Southern States, as far south as New Orleans and Galveston. In the Southern states the colored men working at the trade have taken hold of the organization with avidity, and the result is the Brotherhood embraces 14 unions of colored carpenters in the South.

It is by no means unusual to see colored delegates in attendance at the conventions of the Brotherhood for the organization recognizes no distinction on account of color, race, nationality, religion or politics—its members recognize each other only as American working men. Its constitutions and documents, however, are translated and printed in the German, French, Bohemian, and Scandavian languages.[34]

Not only do these paragraphs signify the fruits of his heroic efforts to organize, but also his awareness of diversity as well as commitment to welcome it among the membership. Segregated locals for blacks in the South would not meet standards of the late twentieth century, but for 1886 the presence of black carpenters in the union bespeaks an advanced level of tolerance. It is fair to point out that P.J. McGuire was ahead of his time in this regard.

AMERICAN FEDERATION OF LABOR

McGuire's part in establishing the American Federation of Labor was crucial. As the secretary of the Saint Louis Trades Assembly, elected in May 1881, he participated as delegate from that body to a conference in Terre Haute, Indiana, consisting of men dissatisfied with the Knights of Labor. Their idea was to form a rival body. McGuire was impatient with what he considered the backward-looking program of the Knights of Labor and, by implication, its leader—Powderly. It was McGuire, therefore, who, as the most able delegate to the conference in Terre Haute framed a call for a convention in Pittsburgh to establish such a body.[35] The convention, duly held in November of 1881, birthed the Federation of Organized Trades and Labor Unions (FOTLU).

McGuire was not present at Pittsburgh, however, due to his trip to Europe as a delegate to the international socialist congress in Coire, Switzerland. Due in part to McGuire's absence, the organization did not get off to a good start, and limped along from one annual convention to another, barely surviving with no full-time officers and little funding. McGuire was preoccupied during this time with building the Carpenters' Union. He was also distracted by the death of his wife, Maggie, in January of 1884.

As conflict between the Knights of Labor and the craft-based unions developed over jurisdiction, national leaders of craft unions felt the need for a central body to coordinate their efforts, one that could be effective where the FOTLU was impotent. The idea arose out of meetings of trade union leaders for the purpose of finding a peaceful solution to difficulties with the Knights of Labor. McGuire's leadership was evident in these deliberations, and his attitude remained conciliatory toward Powderly and his order because of a deep sense of solidarity with all workers. When a treaty proved impossible, plans were made to transform the FOTLU into a viable and effective institution. Walter Galenson tells the story of these proceedings in this way:

When the founding convention of the AFL met in December 1886, McGuire was at the peak of his career. He was the undisputed leader of one of the largest unions in the United States. It was in large measure through his initiative that the constitutional convention of the AFL had been called. It was he who called the first session of the convention to order, and when he declined the temporary chairmanship, the convention unanimously insisted that he take it. He could have been elected to the presidency of the AFL if he had wanted the job.[36]

As it was, McGuire was elected secretary of the AFL and, in the words of historian Philip Taft, in that capacity, "McGuire was a tower of strength to the American Federation of Labor. He directed his own union, and he also contributed innumerable hours to organizing workers in other trades and negotiating with employers on their behalf. Few important decisions were made without his advice."[37] P.J. McGuire's leadership talent, his eloquence, judgment and intelligence, freely given, were essential to the success of the AFL in those critical early years. The numerous obligations he undertook undoubtedly led to the later breakdown of his health.

A sampling of his typical activities as general secretary reported in *The Carpenter*, explains why his traditional vigor eroded. In February 1886, McGuire pushed himself to answer 1,246 letters and 109 postals "as well as prepare this journal, send out circulars to start new unions, keep his books and attend to a score of routine duties." During the month beginning on August 27, 1886, he visited eleven cities in seven states, called on local unions and gave speeches. From May 9 to June 9, 1887, he traveled to twenty-two cities in eleven states on trade union business. Not surprisingly, he began to report absences due to illness: pneumonia (May 1891), influenza (January 1892), flu and catarrah (April 1894), catarrah and la grippe (February 1895). His remarkable constitution was showing the strain.[38]

If his annual reports, regularly published in *The Carpenter* (August or September issue), are any indication, McGuire kept careful and thorough records, usually without additional help.[39] As the frequency of his spells of illness and resulting absences increased, the problem of handling the work mounted. In addition, melancholy set in as his vision of a cooperative society receded beyond hope of realization. The vision was not shared by his fellow members of the general executive board, who were of a more narrow bureaucratic orientation.

FACING OBSCURITY

By the turn of the century, McGuire was forty-eight, and his health was failing. All the traveling, speaking engagements, and other imperatives for building the Brotherhood had taken their toll. In short, he was a burned out case. It is clear that, by then, he was no longer able to shoulder the burden of leading an organization as large as the carpenters' union. In fact, it was probably beyond what any one individual could handle at this stage, let alone one whose health had seriously deteriorated. Furthermore, McGuire had neither formed a cadre of younger men to whom he could delegate responsibility, nor had he groomed a successor for himself.

After devoting himself unsparingly to it for almost twenty years, understandably, McGuire held a proprietary view of the Brotherhood. He did not wish to relinquish control. In addition, his resort to alcohol for relief from his frustrations became a problem. Under the circumstances, a changing of the guard was probably inevitable; however, the manner in which it was handled was, to put it mildly, unseemly.

The unseating of McGuire was engineered by a new breed of business unionists who craved more influence on the policies and direction of the organization. Their tactics were adopted because ordinary democratic procedures would not achieve their ends. Out of gratitude and loyalty for what P.J. McGuire had done, rank-and-file members persisted in supporting his candidacy and policies in elections and referenda.

Having built the Brotherhood into a solid going concern of over 60,000 members at great financial sacrifice and at the cost of his own health and the economic security of his family, he was confronted in July of 1901 with charges of embezzlement by fellow executive board members Frank Duffy and William Huber. Younger men, ambitious, confirmed "business unionists" lacking McGuire's idealism and sense of worker solidarity, they conspired with Francis S. Brown, a wealthy, well-known, antiunion Philadelphia attorney, to indict the founding father of their organization. It is unthinkable that McGuire deliberately diverted treasury funds for his own indulgence. It is conceivable, however, that he borrowed funds entrusted to him to meet his medical expenses, with the intention of repayment upon his recovery. In the condition of failing health of his later years—he had severe rheumatism and liver disease related to use of alcohol, and other problems—it is clear that he was no longer able to keep up-to-date records. In any case, he was suspended from his position as general secretary and, after an out-of-court settlement involving reimbursement by him of $1,000, he gave up his office in the organization.

His last appearance before the union at the convention in 1902 was a sad occasion. A bitter debate over his fate was taking place among delegates. McGuire came to defend himself, but illness prevented even his standing upright. The once powerful voice was barely audible. The always eloquent words, which had stirred workers in cities across the nation, no longer flowed from his tongue. His body and his spirit were finally exhausted. He could do little more than deny the charges. He concluded by resigning from the very brotherhood he had created as a young man and had dedicated himself to until his formidable energies had at last been exhausted.[40]

THE POWDERLY PATH

As a young man, Powderly was thoughtful, ambitious and rather unconventional in his habits. Early on he concluded that the evils of drink exceeded its advantages, and as a member of the Fr. Matthew Temperance Society, decided not only to avoid it altogether himself, but to exhort workmen to do likewise. Temperance became a major theme of his speeches to workers' gatherings. In addition, he was not gregarious. His inclination was toward study and reading. The craft of machinist was challenging and encouraged its practitioners to deepen their skills by improving their mathematics and delving into engineering publications.

Powderly found it satisfying to keep up with the latest developments. His interests, however, were wide. He enjoyed Shakespeare, novels by Dickens and poetry. Tennyson was a favorite. He liked to read history, especially Irish history. He dabbled in verse himself. He lived at his parents home until age twenty. During periods of layoff, he indulged his desire to sleep until noon. Rather less than heroic, his early life was of human proportions, but he had a good mind and saw his youth as a time of preparation for attractive opportunities in the future.

Historians have gained much insight into Powderly's motivation and experience by examining the diaries he kept from the time he was a young man. They have found the diaries differ from his published account in a number of significant respects. His rise to a position of leadership did not occur by accident. It was, indeed, premeditated. Yet, it need not necessarily have been in the direction of labor leadership. In his autobiography, he attributes his interest in workers' organizations to hearing John Siney's impassioned eulogy of men killed in a mine explosion on September 9, 1869, at Avondale near Dunmore—known as the Avondale Massacre. His diary belies this version since it records that he was not in Avondale to hear Siney's speech and, while he must certainly have been aware of the accident, he did not involve himself in union activity until several years later.[41]

Terence Powderly's career was bound up with the coming of age of American railroads. In a variety of ways it was linked to the rise of and reaction to railway corporations—its high and low points were connected to dealings with this industry. The railroads, which had reached the Mississippi River a few years after he was born in 1849, represented America's first large-scale corporations. They were the first enterprises to employ men by the tens of thousands—introducing depersonalized employee relations—a sure cause of worker disaffection. The large administrative structures of railroads required some of the nation's earliest professional managers whose decisions and whims directly affected the livelihood of employees, and inspired employees to make an effort to control their destinies through organization—frequently involving the Knights of Labor.

Railroad executives importuned state and federal legislatures for laws favorable to them in regard to charters, tax assessments or abatements, land grants, loans, and so forth. This was often done by distributing railroad passes, corporate stock at below market prices and straightforward bribery, so that standards of republican government were subverted. These developments stimulated instincts of reform in Powderly and his movement.

Requirements for capital to build the railroads were far larger than those for earlier businesses and led to the institutionalization of investment markets in New York, opening opportunities for financiers, speculators and lawyers, who not infrequently were used to manipulate stock prices, engage in insider trading and attempt to create monopoly, which offended adherents of republican ideals.[42]

Terence Powderly's father became an early employee of the fledgling Delaware and Hudson Railway (a feeder line between mines and the D&H Canal) after failure of his mining venture. Subsequently, he obtained employment for his thirteen-year-old son and namesake with the same firm in 1862. The young Powderly began work in the industry, which lasted until his election as mayor of Scranton in 1878.

After a series of limited skill jobs—switch tender, car examiner, repairman and brakeman—he was (in 1866) apprenticed for three years to James P. Dickson, master mechanic in the D&H railroad shops. One of the first tasks assigned to the young apprentice was to dismantle the famous "Stourbridge Lion," an import from England, which had been the first locomotive to operate on a commercial line in America.[43]

Terence Powderly first became a union member on November 2, 1871, when he joined the machinists and blacksmiths' union, which by that time had a large part of its membership in railroad shops. His diary mentions the event matter-of-factly. It did not happen during a period of strife or as the result of a bout with an oppressive employer. In September of 1872, feeling secure in his craft, he married a hometown girl, Hannah Dever, his wife until her death in 1901. However, the talents he had been honing for some time quickly manifested themselves. He became a leader in short order. By February of 1873, he was elected president of the local in Scranton. A short time later, he chose to become corresponding secretary of the Scranton local, so that his writing skills could be put to good use. In that capacity, he was soon noticed by national leaders of the machinists and blacksmiths' organization, President John Fehrenbatch in particular.

While labor organizations became an avenue for his advancement, he lacked an ideological commitment. The decisive factor in his conversion to an advocate of workers' welfare was the panic of 1873, his resulting layoff and blacklisting. Like McGuire, the prolonged economic downturn affected him deeply. At this time, he was working for the Delaware, Lackawana and Western Railroad. Powderly was rudely apprised of railroad labor policy by Walter Dawson, DL&W superintendent, who chose to discharge him early because of his union offices and proceeded to blacklist him in the Scranton community. At this time he was forced to leave Scranton to find work and discovered that blacklisting by Dawson dogged his tracks everywhere he went. Onset of the severe depression of the 1870s moved him to recognize the shortcomings of capitalism and the necessity for labor reform.

A family tragedy deepened his gloom in the mid-1870s. In December of 1875, he was called home to learn that his infant daughter Margery was ill. She died before the year was out, and the Powderlys were never blessed with another child.

Powderly remained in Scranton and worked as a machinist in spite of further blacklistings (by Dawson), which were overturned through the intercession of William W. Scranton, general manager of the Lackawanna Iron and Coal Company in the city. Scranton was a member of the family after whom the city was named in recognition of its pioneering iron and railroad enterprises, which were responsible for development of the area.[44]

These experiences—perception of the machinations of Franklin Gowen, builder of a transportation monopoly in anthracite through the Reading Railroad; awareness of the antics of Vanderbilt, Gould, Drew and their associates in the stock markets, their corruptive activities in the courts and legislatures—were sufficient to persuade Powderly that republican values were being perverted. The federal government's huge land grants to the railroads was another element of his distrust of large corporations and blended into his Irish passion for land reform.

A receptiveness to antimonopoly movements, monetary reform and cooperative enterprise were for Terence Powderly the legacy of his encounters with economic reality. Therefore, on becoming reestablished in Scranton, he organized a local unit of the Greenback-Labor organization—a third party. In February of 1878, the same year McGuire moved to Saint Louis, Powderly was elected for the first of three two-year terms as mayor of Scranton on the Greenback-Labor ticket. Historian Vincent Falzone credits him with honest government and innovative reforms of advanced character for his day, specifically in the area of tax reform, sewage disposal and health.

In September of the year following his first mayoralty victory, he was elected leader of the Scranton district assembly of the Noble Order of Knights of Labor in which he had been initiated as a member only three years before. His rise was advanced significantly by productive service on the committee on constitution of the 1878 Knights of Labor convention in Reading. He became an influential voice on behalf of lifting the secrecy of the Knights of Labor, a cause of opposition to the Order by the Catholic Church. Finally, in September of 1879, he was elected grand master workman of the Order at a convention in Chicago.[45]

Powderly's dealings with the hierarchy of the American Catholic Church were historically important. They represent his most significant contribution to the development of labor organizations in America. They called for a high order of discretion and diplomacy on his part amidst vigorous pressures from opposing sides of the church and labor issue. On one side, he was bedeviled by Catholic clergy and laymen for his leadership of a quasi-Masonic labor organization. When, largely through his endeavors, secrecy, oaths and rituals were gradually set aside, abuse was heaped upon him by critics of the Church inside and outside the Order (particularly those in the nativist American Protective Association) who charged him with slavishly following the dictates of the Catholic hierarchy. From the time Powderly joined the Order, which had a strong religious orientation (though distinctly not a Catholic one), he was opposed to its policy of secrecy and use of quasi-sectarian rituals with Masonic overtones in initiations and other ceremonies. They were a legacy of Uriah Stephens, founder of the Order, who at one time studied in a Baptist seminary.

Powderly recognized that a large proportion of the work force was Catholic and perceived that these practices were impediments to their joining or remaining members of the Order. He estimated that two-thirds of the membership was Catholic.[46] It is fair to say that most of the clergy, and a majority of the hierarchy, had grave reservations about labor organizations and most especially secret ones. Conspicuous among critics of the Order and especially of T.V. Powderly was Michael Corrigan, Archbishop of New York. They were acutely conscious of the Molly Maguires episode of recent memory. A major conflict between the two institutions impended. Prospects for the conflict heightened in October of 1883, when the Archbishop of Quebec, Alexandre Taschereau, applied to Rome for a ruling on whether the Knights of Labor should be condemned. The conflict blossomed in April of 1886, when Taschereau, without specific Vatican authorization, condemned the Order.

Powderly initiated efforts to contact Cardinal Gibbons of Baltimore, the leading Catholic churchman in the United States. Perhaps only another Irishman could deal effectively with the predominantly Irish hierarchy. He first approached Bishop Keane of Richmond in October of 1886, when the Order was holding a general assembly in the Virginia capital. Keane arranged a meeting with Gibbons on October 28. A second conference was held eleven months later at the invitation of Cardinal Gibbons. In these meetings the issue was resolved when Powderly explained that the Order had dispensed with secrecy and eliminated sectarian rituals effective January of 1882.

His assurances that these steps had been taken and Gibbons's understanding that other objectionable aspects would be removed were relayed by Gibbons to other members of the American hierarchy, who fell in line, albeit reluctantly in a number of cases, notably Archbishop Michael Corrigan of New York. Upon personal representations by Cardinal Gibbons in Rome in the spring of 1887, Vatican thinking moved away from a possible condemnation. Gibbons's view prevailed. The issue was therefore closed. Henceforth, American workers who professed Catholicism need no longer be concerned with any contradiction between their religious faith and their membership in labor organizations.

Gibbons was widely congratulated for the wisdom of his judgment in the matter. The episode is believed to have been a major stimulus to issuance, by Pope Leo XIII, of the encyclical Rerum Novarum in 1891. Rerum Novarum, "On the Condition of Labor," was the first statement emanating from the Vatican that explicitly endorsed the right of workers to organize unions for their economic betterment.[47]

There is a fine irony in the fact that immediately after his successful peacemaking efforts between the Knights of Labor and the Catholic Church, Powderly came to New York City in 1886, and campaigned for Henry George in the mayoralty election that fall, joining Reverend Doctor Edward McGlynn in that third party drive—the same Reverend McGlynn who was temporarily excommunicated for his support of Henry George's single tax plan and for his refusal to go to Rome to explain his position. All this was done under the disapproving gaze of Powderly's old adversary, Ordinary of the New York Archdiocese, Michael Corrigan.

Indeed, Powderly had had his fill of imperious hierarchs. He eventually (in 1901) joined the Order of Free Masons, finding in it, he wrote, "no evidence of all the evil things he had heard about it from Roman Catholic sources."[48] Nevertheless, he never foreclosed all connections with the Catholic Church. In his later years, he continued to have cordial associations with faculty from the Catholic University of America,

near his home, who were concerned with social justice, especially
Reverend William J. Kerby, Professor of Philosophy, with whom he had
numerous conversations.[49] The incredibly rapid growth of the Knights
of Labor and its later rapid decline are both substantially attributable to
Powderly's leadership. In a word, it was a paradox. After a successful
strike in opposition to wage cuts imposed by three railroads controlled
by Wall Street wizard Jay Gould, the operators were found to discrimi-
nate against members of the Knights of Labor by laying them off.
Strikes began on these railroads in 1885. At this point, Powderly,
whose policy was opposed to strikes generally, became directly
involved. He conducted face-to-face negotiations with Gould and with
the railroad operating executives. A peaceful settlement resulted, and
all America was impressed with this labor organization's ability to contend with the powerful baron of the railroads. Men flocked to join the
Order by the thousands.

Only a year later (1886), Gould broke a strike on his railroads by
replacing those on strike, and the Knights of Labor was found to be a
good deal less than invincible. Powderly had taken his usual position of
opposition, vacillated, and then, in efforts to find a settlement, was
hoodwinked by the genius of this accomplished practitioner of financial
manipulation from a century ago. Failure of other strikes now befell the
Order. The flood tide of new members now ebbed with equal speed.[50]

The principles of artisanal republicanism, dating from a simpler time,
were inadequate guides for dealing with large corporate enterprises, such
as railroads, whose destinies were controlled by unfettered Wall Street
finance, rather than by owner-operators of an earlier day. Such principles,
embracing virtue in the form of restraint of self-indulgence or aggrandizement in favor of the common good, to be practiced by worker-citizens,
are (to say the least) incongruous in the face of uninhibited capitalists
such as Jim Fisk, Jay Gould, or the Vanderbilts. These principles contem-
plated neither the changes wrought by large-scale industrial corporations
nor the fluctuations of ever-widening markets. Their influence was a
major source of the limitations of Terence Powderly's leadership.

Powderly's leadership of a greatly diminished Knights of Labor
endured until 1893, when he was unseated by a palace revolt. His life
of thirty years thereafter may be sketched in brief. Unable to return to
his original craft of machinist, he turned to the study of law and was
admitted to the Pennsylvania bar in 1894. His leadership skills now led
him into national politics. In the campaign of 1896, he supported
William McKinley, with whom he had become acquainted in Cleveland
years before. In return, the new president appointed him commissioner general of immigration. He remained a public servant (except for a
brief interlude involving a misunderstanding with Theodore Roosevelt)
until his retirement in 1921.[51] He died on June 24, 1924.

This man, who became a national figure as a pioneer of the labor
movement, was associated with solid ideals of the American republic.
He headed an organization that opposed discrimination based on race,
religion, or nationality. That these ideals were quite imperfectly

observed on Powderly's watch as grand master workman is hardly grounds for serious criticism of the man, since even a century later they were far from adequately achieved by organizations of workers or by American society in general. It was the value of equal opportunity for all that he espoused. If the practice left much to be desired, it was certainly not his fault alone.

A widower at fifty-two, in his seventieth year he married Emma Fickenscher, his secretary, and with his second wife provided a refuge in their home in Washington for an old friend, Mother Jones, famed labor agitator, between her excursions to mining fields to exhort strikers to greater militance.[52] Withal, he was an accomplished amateur photographer, whose voluminous glass negatives are stored in the archives of Catholic University in Washington along with his extensive personal papers.

MCGUIRE'S LAST YEARS

McGuire lived only four years after his tragic departure from the Carpenters' Union. He and his family were forced to accept poverty as their lot. They moved to a small house at 204 Byron Street in Camden from a larger one in that city. The McGuires had lived in a relatively comfortable three-story house at 221 Vine Street, a short walk from the Vine Street Ferry which McGuire had taken each day to reach Carpenter Headquarters in Philadelphia. In spite of his failing health, McGuire was able to obtain occasional work representing the Disston Company, one of the nation's largest manufacturers of saws, which was located in the Tacony section of Philadelphia. The firm had been a regular advertiser in *The Carpenter* during McGuire's editorship. He also found periodic employment as a labor reporter for the Philadelphia *Public Ledger*.[53]

McGuire was obliged to enlist his teenaged daughters and son to help support the family. This remarkable man, on the decline from a life of vigorous physical and intellectual activity, suffered severely from his lowered estate.

His plight is captured in the following fragment of a letter to his sisters in New York in 1904:

Every week or two I write Gompers to put me out as an organizer in this neighborhood so as to be home every night. It would be $25.00 per week. But he keeps putting me off. He has done the same in writing the history of the Federation, for which I was to get $500.00. Duffy too has fooled me on the brotherhood history which was to bring me $500.00 more. Besides that both the Federation and brotherhood have new men out as organizers at $25.00 per week and won't send me out. Well it's a long lane has no turning. Love to you both from us all.

> Your loving brother,
> P.J. McGuire[54]

IMPLICATIONS

The careers of these two men document characteristics hypothesized about Irish-American leadership in the introduction. The choice of their vocation arose out of a heritage of adversity suffered by their parents and previous generations in Ireland and their own work experiences in America. This background engendered a pronounced sense of injustice. They were not disposed to accept conditions as they were. Severe unemployment, especially in the 1870s, affected the outlook of both of them. They developed an idealism and passion for solidarity—an impatience with economic conditions for workers, which was strengthened by memories of the hardships of their families in adjusting to the realities of American society. McGuire's description of the seventeenth ward in New York is especially revealing.

Furthermore, having sprung from parents who crossed the Atlantic Ocean to find a better life, these two leaders were indeed mobile when faced with need of it for both earning a living and pursuing their mission of labor leadership. This trait is most vivid in McGuire's career, but it is an important aspect of Powderly's as well.

Powderly's three terms as mayor of Scranton, beginning when still in his twenties, and McGuire's rise to lead the Committee of Safety in New York and his successful lobbying for LaSallean reforms in Missouri, while yet in his twenties, are indicative of the political acumen of the pair. Their understanding of the institutions of democratic government and the ease with which they emerged in third party circles bespeaks a politically conscious upbringing which can reasonably be associated with the charged atmosphere of Ireland. The same impatience with existing conditions in the economy led them toward reform politics.

McGuire and Powderly came of age at a time when Irish Catholics had become a substantial proportion of the working population. For leaders of organized labor, the Irish represented a substantial part of their potential constituency. On balance, this was favorable to the success of these two leaders. It was also a time when the economy alternated between vigorous growth and serious slumps—the latter phases causing conditions to become desperate for workers. In virtue of their fluency in language, they were able to crystallize the grievances of their fellow toilers. They enjoyed the advantage of having been raised in English-speaking households, learning the value of language and consciously cultivating skill in the use of words, both spoken and written. Much of their success as organizers is attributable to the persuasiveness of their rhetoric, this in contrast with the difficulties of those reared in families where English was not spoken at home. For parents and, to a lesser extent, the offspring of such immigrant families, the language barrier was a serious drawback.

Contributions to the labor movement of these two individuals rest heavily upon their perception of ethnic, religious and even racial divisions in the work force, along with the sophistication they demonstrated in efforts to foster cohesion in organizations made up of diverse elements. Ethnic politicians indeed—operating in an economic sphere. Organizations headed by these men incorporated local units segregated by race. However, they should not be denied credit for failing to measure up to standards of the late twentieth century. The fact is, they were well ahead of their time. Perhaps Terence Powderly was intolerant of orientals, but that merely illustrates the limits of his commendable progress in subordinating a discriminatory impulse.

Pragmatism is evident in these stories. Ideologies such as Greenbackism, LaSalleanism, producers cooperativism, land reform schemes and sundry versions of socialism were tried on for size at different times— and later either soft-pedalled or discarded. These pathfinders of labor ideology had to change direction often in order to grow or merely survive. More than anything else, their experience in the work force of nineteenth century America influenced their ideological outlook. They became pragmatic. It was an Americanizing process.

NOTES

1. Walter Galenson, *The United Brotherhood of Carpenters* (Cambridge, Mass.: Harvard University Press, 1983), 25.

2. Ibid., 33–34. Galenson considers the claim that a certain machinist, Matthew Maguire was the father of Labor Day, but rejects it. However, P.J. McGuire credits Matthew Maguire for joining him in presenting a motion before the Central Labor Union in New York City in June of 1882 proposing that the first Monday in September be celebrated as a labor day holiday. The motion was passed unanimously. See: *The Carpenter*, November 1890, 2.

3 Cecil Woodham-Smith, *The Great Hunger* (New York: Harper and Row, 1962), Chap. 6.

4 Interview with Mrs. Iris Rossell, granddaughter of P.J. McGuire, Collingswood, New Jersey, November 17, 1988.

5. Testimony of Peter J. Maguire, U.S. Congress, Senate Report on Hearings upon Relations between Labor and Capital, Washington, D.C., 1885, 343–44 (Senate Report no. 1262, 48th Congress, 2d Session).

6. Jay P. Dolan, *The Immigrant Church* (Baltimore: Johns Hopkins Press, 1975), 27–44; Robert Ernst, *Immigrant Life in New York City, 1825–1863* (Port Washington, New York: I.J. Friedman, 1949), 48–54.

7. The quotation concerning McGuire's literary output is from Galenson, *United Brotherhood of Carpenters*, 22. Review from *New York Sun* reprinted in *The Carpenter*, May 1887, 2.

8. Interview with Mrs. Iris Rossell, December 1, 1988.

9. David N. Lyon, "The World of P.J. McGuire" (Ph.D. dissertation, University of Minnesota, 1972), 30–31.

10. P.J. McGuire to Gabriel Edmonston, March 21, 1882, Edmonston Papers, microfilm, Pennsylvania State University, University Park, Pennsylvania.

11. Lawrence J. McCaffrey, *Ireland from Colony to Nation State* (Englewood Cliffs, N.J.: Prentice Hall, 1979), 13–22; Kerby A. Miller, *Emigrants and Exiles* (New York: Oxford University Press, 1985), 21–25.

12. Terence V. Powderly, *The Path I Trod* (New York: Columbia University Press, 1949), 5.

13. Ibid., 7.

14. Family genealogy obtained from John Michael Powderly, Rockville, Maryland, July 1988.

15. Powderly, *Path I Trod*, 176–77.

16. William O'Brien and Desmond Ryan, eds., *Devoy's Post Bag* (Dublin: J. Fallon, 1953), Vol. 1, 60.

17. Powderly, *Path I Trod*, 177–79.

18. Eric Foner, "Class, Ethnicity, and Radicalism in the Gilded Age: The Land League and Irish America," *Marxist Perspectives* (Summer 1978): 21–24.

19. Sean Wilentz, *Chants Democratic* (New York: Oxford University Press, 1984), 14; Richard Oestreicher, "Terence Powderly, the Knights of Labor and Artisanal Republicanism," in *Labor Leaders in America*, Melvyn Dubofsky and Warren Van Tine eds., (Urbana: University of Illinois Press, 1987), 34–36.

20. Samuel Gompers, *Seventy Years of Life and Labor* (New York: Dutton, 1925), Vol. 1, 26.

21. Ibid., see Chapter 3 for a fuller description.

22. Philip Taft, *Movements for Economic Reform* (New York: Rhinehart, 1950), 123–27.

23. Gompers, *Seventy Years*, 95–96; Herbert G. Gutman, "The Tompkins Square Riot," *Labor History* (Winter 1965): 44–70.

24. Gompers, *Seventy Years*, 97–98.

25. Diary of P.J. McGuire, 4–5. This Diary (handwritten) is in the possession of Mrs. Iris Rossell.

26. Lyon, "The World of P.J. McGuire," 56–62, 85.

27. Diary of P.J. McGuire, 4–6. A separate page of the diary (with no number) lists both of McGuire's marriages and children, including dates of birth. The background of Margaretta V. "Maggie" Richardson comes from an interview with Mrs. Iris Rossell, November 17, 1988.

28. Diary of P.J. McGuire, 7–9; Lyon, "The World of P.J. McGuire," 120–22; Mark Erlich, "Peter J. McGuire," *Carpenter Magazine* (Supplement), March 1982, 4.

29. Galenson, *United Brotherhood of Carpenters*, 271.

30. "A Chapter in Our History," *The Carpenter*, October 1886, 2.

31. Mark Erlich, "Peter J. McGuire's Trade Unionism: Socialism of a Trades Union Kind?" *Labor History* (Spring 1983): 165–97; John R. Commons and Associates, *History of Labour in the United States* (New York: MacMillan, 1918), Vol.3, 308 (from Part 4 written by Selig Perlman). In *The Carpenter*, February 1894, 8, McGuire presents his view of supplanting capitalism as a very long run goal.

32. *The Carpenter*, February 1984, 4.

33. Diary of P.J. McGuire, no page number; marriage certificate, Church of the Nativity, New York, dated October 6, 1884 (both in possession of Mrs. Iris Rossell).

34. "A Chapter in Our History," *The Carpenter*, October 1886, 2.

35. Diary of P.J. McGuire, 10.

36. Galenson, *United Brotherhood of Carpenters*, 49.

37. Philip Taft, *The AFL in the Time of Gompers* (New York: Harper, 1957), 234.

38. McGuire's workload, travels and illnesses are recorded in *The Carpenter*, March 1886, 4 (workload); October 1886, 4, June 1887, 4 (travels); May 1891, 2, January 1892, 2, April 1894, 1, February 1895, 1 (illnesses). As indicated in the text, this is only a sampling.

39. Annual Reports of the General Secretary in *The Carpenter*, August 1889, 8; August 1891, 2, August 1892, 4; August 1893, 10.

40. Erlich, "Peter J. McGuire's Trade Unionism," 189-95; Galenson, *United Brotherhood of Carpenters*, 88-92.

41. Samuel Walker, "Terence Powderly Machinist: 1866-1877," *Labor History* (Spring 1978): 166, 168, 173-74, 181-83; Oestreicher, "Terence Powderly, the Knights of Labor," in Dubofsky and Van Tine, 32, 34.

42. Alfred DuPont Chandler, Jr., *The Railroads* (New York: Harcourt, Brace and World, 1965), 9-12.

43. Powderly, *Path I Trod*, 20; George Rogers Taylor, *The Transportation Revolution* (New York: Holt, Rhinehart and Winston, 1951), 77.

44. Terence Powderly, Diary entry, December 15, 1875; Powderly Papers, Catholic University of America, Washington, D.C.; Vincent J. Falzone, *Terence Powderly: Middle Class Reformer* (Washington, D.C.: University Press of America, 1978), 18.

45. Vincent J. Falzone, "Terence Powderly: Politician and Progressive Mayor of Scranton, 1878-1884," *Pennsylvania History*, 71 (1974): 288-309.

46. Henry J. Browne, *The Catholic Church and the Knights of Labor* (Washington, D.C.: Catholic University of America, 1949), 241.

47. For a thorough, scholarly treatment of this story see Browne, *The Catholic Church*.

48. Powderly, *Path I Trod*, 371.

49. Falzone, *Terence Powderly*, 191.

50. John R. Commons and Associates, *History of Labour* Vol. 2, 368-74, 382-84 (strikes), 423n (data on decline of Order).

51. Powderly, *Path I Trod*, 286-89, 295-302.

52. Falzone, *Terence Powderly*, 192; Edward M. Steel, ed., *The Correspondence of Mother Jones* (Pittsburgh: University of Pittsburgh Press, 1985), XXXVI-XXXVIII, XLI.

53. Interview with Mrs. Iris Rossell, June 15, 1989; letter from McGuire to his sister Susana McGuire, October 24, 1904 (in possession of Mrs. Iris Rossell).

54. Letter from McGuire to sisters Teresa and Susana McGuire, January 14, 1902 (in possession of Mrs. Rossell).

3

A PAIR OF FENIAN REBELS: MCDONNELL AND RONEY

Among the wave of exiles coming to New York in the wake of the abortive Fenian rising of the 1860s in Ireland were Frank Roney and Joseph Patrick McDonnell. They were destined to play important roles in developing American trade unions. Roney, a molder, eventually migrated to the West Coast where he was a dominant figure in San Francisco labor organizations in the 1880s. McDonnell, a journalist and pioneer of the labor press, remained on the East Coast, operating out of Paterson, New Jersey. Both of them came with experience in organization and leadership gained in the rising. Survivors of British courts and prisons, they emerged with courage and unfailing militance.

Although the two shared much in common, their physical characteristics contrasted sharply. In his autobiography, Samuel Gompers, himself a short man at five feet four inches, graphically described McDonnell as only an inch or so taller with "clean-cut, small features, wonderful eyes and an abundance of red curly hair." Gompers remembered that "he was brainy and very gentle, had a beautiful speaking voice and courage for any venture."[1] Etchings of McDonnell show him with a furry mustache and a neatly trimmed goatee.[2] Our image of Roney comes from Ira Cross, editor of his autobiography and historian of California labor, who first met the aging veteran of labor's wars in Vallejo, California:

Here was a big, broad-shouldered molder in dirty clothes, with rough powerful hands hardened by working in sand and with carrying the ladle. His hair was gray and shaggy; his moustache, large, bushy, and gray. His eyes looked out from under heavy eyebrows. I cannot remember their color, but I think they were dark gray. I know they were kindly, and just a little dulled with age for Roney was in his sixty-third year. His face carried a tired, but sympathetic expression. I felt myself in the presence of one who had found the world filled with misery, poverty, and selfishness, and had tried unsuccessfully to shape it more nearly to his ideals of what it ought to be. Cross said, "He impressed me as still possessing vitality and energy sufficient to wage, if necessary, a good battle for the things in which he believed."[3]

FAMILY BACKGROUND

Young idealists, fearless and willing to take grave risks for their convictions, are the lifeblood of any movement. Frank Roney of Belfast and Joseph Patrick McDonnell of Dublin were two such young men in the Fenian cause. Roney was born on August 14, 1841. McDonnell was born six years later on March 27. Both were from relatively comfortable families in which support for Irish independence varied depending on the individual member. Roney's father, for example, preferred a return to an Irish Parliament as it existed prior to the Act of Union in 1800, but he did not relish Fenianism. The families were both headed by entrepreneurs.

Frank Roney's father completed an apprenticeship as a carpenter and served for a time as secretary of the first carpenters' union in Belfast. After organizing the trade thoroughly and planning carefully, he won a ten-hour day for the craft. This orderly method made an indelible impression on his son. However, the father subsequently became a contractor and prospered in the business.[4] Furthermore, he was originally from a substantial middle-class family in Saul, County Down, which owned land and operated a public house in that community.

Roney's mother sprang from an old Belfast Presbyterian line, which had founded one of the first banks in the city. She converted to Catholicism just prior to her marriage. Her father was a partner in the firm of Johnson and Thomson, tobacconists, but according to a grandniece of Roney, was much more than that—a world traveler and adventurer, whose mementos are housed in the Ulster Museum in Belfast. He was a man whose wife disappeared mysteriously after their two children were born. He placed each child in a separate foster home.[5]

Gordon Augustus Thomson, by name, he died in Sydney, Australia. His daughter never passed on the less savory details of his career to her son, Frank. Apparently misinformed, Frank Roney wrote that his grandfather was a patriot in the United Irishmen rising of 1798 and a Republican who detested the Orange Order and its philosophy. He explained that his grandfather smuggled tobacco in order to deny revenue to the British government as a form of revenge for its oppression. Thus the blood of an adventurer flowed in Roney's veins.[6]

Little is known of McDonnell's parents except that they lived in Dublin and were prosperous enough to send their son to secondary school at the newly established Catholic University of Dublin in preparation for his becoming a priest. (This hope was dashed when he was not admitted to the seminary.) Additionally, his father set up Joseph in a small rope and twine producing business sometime later. Clearly, they were a well-off Catholic family.[7]

Thus, neither McDonnell nor Roney was raised in an atmosphere of poverty. Although McDonnell received his elementary education at the national school in Dublin's Marlborough Street, Roney, after a few years in national schools, was sent to Ellis Academy (a private school) because his parents felt national schools were inferior. At this time, his father was unable to contemplate financing a college education for him, but desired that Frank become a mechanic while his mother preferred white-collar work for him.

As a deeply religious boy of thirteen, Roney worked among the poor on behalf of the Saint Vincent de Paul Society, of which his father was an active member. It was no surprise, then, that he quit his first job in disgust since it consisted of serving eviction notices for a real estate agent. When he finally chose to be apprenticed for seven years as a molder, beginning in 1855, it was because it attracted him as work similar to that learned in a government school of design under the tutelage of an artist named Pichioni. The man had taught him to make castes for production of religious articles at which he became adept. He found great satisfaction in it.

Thus, he became a manual worker out of choice rather than necessity. Roney tells us that he found his fellow apprentices rough and vulgar and remained aloof from them because he was accustomed to the refined atmosphere of his home. For one whose life was spent as a trade union leader, it was a rather strange beginning.

BREAKING AWAY

The rebellious impulse of youth surfaced for the two Irishmen in their teenage years. Midway through his apprenticeship, Roney ran away to Dublin intent upon reforming the world. He even managed to publish a piece on improving reform schools in a newspaper called the *Examiner*, founded by Denis Holland, who later established the nationalist *Dublin Irishman*.[8] Exposed to some of the world's vices until his money ran out, the lad took refuge with a friend of his father's, Mr. Shanley, who took him in and got him a job in a foundry until his father came to bring him home to Belfast. But the boy refused to go until his father promised to keep him from going to jail for the crime of being a runaway apprentice—which the elder Roney accomplished through a lawsuit at considerable expense.

McDonnell's impatience with the status quo became evident at the Catholic University of Dublin, an institution recently launched by Ireland's Cardinal Cullen, who installed John Henry Newman (later Britain's Cardinal Newman) as rector.[9] This institution boasted a largely British faculty. Blossoming as a speaker, he became known as "Little McDonnell, boy orator," offering words of passionate nationalism. On one occasion, he was chosen to speak before visiting Archbishop John Hughes of New York City. Then in Europe, the archbishop was on a mission for President Abraham Lincoln, the purpose of which ostensibly was to counteract influence of Confederate representatives Mason and Slidell, who were courting support from England and France. The prelate, a native of County Tyrone, complimented the young man and assured him he could one day become a great bishop.[10] When the British government appeared ready to declare its support for the Confederacy over the Trent Affair, in which Mason and Slidell were seized by an American naval vessel from a British mail packet, Frank Roney participated with five thousand others in a meeting at the Dublin Rotunda which resolved to aid the Northern states if Britain dared to end its policy of neutrality.

While attending the Catholic University of Dublin, the articulate Joseph had joined a discussion club concerned with Irish freedom called the Brotherhood of Saint Patrick. It had been organized in 1861 at the home of Samuel McEvatt, a patriot and owner of a boot and shoe firm, who would one day become his father-in-law.

Meeting in a hall over a restaurant in Marlborough Street near the Liffey, the brotherhood was regularly addressed by able speakers, such as Charles G. Doran, a Dublin architect, and Thomas Neilson Underwood, the nephew of United Irishman Samuel Neilson. It was, in fact, a breeding ground for Fenians. Responding to this atmosphere, McDonnell's tongue became more incendiary and his pen more intemperate. University authorities threatened him with expulsion several times. In one instance, he was spared only by the intervention of his uncle, a member of the board of education for the national schools.

Another escapade finally led to McDonnell's expulsion according to John Devoy, then a fellow student and later a Fenian comrade. The university and loyalist merchants displayed signs celebrating the marriage of the Prince of Wales in 1863. In an outburst of nationalist sentiment, McDonnell led a group of students who tore down these signs, thereby infuriating the institution's mainly British faculty, as well as its administration. Not content with this display of patriotism, nor dismayed by its aftermath, McDonnell and Charles G. Doran, secretary of the Saint Patrick's Brotherhood, toured Dublin later the same year on the occasion of a visit by the Prince and his bride, closing valves on gas mains to prevent illumination of the city in his honor, and they distributed handbills urging people to stay inside their homes and refrain from welcoming the future king. It was the last straw for university authorities. McDonnell was thrown out.[11]

FENIAN ACTIVISTS

By 1863 the two young men had become members of the Fenian Brotherhood. Roney, reinstated in his apprenticeship at Combs Foundry in Belfast, had completed it and become a journeyman. After an impromptu speech before the anti-British Ulster Patriotic Association on a Sunday afternoon, Roney had been approached by John Nolan, a Dublin draper and traveling salesman, who was recruiting for the Fenian

Brotherhood. Nolan, later known as "Amnesty Nolan" for his effective campaigning in Dublin demanding release of Fenian prisoners, administered the secret oath to the twenty-one-year-old Roney in 1862. Together they began organizing, and Roney was subsequently appointed a "centre" (colonel) in the province of Ulster when James Stephens ("Head Centre") visited Belfast. Stephens with Thomas Clarke Luby founded the Irish Republican Brotherhood in March of 1858.[12]

As a soldier of the projected Irish Republic, Roney was instructed to recruit five thousand men, obtain arms, and secure military training for them within three years, all to be done secretly. Together Nolan and Roney enlisted numerous recruits, including a sergeant of the County Antrim militia, William Harbinson, who not only drilled members in military methods, but also provided access to the militia's arsenal. Members trained in locations in the countryside varied regularly to avoid the notice of loyalists and British authorities. A "circle," the basic unit of the organization, consisted of nine men. A "centre" (or colonel) chose nine men called captains, each of whom recruited his own circle of sergeants, and they in turn each enlisted a circle of men who made up the privates of the Fenian Brotherhood. To maintain secrecy, identity of the "centre" was to be known only to his nine captains, each captain to be known only to his sergeants, and so on.

McDonnell and Roney had to contend with clerical opposition to the Fenian movement. The Irish Catholic hierarchy equated the secret brotherhood with anticlerical republican movements on the Continent. They feared it would antagonize British Liberals who had agreed to accept denominational education in Ireland.[13] Cardinal Cullen issued a pastoral in 1864 directing parish priests to deny sacraments to all known members of the Fenian Brotherhood. It was, however, not uniformly observed by members of the local clergy, a significant number of whom were sympathetic to Fenianism. Being a member had, as mentioned above, the effect of preventing McDonnell from studying at Maynooth. Fenians accused ecclesiastics of bias inspired by British government grants of 30,000 pounds annually to the seminary from the time of its founding in 1795.[14]

Roney described an interview with the bishop of County Down arranged by his father (who did not support Fenianism) on the pretext of discussing some iron castings. It turned out to be a heated confrontation in which the bishop denounced the movement and Roney's involvement. Needless to say, it merely reinforced his commitment to the brotherhood, but weakened his religious faith. The Church, which had profoundly influenced both Roney and McDonnell as boys, now began to lose their allegiance. Roney tells that, because of the experience, "I became a freethinker on religious matters, but never a zealot in advocating my views."[15] In McDonnell's case, it undoubtedly made him receptive to the influence of Karl Marx a short time later.

According to Roney, the organization spread throughout Ulster among both Protestant and Catholic opponents of British rule. He reported some resistance on each side to joining with members of an opposing religious faith, but nothing insuperable. Shortly, his importance to the movement was recognized. He made periodic visits to Dublin to consult with other leaders, Jeremiah O'Donovan Rossa in particular. Rossa was then staying in the Dublin home of Maria Shaw, a kind of mother confessor to Fenian activists. At dinners there Roney met not only Rossa, but also "Pagan" O'Leary (who recruited among Irishmen in the British Army), James O'Connor and Pierce Nagle. Rossa, O'Connor and Nagle were all associated with the *Irish People* newspaper, founded by James Stephens as the mouthpiece for the Fenians. Nagle, however, proved to be a British agent who obtained documents leading on September 15, 1865, to a raid on the paper and arrest of those associated with it.[16] Joseph McDonnell was a contributor to the paper and a friend of Rossa, but there is no evidence that he ever met Roney. John Devoy, a Fenian comrade and friend of both McDonnell and Rossa, however, met Roney in Dublin, referred to him as Frank Rooney and described him as "a splendid fellow."[17]

After being denied admission to the Maynooth Seminary due to his refusal to take an oath to report any knowledge of secret societies seditious to British authority, McDonnell, having taken the Fenian oath while at the university, devoted his attention to the movement. His talent with words enabled him to become an editor of the staunchly nationalist *United Irishman* newspaper, and at the same time, contribute to the *Irish People*. He shortly became a member of the Provisional Council of the Irish Republican Brotherhood.

The Fenian rising, planned for 1865, was postponed by James Stephens because he was convinced that insufficient arms had been acquired to give it a chance to succeed. In February of 1866 the iron glove of John Bull fell on the movement. Approximately two thousand suspected Fenians were rounded up and jailed. The act of Habeas Corpus was suspended so that the prisoners could be held without trial. Among them were Joseph McDonnell, seized at his father's house, and Frank Roney, then staying in a Dublin hotel. Both of them, as well as McEvatt (McDonnell's mentor), were held in Mountjoy Prison.

Fenian John Devoy, charged with organizing Irish soldiers in the British Army, occupied a cell next to McDonnell. He recalled that a clipping reporting the brutal flogging of Corporal William Curry (arrested after betrayal by an informer) was passed to him by McDonnell after being smuggled in inside a boiled potato.[18] This attests to McDonnell's importance to the organization, as does evidence discovered by Cormac O'Grada of University College, Dublin, in records of the police files of that city describing McDonnell as an important Fenian leader whom it would not be safe to release. These records also report that he made overtures to provide information about the organization in return for his release, but was refused because he promised to reveal only what was already common knowledge. The offer was considered merely a ruse to secure his freedom.[19]

After McDonnell's arrest, stories appeared in London newspapers, according to his wife, announcing that the "head centre" of the movement (James Stephens) would soon be found now that the "sheet anchor" (McDonnell) was in custody. Stephens had been arrested on November 11, 1865, but made a dramatic escape from Richmond Jail two weeks later aided by John Devoy and jailers secretly dedicated to Fenianism. Stephens later fled to France. O'Donovan Rossa, Luby, O'Connor and several others were convicted of high treason and given long sentences. McDonnell was released in late 1866, never having been put on trial. At this point, his long-suffering father established him in a rope and twine manufacturing business. The enterprise, however, was short-lived due to the preoccupation of its proprietor with the Fenian movement.[20]

When rounded up, Frank Roney was staying in a hotel in Dublin called Caseys, frequented by Irishmen who had returned to participate in the rising after service in the American Civil War. He was put in Mountjoy Prison after a brief stay in Kilmainham Jail, where he devised a plan of mass escape which could not be executed before he and fellow prisoners were transferred. McDonnell was a fellow Mountjoy prisoner at this time. Roney recalled that while there he was regularly consoled and encouraged by letters from Maria Shaw, whom he knew from meetings with O'Donovan Rossa at her home. Like McDonnell, he was released late in the year without having been tried (due to suspension of the act of Habeas Corpus).

In Mountjoy frequent hints were dropped that suspected Fenians could obtain freedom if they agreed to depart for America, but Roney would have none of it because of his loyalty to the cause. When, nevertheless, he was freed he returned to Belfast, secured a foundry job, and secretly began to rebuild the movement there. His reorganization plan called for a director for each province. For Ulster he proposed that a Protestant barrister from Strabane—Thomas Neilson Underwood, a one-time colleague of McDonnell in the Brotherhood of Saint Patrick— become director. Underwood accepted willingly.

These ambitious plans, however, were forestalled by a second arrest of the twenty-five-year-old Roney. Held for three months in the county jail in Belfast, he was then transferred to Dublin's Mountjoy Prison, where, after several more months, he agreed to migrate to America in return for his release. It had all been arranged by his father, who had learned that an informer had surfaced whose testimony would undoubtedly convict his son in a soon-to-be-expected court appearance. The elder Roney was informed because of his well-known loyalty to the government, his reputation as an honest businessman and his friendship with the director of prisons through the Saint Vincent de Paul Society. Frank Roney left from Queenstown in 1867, with the Irishman's classical lament in bidding adieu to his native land: "I never was so utterly depressed. It was like breaking the ligaments of my heart, for we were never to return."[21]

In 1867 McDonnell moved west from Dublin to the town of Mullingar in County Westmeath, where he undertook ventures more suited to his journalistic inclinations. He opened a news agency and tobacco shop there and began to publish the *Irish Star*. His establishment, a front for Fenianism, was closely watched and regularly searched by police in the town—so much so that he was obliged to abandon it after twenty months. While in Mullingar his efforts were aided financially and otherwise by a Reverend Christopher Mullen, Canon Curate—a friend of O'Donovan Rossa and, rare among the clergy, an organizer for the Fenians—whom McDonnell knew from earlier associations. The curate was subsequently reassigned to a parish in County Meath by his bishop.[22]

MCDONNELL IN LONDON

In 1868 McDonnell shook the dust of Mullingar from his feet and left for London where his old mentor Samuel McEvatt now resided. There he continued his lifelong journalistic calling as summary editor of the London *Evening Standard*, as well as correspondent for the *Dublin Irishman* and as an editor of *Universal News*, an Irish nationalist paper published in the city. He also began to make his presence felt through speeches in public—first at a gathering to welcome George Francis Train, a wealthy, eccentric American, notable lecturer and an advocate of Irish freedom. Train's ventures brought him in contact with McDonnell and Roney on both sides of the Atlantic. The occasion was Train's return from imprisonment in Dublin, where he was jailed for lecturing on behalf of Irish independence. There followed large happenings of expatriate Irish, demonstrating in behalf of amnesty for Fenian prisoners. Their instigator, McDonnell, organized the English Amnesty Committee in 1869 for that purpose. It was the counterpart of John "Amnesty" Nolan's impressive efforts in Dublin. These open-air meetings, said to be spectacularly large, were usually addressed by McDonnell, often under the "Reformer's Tree" in Hyde Park.

At that location on October 24, 1869, a request for amnesty for Fenian prisoners was formulated and forwarded to Prime Minister Gladstone who proceeded to refuse it. Gladstone's refusal generated a discussion of the Irish question at a meeting of the General Council of the International Workingmen's Association (IWA) or "First International."[23] Karl Marx, who dominated the council, and Friedrich Engels had long believed that independence for Ireland was a key to eventual overthrow of capitalism in its citadel—England. McDonnell's activities thus brought him to the notice of Marx and Engels.

At some point during this period, Marx and Engels became personally acquainted with McDonnell. The acquaintance most likely began after their attendance at one of the "monster" amnesty meetings which he conducted. Impressed with his oratorical and organizing abilities and having for some time recognized the potential value of the Fenian agitation to the objectives of their own movement, they invited McDonnell to join the International Workingmen's Association. On June 21, 1871, Marx and Engels nominated McDonnell for membership on the General Council of the IWA. The council acted as a liaison between IWA sections in each country, facilitating support by workers in one country for strikes in another, including prevention of the export of strikebreakers. In nominating McDonnell, Marx and Engels were obliged to defend him against critics who charged irregularities in his handling of Amnesty Committee funds and selling Irish votes in local elections, among other things (which they did successfully since no evidence was adduced to support the charges). To Frederich A. Sorge, the IWA leader in New York, Marx wrote, "We want above all influence on the Irish in England, and that for that purpose there exists, as far as we have been able to ascertain, no better man than McDonnell." He was duly elected to the position in August of 1871 and appointed corresponding secretary for Ireland on October 2, 1871.[24]

With customary vigor, but less than profound grasp of Marxian theory, McDonnell plunged into the work of the IWA. There is no evidence that he had studied Marx's work or that he had time to do so. By birth a creature of the middle class rather than of the working class, his receptivity to the socialist cause undoubtedly owed something to the vehement denunciation of Fenianism by Cardinal Cullen and most of the Irish clergy. He organized Irish branches of the IWA in London and reported establishment of them in Dublin, Cork, Belfast and elsewhere in Ireland. In Cork, the IWA branch organized by John DeMorgan—a kind of wandering elocution teacher—became involved in a coach builders' strike and was denounced by clergy and the business community.[25] McDonnell faithfully supported Marx and Engels in meetings of the council and congresses of the IWA more out of personal loyalty than doctrinal concurrence. He attended thirty-one council meetings and was the Irish delegate to the Hague Congress of the IWA in September of 1872.

At the Hague Congress, anarchist Mikhail Bakunin was expelled from the International, but Karl Marx's fear that Bakunin's supporters might obtain a majority on the General Council led him to move the General Council to New York out of their reach. The Hague Congress was the last one held by the IWA. The organization was formally dissolved at Philadelphia in 1876. While in Holland, McDonnell orchestrated one of his "monster meetings" in the city of Amsterdam for the purpose of denouncing British imprisonment of Irish political prisoners and demanding their release "in the name of the working people of the world."[26]

By this time J.P. McDonnell had become adept at the art of assembling massive public demonstrations. He had tweaked the British lion's nose on the fourth of July 1869 by organizing a well-attended excursion to Rye House to celebrate the eighty-third anniversary of the Declaration of Independence, moving the mostly Irish crowd in horse-drawn vans with Irish and American flags flying. On the twenty-ninth of the next month he again managed a successful excursion, this one by steamer from London to Gravesend, to honor the memory of the heroic defense of Limerick against the British siege of 1690. His finest effort in London was a mass demonstration held during 1872 in Hyde Park to demand the right to hold meetings and enjoy free speech in public parks. McDonnell, John DeMorgan and five other speakers were arrested for violating an act prohibiting such an assembly without a permit. Their trial aroused much sympathy throughout England. Found guilty, they appealed the case to the House of Lords which found the Parks Law to be an unlawful enactment.[27]

In the course of his London ventures, on March 15, 1871, McDonnell married Mary McEvatt (daughter of Samuel McEvatt) in the Franciscan church of Peckham, London. The marriage proved to be an enduring and happy one, but produced no children.

One of McDonnell's activities in this period was to recruit a brigade among Irishmen in London to fight for France in the Franco-Prussian War in 1870. This was arranged with a certain General McAdaras who had contrived to obtain that rank in the French Army by devious methods, although his experience was as a noncommissioned officer in the British Army. Done under the guise of organizing an ambulance corps, the brigade's purpose was to provide arms and experience for men who would then apply them to the fight for Irish independence. McAdaras was to deliver funds from France to repay expenses of raising the brigade, but failed to do so, leaving that responsibility to McDonnell. Word of the plan came to the German ambassador, who lodged an official protest with British authorities causing McDonnell's arrest for violation of the foreign enlistment act. A prison stay of over two months ensued.

McDonnell found conditions in Clerkenwell Prison intolerable. He published letters in London papers vehemently protesting these conditions. As a result, he was transferred to Newgate Prison, where his treatment improved. While confined he was arraigned, but his trial was suspended. Finally, he was released on bail, and the trial was never resumed. Defense costs and the financial obligations of raising the brigade were well beyond his means, and except for help from friends he would have been left destitute.[28]

Therefore, hardly a year and a half after becoming a member of the General Council, McDonnell, in early December 1872, left with his wife for America.

When Frank Roney arrived in New York in 1867, he became a harshly critical observer of the new land because of the contrast between the idealized image of the American republic carried in his head and the reality he found in his travels. Immediately upon disembarking he was appalled at the brazenness of a madam who nearly succeeded in kidnapping into prostitution a naive young Irish girl, a shipmate of Roney, until his decisive intervention prevented it. He was disgusted with American politicians when they arranged for him to become (illegally) an instant American citizen—as they had done for hundreds of other immigrants (then hastily registering them as Democratic voters). He refused to go through with it. He was dismayed at the attitude of the American Irish, nearly all Democrats with hostile feelings toward his hero, Abraham Lincoln, and loyal to the party of the Southern states which England—oppressor of their native land—had covertly aided during the Civil War. Roney preferred the Republican party and was a founder of a Republican Club among New York Irish immigrants.

Perhaps he was most critical of what he called "Molding in America," which he observed in New York, Saint Louis, Chicago and elsewhere. Work in foundries was done at a breakneck pace, for long hours, often on a piecework basis, with each man competing for the favor of the foreman. This was strikingly different from the orderly system to which he was accustomed in Belfast, where a businesslike molders' union (of which he had been a member) was generally present to insist upon decent working conditions. The conception of equality he expected to find in America underwent drastic revision. It was a time for shedding illusions.

During his two-month sojourn in New York, Roney made contact with John O'Mahony and other leaders of the American wing of the Fenians. He devoted time to revitalizing the organization, but after leaving the city seems to have gradually detached himself from the cause that had once absorbed him completely. By 1875, when he became an American citizen, he decided to "sever all connections with Irish revolutionary organizations on American soil."[29] By then he considered such associations, as well as those with Irish-American political clubs, contrary to his obligations as a U.S. citizen.

This drastic departure from his devotion to Irish nationalism is curious—McDonnell made no such renunciation. However, Roney's attitude was consistent with his great admiration for Abraham Lincoln and his resentment at hostility toward the late president evident in many Irish Americans he met (who were usually Democrats—and often ambivalent about his having freed the slaves). He opposed Irish-American and other nationality clubs as sources of division in the American republic—a republic preserved by Lincoln's tenacious conduct of the Civil War. Experience had convinced him that corrupt politicians manipulated such organizations for purposes contrary to the principles of a democratic republic. It is evident from his autobiography that Roney not only was independent-minded, but also possessed a rather contrary personality.

Nevertheless, his moves to Saint Louis, Chicago and Omaha and the jobs he obtained were at the invitation of old Fenian comrades or members of his trade who had emigrated from Ireland earlier. In 1868 he settled in Omaha encouraged by John Quinn, a fellow apprentice from Belfast, who obtained a molder's job for him there. Construction of the Union Pacific Railroad, then under way, had made this frontier community a thriving one. He first became involved with American trade unions in Omaha, where he joined Molders Local 190, and following a pattern repeated often in his career, was shortly thereafter elected secretary and subsequently chosen president.

When an organizer from the National Labor Reform party visited Omaha, Roney joined it and dropped his Republican party affiliations.

He began to propagandize for the new party, an arm of the National Labor Union, both of which were dominated by William Sylvis who was also president of the Iron Molders' International Union. Roney became president of the local chapter of the Labor Reform party and, in this capacity as well as in his leadership of Local 190, carried on a limited correspondence with William Sylvis until that pioneer labor organizer died in July of 1869. Richard Trevellick, successor to Sylvis as president of the National Labor Reform party, joined Roney for a speaking tour of Nebraska which Roney credited with fostering progressive politics in the state.

Roney lived in Omaha for several years. He seriously considered settling there permanently. He married a woman named Butterfield and wrote on National Labor Reform party activities for the *Omaha Herald*. His columns vigorously advocated greenbackism, a major plank of the party platform. When *Herald* owner George L. Miller offered him the city editorship, he declined, and later regretted it. He was urged to become a lawyer by early Labor Reform party member Judge Clinton Briggs, but rejected that idea as well as Briggs's proposal that he join him and others in a railroad venture, which he learned later made its founders wealthy. Roney left Omaha convinced that its prospects were poor after completion of the Union Pacific, in spite of financier George Francis Train, an original investor in the road and in land in Omaha, who tried to persuade him of its glorious future. He lived to regret the decision. There followed a brief career in Salt Lake City plying his molder's trade and establishing a molders' union there. In the same period he developed a distaste for the Mormons.

MCDONNELL ARRIVES

On New Year's Day of 1873, the same year Roney came to Salt Lake City, Joseph McDonnell arrived in New York.[30] His arrival followed by only one year that of Samuel McEvatt, who was now living in New York City. Strapped financially, the McDonnells had come steerage class on the *Erin*, a vessel of the American National Steamship Company. Seizing opportunity from adversity, McDonnell spent most of his time on the twenty-eight-day voyage making notes on the conditions endured by steerage passengers. Keeping a diary when confined was a habit of his dating at least from his London jailing. Usually protests about foul conditions were forthcoming thereafter. This was the case in the Clerkenwell episode, and so it was with his passage in steerage on the *Erin*.

Beginning on January 27, 1873, a series of lengthy letters from McDonnell appeared in the *New York Herald*. They told of seriously inadequate sanitary facilities, complete lack of privacy for the sexes, bad food, ill treatment of non-English-speaking passengers collected at Le Havre, unseaworthy conditions of the ship and numerous other problems. The missives called for reforms to protect steerage passengers from such abuses. They were followed by a letter to President

Grant on February 11, which elicited a response from Secretary of State Hamilton Fish assuring McDonnell that negotiations with countries from which the bulk of immigrants came were under way to eliminate such evils. *Herald* editorials took note of McDonnell's account and expressed serious concern.[31] But weeks into his stay in America, he had gained public notice and had associated his name with reform.

AMERICAN ENDEAVORS

The 1870s decade in New York which McDonnell entered was one of economic depression, unemployment, labor turmoil and contesting social theories. The period was a highly formative one for the American labor movement. Manhattan was an arena for contending ideas brought by exiles and refugees from Europe, such as IWA activist Friedrich A. Sorge and by native radicals such as Peter J. McGuire. McDonnell assumed the position of corresponding secretary for the New York Council of the IWA, which met regularly and ventilated these ideas at the Tenth Ward Hotel at Broome and Forsythe Streets. More intensive debate, however, took place among an inner circle of ten men, including McDonnell, Samuel Gompers and McGuire. In his autobiography, Gompers recalled that "from these men who were genuine revolutionaries in thought and in deed, men to whom principles meant something, I learned the fundamentals of the labor movement. They were men who did not hesitate to risk something to accomplish a purpose."[32]

All but Gompers himself were IWA members. In their wide-open, late-night seminars, Marxian, LaSallean and Utopian socialism, anarchism and other isms were assessed for their relevance to American workers. From these origins, permanence in the form of the American Federation of Labor eventually emerged, but not before numbers of other organizations and ideologies had been tried. From Marxism, Gompers and Adolph Strasser, both cigar makers, and McDonnell accepted thorough economic organization of workers as the essential foundation for undertaking anything further. So, also, did P.J. McGuire but not until considerably later after becoming disenchanted with the method of a labor party as a result of his experience with it.

Conditions which Roney encountered on arriving in San Francisco in 1875 resembled those McDonnell experienced in New York. With a population of about two hundred thousand, San Francisco was much smaller and tended to be isolated from the eastern part of the country; however, by that time, the depression had spread to the Golden Gate, unemployment was severe, and demands for relief were growing. Unemployment had intensified, due to a continuing influx of Chinese immigrants and workers from the East taking advantage of recently completed transcontinental railroads, hoping to escape depressed conditions elsewhere by coming to San Francisco. The trade union movement had not yet crystallized and, although the IWA was not present as a catalyst, there were anarchists, German socialists, anti-Chinese agitators and other theorists of remedy, such as Henry George. In Roney's words, "A universal chaos of ideas prevailed and yet all desired something different from what existed."[33]

Frank Roney at once faced a personal crisis caused by economic conditions in San Francisco. With a wife, who was expecting, and two small children, he was unable to find steady employment in his own trade or any other. He recorded his ordeal in a daily diary, similar to what McDonnell had done on board ship. An analysis of it by Neil Shumsky suggests that, as an outlet for his anxieties, it had a therapeutic effect. Roney was forced to borrow from friends and from his lodge, the Odd Fellows. This was against his principles as was spending money on drink, but, in his desperation, he did both. A less tenacious individual might have collapsed emotionally or become an alcoholic. By selling nearly all their furniture, moving frequently and going into debt, the family survived, but not unscathed. Under the circumstances, Roney did not become active in trade unions or politics for some time.[34]

The leadership and organizing skills of McDonnell and Roney, honed in their youthful adventures as Fenians, began to be felt on both coasts in the latter half of the 1870s. McDonnell leaned more heavily on his journalism and oratory, while Roney depended more on his powers of personal persuasion and talent for designing organizational structures. Initially, McDonnell with some IWA associates, circa 1875, established the United Workers of America. They endowed it with the principles of and affiliation with the First International. It was not a success. At Philadelphia, in the summer of 1876, the First International was officially dissolved—the United Workers of America survived not long thereafter.

But other organizational ventures were launched by McDonnell and his allies, who insisted upon effective economic foundations before all else. In April 1876 they formed the Central Organization of Trades and Labor Unions of New York, a city federation of local unions. At the same time, they took control of *The Socialist*, a radical English language newspaper and made it the journalistic arm of the New York federation, installing McDonnell as editor. A short time later, they changed its name to the *New York Labor Standard*. Henceforth a *Labor Standard* paper was identified with McDonnell throughout his career—though it emanated from several different cities.

With the demise of the First International in Philadelphia in 1876, a new organization arose immediately from its ashes. The new organization attempted to unify all socialists and related movements. The organization was born in Philadelphia on July 19, 1876. Calling itself the Workingmen's party of the United States, it nevertheless adopted a constitution that restricted involvement in election campaigns. This reflected the influence of the trade unionist faction, and was opposed by P.J. McGuire who favored immediate political involvement. The new organization designated the *Labor Standard* under McDonnell's editorship as its English-speaking voice (it had several German language organs as well). McGuire attempted to replace McDonnell as editor at this time, but failed.

The party was promptly beset by bitter factional struggles between the political-action-now (or LaSallean) wing and advocates of trade unionism first. Political actionists got an unexpected boost for their cause from outbreak of the great railway strikes across the nation during the summer of 1877, one year after the new organization began. Convinced that a great opportunity for political victories had presented itself, they soon gained control of the Workingmen's party, and in December of 1877, at a Newark convention, changed its name to the Socialist Labor party (SLP) with McGuire in a leading position.

Wasting no time, the newly named party began laying plans for political campaigns. In doing this, the political wing alienated numerous leaders of trade unionist orientation, including McDonnell, who parted company with the SLP at the time of its inception. Meanwhile, he was having his own difficulties with colleagues in the camp of the trade unionists. Some of them—Ira Steward, George McNeil and George Gunton—were reformers in the New England tradition of abolitionist William Lloyd Garrison. Steward had built an entire theory of social reform on the basis of shortening the hours of work. Preoccupied with the campaign for shorter hours, they had previously collaborated to form the Boston Eight Hour League and similar associations. The revolutionary tone of McDonnell's editorials in the *Labor Standard* made them uncomfortable. They determined to move the paper to New England and make it more of a vehicle for promoting state eight-hour laws.[35]

In this endeavor, the eight-hour triumvirate was partially successful: the *Labor Standard* was relocated to the textile manufacturing town of Fall River, Massachusetts, in August 1877, and McDonnell accompanied it as associate editor, somewhat of a comedown. His wife recalled that in Fall River he was "dictated to" on matters of policy. Needless to say, the volatile journalist chafed at these conditions. While there a rift of sorts erupted, and McDonnell returned to New York to resume publishing the *Labor Standard*.[36] At the same time, a short-lived *Boston Labor Standard* began to appear. The rift was not permanent, since we find the same four men jointly engaged in establishing the International Labor Union at the beginning of 1878.

The International Labor Union is significant as one of the first attempts to organize unskilled workers in manufacturing. The union lasted until 1883, and at one time its president, George McNeil, claimed nearly eight thousand members.[37] Its efforts were concentrated in the New England, Cohoes, New York and New Jersey—locations of America's oldest mechanized industry—textiles, which at first utilized a work force of New England farm girls, but was by now employing immigrants, mainly women and children. Attention to the textile industry drew McDonnell to Paterson, New Jersey, one of America's oldest manufacturing towns, by then a community of approximately fifty thousand and known particularly for its silk mills. A strike had broken out at a textile mill, and the ILU offered support. Bringing the *Labor Standard* along, McDonnell had at last found a permanent arena for his endeavors and spent the rest of his life—some twenty-eight years—in

Paterson with, on balance, quite satisfactory results. When George Francis Train came to Paterson to address a gathering of silk workers, he was met by Mayor Beckwith and McDonnell, to whom his first words were: "What, you who stirred up all England and parts of Europe, here in a little village."[38]

RONEY IN CALIFORNIA

One of Frank Roney's first efforts on the West Coast came early in 1878 when he served as temporary chairman of the first state convention of the Workingmen's party of California, an organization led by the notorious sandlot orator Denis Kearney.[39] Kearney, an Irish-born, former seaman, now a small businessman in San Francisco, was standing trial for inciting to riot when the convention opened, but after his acquittal a day later, he rushed triumphantly to assume command of the convention from Roney.

In 1877 Kearney had transformed himself from a conventional self-made small businessman and bumbling amateur speaker into an anti-establishment rabble-rouser. He had capitalized on anti-Chinese sentiment and a new-found capacity for demagoguery to build the party which began to threaten the dominance of the two major parties in San Francisco.

Roney was drawn to the new party by the injustice of Kearney's arrest.[40] Nevertheless, always dubious of the man's intemperate speeches and tyrannical mode of leadership, he clashed with him repeatedly, finally splitting from the party altogether. Furthermore, Roney was ambivalent about the Chinese issue. As a union activist, he objected to the depressing effect on wages and working standards of the incoming stream of Oriental labor, but he considered the vilification of the Chinese character to be brutal and contrary to his humanitarian principles. In this, he was mindful of its resemblance to the vicious prejudice against Irish immigrants and the Anglo–Native American view of the Irish as less than civilized. However, he saw the party as a potential means of advancing labor organizations on the West Coast. Roney records that, at the party's convention, he "proposed the resolution which a few weeks later called into existence the trades and labor assembly which Kearney thoroughly disliked."[41] This was the San Francisco Trades Assembly, a central labor body which functioned from 1878 to 1882.

Roney expressed definite ideas about structuring the union movement in *The Working Men's Advocate* in 1869 while still in Omaha. An innovator, he advocated that craft local unions composed of workers from a specific industry should be joined in a council in each locality—such as an iron trades council, a building trades council and so forth. Each local craft union should also be affiliated with the appropriate national union, and these should be gathered in national trades councils corresponding to those at the local level.

This plan was outlined in 1881 at the founding convention of the Federation of Organized Trades and Labor Unions (which became the AFL in 1886), but it was not adopted at that time.[42] Later, however, such structures were incorporated in the AFL without acknowledging their origin. Furthermore, Roney himself established the Federated Iron Trades Council of San Francisco, implementing his own design. He was at various times a leader or founder of a number of other organizations—specifically, the Seaman's Protective Association, the San Francisco Trades Assembly, the Vallejo Labor Council and, most important, the Federated Trades of the Pacific Coast, a central labor council for San Francisco, of which he was president from 1886, when it was founded, until 1887. By calling a labor convention on the Chinese issue, always a strong draw, he proceeded successfully to form the Central Labor Council for the city. On other occasions, he reported initial meetings of a nonexistent labor organization and published them in a local newspaper. Sufficient numbers of the curious attended subsequent meetings he had advertised, and the body gained permanence. Such was the cunning method of a consummate organizer. But unlike McDonnell, Roney—always a craft unionist—never interested himself in organizing unskilled workers.

In the early 1880s prosperity returned to San Francisco. Trade unions made a strong comeback with aid from energetic efforts by leadership of the city's Trades Assembly. Chinese immigration also rose sharply at this time. During the twelve months Frank Roney served as president of the Trades Assembly (beginning in August 1881), a bill was passed in the U.S. Congress prohibiting Chinese immigration for twenty years. When President Arthur vetoed it, the Trades Assembly called a statewide convention on the issue, which formed the League of Deliverance to effectuate its anti-Chinese goals.[43] As president of the league, Roney employed an old Irish device, the boycott, using it against retailers who handled goods made by Chinese labor. He and his associates picketed stores until they capitulated. When one picket was arrested, another took his place. This process was repeated again and again. Though effective, Roney recognized how vulnerable to abuse it was. His disappointment was slight when the league died of disinterest after a more moderate version of the Exclusion Act was signed by the president in May of 1882.

In the summer of 1886, Roney made a swing around the East on the occasion of his being chosen a delegate to the London, Ontario, convention of the International Molders Union. He was much in evidence as the mover of numerous resolutions, including one that annual conventions be replaced with biennial ones, as he felt much money and time of the union was wasted at conventions. He was nominated for president of the molders and ran third in a field of four, but he was elected vice president in a field of three.[44] As secretary of the Committee on Constitution and By-laws, he was persuaded to spare the convention his report on the small proportion of molders who were actually members of the union (less than 25 percent) as it could be demoralizing.

On the same trip, he met briefly with Samuel Gompers who, he says, was relieved to learn that Roney was not interested in running for AFL president. In contrast to McDonnell's admiration for Gompers, Roney was not impressed. Stopping in for a beer together, he noted that Gompers ordered a brand on the union unfair list and even smoked a cigar without a union label. Also in New York he visited old Fenian comrade O'Donovan Rossa for whom he felt pity on account of the man's continued effort on behalf of Irish independence, which by then Roney believed futile. Clearly Roney was capable of his share of wrong-headed perceptions.

Roney's term as president of the San Francisco Federated Trades Council (his own creation) marks the high point of his career. Not long after his retirement from that post in early 1887, he was denounced by the organization as a traitor to organized labor for criticizing (in a private conversation later publicized) a boycott conducted for the sake of organizing San Francisco breweries. A subsequent decade spent working at the Mare Island Navy Yard in Vallejo was punctuated by the death of his first wife in 1904, a second marriage to a woman named Jones (with whom he never lived for reasons never revealed), and a first meeting with Ira Cross. His departure from the Vallejo Labor Council, of which he was a founder and had served as president for one term, was the inauspicious result of internal quarrels.

After he left Vallejo in 1909 due to serious illness, his life alternated between working sporadically and poverty. Migrating south he lived in Watts for a time, then lived in Los Angeles with one of his sons for several years and spent his last days in Long Beach. A final connection with trade unions was a term as secretary-treasurer of the Los Angeles Metal Trades Council. His second wife died in 1912, but he married a third time in the early 1920s to a woman Cross was unable to identify, and who became his widow on January 24, 1925, in Long Beach.

Frank Roney's long and arduous efforts on behalf of social justice were not rewarded with the gratitude of his fellow workingmen, or even their remembrance. He would have disappeared into the ranks of labor's unknown soldiers, except for Professor Cross's insistent urging that he record his recollections. Yet, according to Cross, he never became embittered.

MCDONNELL IN NEW JERSEY

For an account of J.P. McDonnell's work in Paterson, New Jersey, we draw heavily on a study by the late Herbert Gutman, who investigated it intensively. He found in the story evidence that citizens of this industrializing town were not yet ready to adopt the discipline imposed by factory production, nor the ethos of the industrial leaders. Far from ostracizing the Irish radical they accepted him, read his newspaper (which had wide local circulation) and even paid tribute to him on at least one occasion.[45]

The maiden issue of the *Paterson Labor Standard* appeared in October of 1878, whereupon McDonnell was charged with libel. In print he had called some employees of the R. and H. Adams textile firm scabs for crossing the picket line during a strike. A jury of local citizens found him guilty. The judge imposed a fine of five hundred dollars and court costs of sixty-eight dollars. Nevertheless, the financial burden of the editor was relieved when his supporters immediately raised sufficient funds to pay it. Far from cramping his style, the experience appears almost to have whetted his appetite for controversy. He contrived to print a broadsheet containing the statement of his conviction and fine with an engraving of himself above it, below which is printed, "The Attempt to Crush Labor—the Memorable Blood Money Bill."[46]

Less than a year later, McDonnell fearlessly published a letter from an employee at a local brickyard who complained of treatment by his employer, Van Blarkam and Clark. This employer provided, the letter said, rotten bread, rancid butter, tainted meat and coffee equally appetizing. Working hours lasted from 4:00 a.m. to 6:00 p.m., with housing and toilet facilities no better than leaky wooden shacks. Employees became ill as a result, but were cared for badly. Such conditions were reminiscent of those experienced by McDonnell on his passage across the Atlantic. Once again, a local firm sued the doughty editor for libel. A jury duly convicted him. The judge, noting that a fine alone would not deter McDonnell, sentenced him, along with the letter writer (Michael Menton), to two months in the Passaic County Jail.

Had Paterson industrial employers finally silenced his disturbing voice? Not at all. In fact, the jail episode, served in February and March of 1880, proved more of a triumph than a chastisement. McDonnell, with the full approval of sympathetic Warden John Buckley, continued to edit the *Labor Standard* while confined. His meals were delivered from a local boardinghouse by his newly hired printer's devil, George Leonard McNeil, son of McDonnell's old associate George McNeil. Paterson saloons provided him with a fully adequate supply of wines, liquor and cigars during his stay—and special dinner celebrations materialized for both his birthday and Saint Patrick's Day. Visitors were numerous and welcomed hospitably, often in the warden's office. Old friends Samuel Gompers of the Cigar Makers' Union and O'Donovan Rossa of Fenian days came, as well as Terence Powderly, mayor of Scranton, soon to become leader of the Knights of Labor, and prominent journalist and friend of labor John Swinton, whom he also knew from New York.

The climax of his second Paterson conviction was a demonstration on his behalf by townspeople on April 1, 1880, the day of his release. A multitude, estimated to have consisted of from fifteen to twenty thousand, greeted his return to freedom, feted him with a banquet and presented him with a gold watch suitably inscribed. While workers made up the bulk of the crowd, numerous small businessmen and professional people participated as well. Freedom of the press was recognized as at issue in both trials. Lawyers for his defense were men of substance from respected families in Passaic County who had been in politics (from both parties) and business. Evidently, important elements of the community, in addition to its workers, were favorably disposed toward this thirty-three-year-old critic of the evils of industrialism.[47]

One of the first things that McDonnell did when he arrived in Paterson was to join with other trade unionists, socialists and reformers to establish an annual New Jersey Labor Congress. The congress met each year usually in the state capitol (Trenton) before the legislature convened and interested itself in legislation affecting workers in New Jersey. In time it became a vehicle for promoting labor reform laws through nonpartisan politics. McDonnell took a leading role in it and was the loudest voice advocating a permanent, year-round agency to promote the interests of organized labor in the state. This was accomplished in 1883 with establishment of the Federation of Organized Trades and Labor Unions of New Jersey. McDonnell became chairman of its legislative committee.

Among McDonnell's noteworthy achievements were pioneering labor reform bills he was responsible for drafting and the effective nonpartisan political methods he utilized to advance them through the state legislature. For this purpose, he mobilized the voting strength of workers in industrial cities of the state, such as Newark, Paterson, Jersey City and Camden. He had to focus it on candidates, regardless of party, who could recognize the importance of the labor vote in their own district. A favorite method was to submit a questionnaire listing bills advocated by the New Jersey Labor Federation and ask if the candidate would back them if elected. If the candidate's response was positive, the federation would endorse him and support his campaign. This was followed up by lobbying during sessions of the legislature to make sure the bills were introduced and that those who agreed to support them actually did so. It also involved testifying in favor of them when hearings were held. According to Gutman, McDonnell spent the winter months in Trenton for fifteen years as a lobbyist for this cause.[48]

The fruit of these efforts was passage of an impressive series of laws over fierce opposition of industrial employers. Indeed, they were enacted between 1883 and 1892 before onset of the progressive movement quickened the social conscience of America. Without exhausting the entire array of them, mention can be made of those restricting child labor, requiring safety standards in industry, limiting the workweek to fifty-five hours in manufacturing, prohibiting Pinkertons from being deputized as law officers and those restricting the use of convict labor. On April 6, 1887, New Jersey became the first state to make Labor Day a legal holiday due primarily to the strenuous efforts of McDonnell. It also passed an early compulsory education law for children during his tenure as lobbyist.

In the course of his political activities, McDonnell received appointments to the position of deputy factory inspector and, in 1892, to membership on the state's (briefly existing as it turned out) Board of Arbitration and Mediation. The Arbitration Board elected him chairman, and he involved himself in numerous labor disputes around the state as his meticulous records show, much to the displeasure of many employers who soon prevailed upon the legislature first to curtail his travel expenses and later to abolish the board. The board nevertheless represented an advanced approach for its time for dealing with strikes and owed its energetic operation to McDonnell.

McDonnell's myriad undertakings raises the question of how he found time and energy for all of them. In addition to those already mentioned, he was the founder in 1884 of the Paterson Trades Assembly, a central federation of local unions in the city, and two years later he established Typographical Union 195 in Paterson, in which he retained membership for the rest of his life. As recounted above, Samuel Gompers, in his autobiography, wrote warmly of his friend McDonnell. Gompers first met McDonnell in the office of Patrick Ford, editor and publisher of the *Irish World*, shortly after McDonnell arrived in New York.[49] Their friendship endured. When the Labor Press Association was founded by a group of journalists inspired by Edward Bellamy's *Looking Backward*, McDonnell became its first chairman and was called by Gompers "The Nestor of Labor Journalists." Gompers went so far as to write that McDonnell "was to take a leading part in the development of the American trade union movement."[50]

LEGACY

The various affiliations of these two Irishmen mirror much of the evolution of trade unions in America after the Civil War. They both exchanged the ideal of an Irish republic for that of an America where workers could enjoy dignity in a rapidly industrializing age. At one time or another they subscribed to most of the movements circulating in this formative period of labor history. Roney, while his adherence to molders' craft unionism was constant, never seemed to find it enough by itself. In Omaha he opted for the Labor Party approach and was much influenced by the ideas of William Sylvis. After his involvement with Kearney's party, he joined the socialists, whose ideas and fraternity he enjoyed until finally deciding their program "was excellent but not capable of being realized except through a long period of education."[51]

McDonnell came to New York steeped in the ethos of the IWA. His effort in textiles was very much in that vein. He consistently employed its rhetoric, but proved not to be a doctrinaire Marxist in spite of the strong personal influence of Karl Marx. Rather he, like Roney, was something of a lifelong pragmatist. For example, by the time he participated in founding the New Jersey Federation of Trades and Labor Unions in 1883, he had joined the Knights of Labor whose philosophy of uplift and reform had much in common with that of the New England triumvirate of Steward, McNeil and Gunton. A majority of his cofounders of the New Jersey Federation were also Knights. John W. Hayes, first presiding officer of the federation, had, in fact, been secretary-treasurer of the Knights of Labor, editor of its journal and a close personal friend of Terence Powderly until their falling out in 1893.[52]

Roney also had dallied briefly with the Knights as a member of the San Francisco Local Assembly after earlier accepting a position of organizer "in order to keep it out of San Francisco" because of his skepticism about its true nature.[53]

As time went on, conflict developed in New Jersey between factions representing the Knights of Labor and those converted to the craft union mentality. By 1890 the conflict had been resolved in favor of the craft unionists; McDonnell himself had moved toward that point of view. The New Jersey Federation secured a charter from the AFL in 1892. McDonnell's conversion to AFL style unionism was by no means complete. His emphasis on labor reform legislation is not consistent with the voluntarism or opposition to government involvement which became the watchword of the AFL. His continuing interest in organizing the unskilled in textiles did not fit the pattern either. Nevertheless, he was a general organizer for the AFL from 1888 on and a lifelong friend of Samuel Gompers from the time they met in 1873. Perhaps it is also worth mentioning that the McDonnell Papers include a certificate of membership for him in the Anti-Poverty Society signed by Edward D. McGlynn, president, and Henry George, vice-president, dated May 10, 1887.

The careers of Joseph McDonnell and Frank Roney stand as classic examples of how idealistic young men devoted to the cause of Irish independence were transformed into passionate campaigners for organized labor in America. They were resourceful, imaginative and flexible enough to adapt reasonably well to the realities of the American scene without ever losing their concern for the dignity of working people.

Professor Cross says of Roney that: "he dominated the labor movement in San Francisco during 1881–1886."[54] He found Roney's leadership remarkable for its dedication and willingness to sacrifice for the trade union cause. Roney passed up numerous opportunities to profit from business ventures and other chances for accumulating wealth. McDonnell never changed careers for the sake of more lucrative pursuits, which unquestionably were available for someone with his talents.

On at least four occasions, Roney was fired by San Francisco's Union Ironworks for union or union-related activity. In the first instance, he was also blacklisted and forced to find work for three months at a foundry in Pioche, Nevada, a mining camp. In May of 1882 he had to retire from trade union activity temporarily due to mounting indebtedness. Physical and mental exhaustion were the cause of his refusal to run for reelection as president of the Federated Trades Council in 1886. McDonnell's trials for libel and imprisonment speak for themselves. Above all, they were both unfailingly militant, lived modestly and were without wealth at the time of their deaths. It was a way of life learned in youth as soldiers for the Irish Republic.

NOTES

1. Samuel Gompers, *Seventy Years of Life and Labor* (New York: Dutton, 1925), vol. 1, 88. The source for Gompers's height in Benjamin Stolberg, "The Greatness of Devotion," in *Gompers*, G.E. Stern, ed. (Englewood Cliffs, N.J.: Prentice Hall, 1971), 162.

2. *National Labor Standard*, January 20, 1906, 1.

3. Frank Roney, *Frank Roney, Irish Rebel and California Labor Leader, An Autobiography*, ed. Ira B. Cross (Berkeley: University of California Press, 1931), xii.

4. Roney, *Autobiography*, xxvi–xxvii, 1–3. All information about Roney is drawn from his autobiography except as otherwise noted. Only direct quotes from it are footnoted hereafter.

5. Letter to author from Mary Scott Rooney of Belfast, Northern Ireland, May 28, 1983. Ms. Rooney points out that Reverend John Roney, S.J., of Riverview College, Sydney, Australia, was a brother of Frank Roney.

6. Gordon Augustus Thomson could not have been a United Irishman since he was born in 1799; however, his father, John Thomson, might well have been, having lived from 1766 to 1824. See letter to author from Dr. W.A. Maguire, Department of History, Ulster Museum, Belfast, August 7, 1986.

7. Biographical sketch of McDonnell dictated to Clara Commons (sister of John R. Commons) by widow of J.P. McDonnell, 1908, McDonnell Papers, State Historical Society of Wisconsin, 1–2.

8. The *Examiner* was founded in Belfast by Denis Holland and Richard Pigott. Later, these two men moved to Dublin and founded the *Irishman*, which had a strong nationalist editorial policy. In 1899 Pigott confessed to having forged letters which, if genuine, would have discredited Charles Stewart Parnell, champion of Irish freedom in Britain's Parliament, Roney, *Autobiography*, 38–40.

9. During the frustration and failure of the seven years (1851–1858) of his rectorship of the university, Newman composed the essays which comprised his classic *The Idea of a University*, not published as a book until 1873.

10. John Devoy, *Recollections of an Irish Rebel* (New York: Charles D. Young, 1929), 14; Sr. M. Jane Coogan, B.V.M., "A Study of the John Hughes, Terence Donaghue Friendship, " *Records of the American Catholic Historical Society of Philadelphia*, March–December, 1982, 68–70; biographical sketch, McDonnell Papers, 1.

11. Devoy, *Recollections*, 15, 33–34; biographical sketch, McDonnell Papers, 1, 7.

12. William O'Brien and Desmond Ryan eds., *Devoy's Post Bag* (Dublin: C.J. Fallon, 1948), vol. 1, xxx, 1, 57.

13. Lawrence J. McCaffrey, *Ireland from Colony to Nation State* (Englewood Cliffs, N.J.: Prentice Hall, 1979), 92–93.

14. John W. Boyle, "Ireland and the First International," *Journal of British Studies* (May 1972): footnote p. 50; the amount of the grant is mentioned in Roney, *Autobiography*, 70.

15. Roney, *Autobiography*, 148.

16. In addition to those mentioned, Thomas Clarke Luby, Charles Kickham and John O'Leary of the editorial staff were arrested. See Devoy, *Recollections*, 33.

17. Ibid., 33.

18. Ibid., 148–49.

19. Cormac O'Grada, "Fenianism and Socialism: The Career of J.P.

McDonnell, " *Saothar: Journal of the Irish Labour History Society* (May 1975): 33–34.

20. Devoy, *Recollections*, Chap. 13 (entire chapter on Stephens's escape); biographical sketch, McDonnell Papers, 2–3.

21. Roney, *Autobiography*, 167.

22. O'Grada, "Fenianism and Socialism," 34; biographical sketch, McDonnell Papers, 3.

23. McDonnell, Ibid., 3–4; Boyle, "Ireland and the First International," 46–47. An amnesty act was finally passed by the British Parliament in 1870, and Fenian prisoners were subsequently released on condition they be deported.

24. *Karl Marx and Frederick Engels on Ireland* (London: Lawrence and Wishart, 1971), 298–99; O'Grada, "Fenianism and Socialism," 35.

25. Boyle, "Ireland and the First International," 53-58.

26. *National Labor Standard*, Obituary, January 20, 1906, 1.

27. Ibid.; biographical sketch, McDonnell Papers, 4-5; *Marx and Engels on Ireland*, 308.

28. Devoy, *Recollections*, 337–38; Boyle, "Ireland and the First International," 57; biographical sketch, McDonnell Papers, 7.

29. Roney, *Autobiography*, 264.

30. *Paterson Labor Standard*, November 24, 1898, 1.

31. *New York Herald*, January 27, 1, February 4, 1, March 6, 1-2 , 1873. It is likely that the prominent publication of these letters by the *Herald* was aided by the presence of John Devoy on its editorial staff.

32. Gompers, *Seventy Years*, 88.

33. Roney, *Autobiography*, 327.

34. Neil Shumsky, "Frank Roney's San Francisco—His Diary: April 1875–March 1876," *Labor History* (Spring 1976), 244–64.

35. This episode is described in detail in Eugene Lyons, "The World of P.J. McGuire" (Ph.D. diss., University of Minnesota, 1972), 58–65; and in John R. Commons and Associates, *History of Labour in the United States* (New York: Macmillan, 1918), vol. 2, 304.

36. Biographical sketch, McDonnell Papers, 8.

37. Commons and Associates, *History of Labour in the United States*, vol. 2, 304.

38. Reminiscences of Mrs. McDonnell (no date), McDonnell Papers.

39. Alexander Saxton, *The Indispensable Enemy* (Berkeley: University of California Press , 1971), 121. This convention might never have opened except for Roney's deception of police who had been ordered to enforce the mayor's ban on public gatherings. On notices of the convention Roney had listed a given location, but when delegates arrived they were directed to a different hall where it was actually held. By the time police found it the first day's proceedings were nearly over, having been handled in a very orderly manner by Roney, who persuaded police not to interfere.

40. Ibid.

41. Roney, *Autobiography*, 287.

42. This plan and the history of it were outlined by Roney in *The Molders' Journal*, March, 1900, 214–15, as well as in his *Autobiography*, 230–33.

43. Saxton, *The Indispensable Enemy*, 172–76.

44. *International Molders' Journal*, July, 1886, 60–61.

45. Herbert Gutman, *Work, Culture, and Society in Industrializing America* (New York: Knopf, 1976), 260–62.

46. Broadsheet included in McDonnell Papers.

47. Biographical Sketch, McDonnell Papers, 8; *Paterson Daily Guardian*,

March 30, 1900 (story on twentieth anniversary of the occasion). Clipping in scrapbook included in McDonnell Papers; *National Labor Standard*, April 1, 1905, 1 (article by George Leonard McNeil recalling the occasion); Gutman, *Work, Culture, and Society*, 252–53.

48. Gutman, *Work, Culture, and Society*, 270–71, 284–86; *Report of Ninth Annual Congress of N.J. Federation of Trades and Labor Unions*, September 15, 1887. (Reporting enactment of first state law making Labor Day a legal holiday), McDonnell Papers. Leo Troy, *Organized Labor in New Jersey* (Princeton, N.J.: Van Nostrand, 1965), 157.

49. Galway-born in 1835, Ford was brought to America as a seven-year-old orphan. Educated in Boston public schools and apprenticed in printing shop of William Lloyd Garrison, he worked as a journalist, served in the Civil War, and opened the *Irish World* in 1870 to promote Irish independence. See *National Cyclopedia of American Biography*, vol. 22, 317.

50. Gompers, *Seventy Years*, 103, 128.

51. Roney, *Autobiography*, 346.

52. Troy, *Organized Labor*, 53–61.

53. Roney, *Autobiography*, 325–26, 434.

54. Ibid., x.

4

P.H. MCCARTHY:
LORD OF THE BUILDING TRADES

Patrick Henry McCarthy, twenty-six, an Irish immigrant and journey-man carpenter, walked south on Kearny Street on a fine morning in June of 1886. Reaching Market Street, he and his two traveling companions from the American Midwest "were the recipients of a most delightfully refreshing breeze which was coming in over the city from the ocean." All three young men were reluctant to return to a sweltering Midwestern summer, but only McCarthy decided to remain, having "learned to like San Francisco and California very much."[1] It was an impulsive decision, uncharacteristic of McCarthy, who even as a young man carefully weighed the pros and cons before making up his mind. It was, however, a decision he never regretted, and the remaining forty-seven years of his life were spent in San Francisco, over half of them as the awesome "labor baron" figure in the building trades of the city and the State of California. Indeed, two of these years were spent as mayor of San Francisco in a Union Labor administration during which he claimed credit for bringing the Panama Pacific Exposition to the city. Commonly known as "P.H." to friends and associates, predictably he was labeled "Pinhead" by opponents, of whom he had his share. But detractors could not disguise the fact that he became one of the ablest and most powerful labor leaders on the West Coast during his time.

In virtue of good fortune and perhaps good instincts, as manifested in his impulsive decision, McCarthy came to settle in a community where opportunities for an immigrant carpenter from Ireland with aspirations to labor leadership could hardly have been more promising. The city was in a period of phenomenal growth from one hundred fifty thousand in 1870 to more than a third of a million in 1900—a condition particularly advantageous for building tradesmen. Furthermore, it was a city which, even by 1886, had a tradition of trade union organization, particularly in the construction industry. Additionally, it had a substantial Irish population amounting to a quarter of its total, and this may have contributed to McCarthy's career most of all.

By this time, the Irish community in the city had already produced leaders in politics, such as U.S. Senators David Broderick, Eugene Casserly and John Conness, and Democratic party chief Chris Buckley, among others. It was no less visible among movements of workingmen as evidenced by sandlot orator Denis Kearney and Frank Roney, president of the San Francisco Trades Assembly. The ascent of the Irish in San Francisco benefitted from the absence of an established WASP elite to stand in its way. Indeed, a disapproving Anglo-American Protestant aristocracy constituted a serious barrier to upward mobility in cities along the East Coast. As a group, the Irish in San Francisco typically had been seasoned by experience in other large American cities, and this was a distinct asset in their contest for power on the West Coast.[2] It was certainly true of McCarthy who first came to America in the spring of 1880 and had tried his hand at organizing workers in both Chicago and Saint Louis before arriving at the Golden Gate. Due probably to its remote geographical location, this city did seem to attract the most venturesome, confident and mobile of the Irish immigrants.[3] Such adjectives describe McCarthy very well.

The Irish were therefore present at the creation of this "instant city" which had been no more than a sleepy village of less than a thousand people before the Gold Rush of 1849. They participated in its building, banking and politics as it grew. With a vigorous predilection to register, the Irish were recognized early as the most potent of the foreign-born voters, constituting over a fifth of its electorate. Combined with American-born Irish, they gave the Democratic party a strong edge. Indeed, McCarthy began as a Democrat, and, after being nominated by Democratic Mayor Phelan, was elected a member of the Freeholders Board, which rewrote the city charter in 1898. Political advances in San Francisco came well before those of the Irish in Boston, New York, or Philadelphia. Exercise of such political influence, assuming the role of broker among diverse ethnic groups and forming political machines, was bound to bring out nativist attacks on Irish Catholic "bossism" and corruption. It did. But the impact of these attacks was limited since nativists did not enjoy the support in San Francisco that they had in places such as Philadelphia and Boston. Appeals to ethnic and religious prejudice were not very popular in this pluralistic, cosmopolitan city. The glaring exception was the attitude toward Orientals. Orientals were subjected to a virulent exclusion movement in the city for much of its history, a movement of which Irishmen were often leaders.

A study of the San Francisco Irish by Robert A. Burchell effectively demonstrates Irish occupational progress using data from census manuscript schedules.[4] A significant decline in the percentage of Irish-born men in unskilled employment is evident from 1852 to 1880, as is a rise in the proportion of them employed in semiskilled occupations and, more important, in white-collar jobs.

Furthermore, occupational distributions comparing first- and second-generation Irish in the city offer dramatic evidence of upward mobility. Data on occupational structure of the Irish community, broken down by political ward, make it abundantly clear that the Irish were not consigned to an inner-city ghetto, but spread widely as the city grew and did not correspond to the traditional caricature derived from Eastern cities. A remarkably small proportion of them lived as unattached single lodgers and boarders. Typically, they were found in stable family groups which contributed few recruits for urban gangs. Endogamous to a large extent, families passed on traditional Irish values to their young, chief among them being Roman Catholicism. The church, in turn, was an important supportive institution, which aided the immigrants' adjustment and reinforced their endogamous tendencies with its strictures against mixed marriage.

P.H. McCarthy and his reign of twenty-four years as president of the San Francisco Building Trades Council are well known to historians of the Bay Area and to those who specialize in labor history,[5] indeed, unkindly so. His principal chronicler, Frederick L. Ryan, learned about him "that he was selfish and domineering; that power went to his head; that he was determined to 'rule or ruin.'"[6] Only grudgingly does Ryan acknowledge that "there was never any evidence of the use of bribery or the levying of 'strike insurance' by officials connected with the Building Trades Council or any of its affiliated unions."[7] The absence of these practices is, nevertheless, remarkable, since they flourished scandalously in the building industry in Chicago, New York and elsewhere during this period. Ryan readily concedes that "P.H. McCarthy's ability was beyond question; he was an able organizer and administrator."[8] In discussing a famous 1901 agreement between the Bay Area Planing Mill Operators and the Building Trades Council, Ryan goes so far as to assert, "In many respects, McCarthy deserved the adoration that came to him from his faithful followers. The idea of the mill owners' agreement was a brilliant one, and it was excellently executed."[9]

Ray Stannard Baker, celebrated muckraking journalist known for his exposé of corruption in the building trades, paid a visit to San Francisco in 1904 and found an "absolute dictator" of the building industry—P.H. McCarthy—without whose permission "neither employer nor employee can turn a hand."[10] He deplored the monopolistic arrangements with contractors cultivated by McCarthy and the subversion of democratic procedures used in order to control the Building Trades Council. Yet Baker also noted that, unlike New York, there was a curious absence of terrorism, intimidation and bribery in the San Francisco building industry. Although he judged it strange that McCarthy received no salary as president of the Building Trades Council and relied on his job as building superintendent of the California Hotel to earn a living, Baker was unable to discover a "source of graft" for the man. Even Baker felt compelled to attest that, while McCarthy "ruled with a hand of iron, his generalship has been highly effective in materially benefitting his followers, and he has even endeavored apparently to deal with employers on a reasonable business basis."[11] However, our purpose is not to catalogue the often dichotomous assessments of McCarthy's numerous critics, chroniclers and devotees. Rather it is to explore his own side of the story as told in memoirs which he recorded after retiring from the labor wars in 1922. San Francisco's reputation as a citadel of the closed shop on the West Coast early in the twentieth century is traceable to the organizing skill of P.H. McCarthy and a small number of his contemporaries, such as Michael Casey of the Teamsters' Union and Andrew Furuseth of the Sailors' Union. It is fortunate, therefore, that McCarthy has provided us with a personal account of his career. Such records by men in organized labor are rare. While necessarily subjective and, in this case, self-laudatory, even triumphal (such was McCarthy's nature), his memoirs afford insight into his personality and provide details found nowhere else.

Tall, handsome, luxuriously mustachioed, and above all, a spellbinding speaker with piercing eyes and Irish glint, P.H. McCarthy in celluloid collar and bow tie was the very model of a labor aristocrat from the Edwardian era.

EARLY YEARS

Patrick Henry McCarthy, future dean of the San Francisco Building Trades, was born in Killoughteen outside Newcastle West, in County Limerick on March 17, 1860. He tells us, in one of the minor vanities appearing in his memoirs, that it was 1863, but the parish register of Newcastle West records the baptism of Patrick, child of Ellen Hough and Patrick McCarthy, on March 18, 1860.[12] The baptismal records of the other children, beginning with Michael in 1844, show Patrick to be the fourth son and second youngest child. His mother, Ellen Hough, of nearby Dually was—according to local historian R.V. Cussen, Sr., of Newcastle West—the daughter of a well-known family of "strong farmers" in the region whose roots in it go back innumerable generations.[13] The name of McCarthy, on the other hand, is not very old in the region, and Cussen speculates that the elder McCarthy may have been an itinerant tradesman who came to do carpentry work for several farmers in the area and remained to marry the daughter of one of them. Kevin Danaher, the Irish folklorist and also a Limerick man, confirms that the name McCarthy is relatively recent to this area.[14]

As a skilled tradesman, in Cussen's opinion, McCarthy's father would have been acceptable as a prospective son-in-law for such a family, whereas an agricultural laborer would not. There is no evidence that he was a carpenter, but several of his sons, including Patrick, exhibited marked inclinations toward the building trade. In any case, the senior McCarthy, like many Irish fathers, conveyed to his children a story of the family's noble origins. His son Patrick recalled that: "My father was a McCarthy Moor and as such as, of course, according to the records of the genealogists, entitled to at least one of the thirty-five thrones at one time occupied by as many kings in the Province of Munster, named McCarthy."[15] That his father appeared on the scene some generations too late to claim his title to the throne did not disappoint his youngest son, whose career as a labor organizer might well have been "very much restricted by the . . . belief in the divine right of kings by the people of those times."[16]

Whatever his initial occupation or lineage, McCarthy's father supported the family as a tenant dairy farmer on eighteen acres in Killougheen leased from the estate of the Dowager Lady O'Brien,[17] a relative of William Smith O'Brien. The family was certainly not poor by the standards of nineteenth-century Ireland. The thatched cottage in which McCarthy was born and spent the first sixteen years of his life stands today, although it was gutted by fire in 1974, only a few years after the death of its last occupant, Michael McCarthy, a nephew of Patrick.[18] It is located on level grassland as fertile as any to be found in this rich dairying country, not the sort of marginal acreage that one would expect to find occupied by recent settlers.

In his ninth year, Patrick's family was overtaken by tragedy. An older sister died, shortly to be followed by the death of his father and mother. Tuberculosis, in Cussen's opinion, was the likely cause. Although two older sisters had already emigrated to the United States, the remaining members of the family retained the farm and kept the family together. By the terms of his father's will, Patrick was placed under the protection of Michael, his oldest brother, and a Father John Carrick, curate of the parish in Newcastle West. At the time a pupil in the small national school at Killougheen, less than fifty yards from his home, Patrick appeared to be completely engrossed in his studies except for, in his words, "my indulgence in all kinds of boyish sports, of which I was very fond."[19] McCarthy seems to have done well at Killougheen school[20] and in the course of his last few months there, his guardians informed him of their plan for his career. He did not like it. A contest of wills ensued. The issue was at length resolved in favor of McCarthy's wishes.

Encouraged by the promise he displayed in his schoolwork, the guardians laid out a program of studies leading to a career in law. In itself, this choice of occupation suggests that the family had at least some means to finance the necessary schooling and is further evidence that it was not poor. But the young man was not impressed with the glowing accounts of his future: "They had it all set up for me. I was to study law and be an attorney like my namesake, Charles McCarthy. He was a very wonderful man and, of course, I must be still better than he. Well to me, Mr. Charles McCarthy was just a small town lawyer and no more."[21] His guardians, particularly the Reverend Carrick, were not easily dissuaded by this precocious independence of mind, and numerous conferences with them as well as a threat to "break away, leave the country" were necessary before they would unbend. Apparently, in his school days, McCarthy had learned skill in debate and developed the tenacity that became characteristic of his entire career. Early in these confrontations, he had revealed his own choice. He would become a house carpenter.

Through the good offices of his guardians, McCarthy was apprenticed to one James McCormack of Knockaderry, County Limerick, a

man McCarthy came to consider "one of the best and keenest minds
engaged in the building business in all Ireland at the time."[22] For this
fatherless young man, the first meeting with McCormack, on April 12,
1876, was "one of the happiest days of my life," because it was on this
occasion that he became an apprentice in the carpenter trade to a man
who "from the moment I laid eyes on him, I was completely carried
away with him as was also my brother and Father Carrick."[23] McCarthy
entered four years of a master-apprenticeship relationship under the
traditional system established by English law under which he was
bound to the master, who supplied lodging, board and training, but no
wages at all. In those days, the apprentice necessarily learned every
aspect of the trade because "the carpenter engaged in the building
industry did by hand everything that was to be done in that department. He made the frames, doors, sash, moldings and everything connected with the building."[24] For the master there was ample incentive
to provide the apprentices with the best possible training in the short-
est possible time "since when he was thus trained, all of his earnings
rebounded to the benefit of his employer."[25]

As a substitute for his real father, McCormack apparently was more
than satisfactory. McCarthy remembered him affectionately as "an
exceptionally fine man; good hearted, kind in the extreme; joyful, so
much so that he made all those around him happy."[26] Like a good
father, his absences were mourned and his returns welcomed. In
McCarthy's own words: "Personally, I always felt better, more happy
and contented, when he was in evidence, than otherwise. He, of
course, had to be away a great deal, yet on his return, men and apprentices alike felt extremely happy at his coming back to them."[27]
Furthermore, McCormack was remembered as a fine teacher—patient
and interested in developing the ability of his young men. An elderly
member of the Ballingarry Parish recalled stories about him handed
down from the time when McCormack did carpentry work on the
Catholic church there. One story, which illustrates his patience, concerns an apprentice found butchering a piece of lumber. His response
was: "If we can't make a coat of it, we'll make a waistcoat."[28] His methods included awarding prizes for the best answers offered by his
apprentices to questions about the trade: "those trophies were fought
and battled for and we apprentices studied as tho [sic] we were preparing for an annual competitive examination."[29]

Although McCarthy recollects his apprenticeship years as passing
quickly and happily, given his personality, they were not without their
share of conflict. Most dramatic was an event that occurred in the
course of work on a church, not named by McCarthy, which would
certainly be the one in Ballingarry, County Limerick.[30] An imposing
structure of Foynes limestone, whose monumental sculpture in
imported Caen sandstone was done by the father and brother of
Padraic Pearse, this church was built on an attractive plateau on the
northwest edge of the village. It was constructed during a period
when Ireland seemed on a church-building spree in response to con-

tinuing relaxation of penalties for practicing the Catholic faith. Like many Catholic churches built at this time, it was clearly beyond the financial means of the small community that undertook it. Money for its construction had been raised, initially, by Reverend James Enraght who had spent much of his priesthood as a fund-raiser and was in America in that capacity at the time of his appointment to the parish in Ballingarry. He began the new church, but completed little more than the foundation when his funds ran out. Weary and discouraged, he applied for a new assignment and was succeeded in 1874 by a younger man, Father Timothy H. Shanahan, who was expected to finish the job. Shanahan immediately enlisted his brother, Reverend Denis Shanahan, as curate and promptly dispatched him to the United States to promote funds for the work.[31]

This account of the Shanahans, drawn from James Begley's history of the Limerick Diocese, coincides with McCarthy's memoirs in which he refers to working on a church for which "a certain clergyman and his brother, also of the clergy, collected quite a sum of money in the United States."[32] His description of the parish priest also corresponds to the character of Timothy Shanahan who earned the reputation of a very demanding and rather officious man. It was Shanahan who also built the substantial dwelling that became the convent of the Sisters of Mercy in Ballingarry. Legend has it that, while this structure was being built, he visited the site daily and, more often than not, required that several courses of brick be taken down by the masons because he insisted they had been laid improperly. His initials appear on the post of an attractive hardwood staircase in the convent, crafted by James McCormack.[33] It was with Timothy Shanahan that P.H. McCarthy had a second momentous contest of wills.

Since the work on this church had been discontinued once already, it is understandable that for its current pastor "the urge to finish at some certain date became all absorbing."[34] Accordingly, the man appeared one morning "like a cloudburst out of a clear sky" and "informed those in charge that . . . it became necessary for him to issue an order that they must begin at once, yes, that same night, working overtime until at least 11 o'clock."[35] McCormack was away for several days at the time and, in his absence, the superintendent, carpenter foreman and journeymen were not willing to risk an outright refusal of the priest's order. McCarthy, however, was not so cautious. He had an entirely different idea and was not hesitant about proposing it. He insisted that "other men were walking the streets idle, who if employed on the job would accomplish the result sought by the clergy."[36] McCarthy persuaded his three fellow apprentices, but they felt powerless without support from the journeymen. He then called a meeting in which, he explains, he succeeded in selling the mechanics on his solution and "all of the men left for their homes and the strike against night-work overtime was on."[37]

The time came for the apprentice to face his clerical adversary. McCarthy remembers that when they met "what he said to me would fill quite a book" and "according to his viewpoint the jail doors opened for me." Unawed, the upstart apprentice stood firm, replying "that I would not work nights for him or anybody else, unless Mr. McCormack told me to and that I felt quite sure he would not order me to work nights, while there were carpenters walking the streets idle."[38] The priest then ordered him off the job, but he "just as religiously declined to go off the job."[39] McCormack, then, was summoned, as was McCarthy's older brother. Conferences were held, facts ascertained, and in the end McCormack affirmed the stand taken by his apprentices. He hired more carpenters. The strike was over, and P.H. McCarthy's first venture as labor organizer had succeeded. Indeed, "the church was finished on time and everything treated in the best possible form."[40]

The four years of P.H. McCarthy's apprenticeship were scheduled to expire on April 12, 1880, but well before that time he entertained the notion of emigrating: "I had a strong liking to go to Dublin, Ireland, to England and Scotland, where I understood building construction was of a somewhat different type of style, and then again, the United States had a tremendously powerful call on me from the same standpoint."[41] His choice was finally based upon his perception "that the United States, after all, presented the deeper, broader and more elaborate field for the future of the building industry."[42] His departure, therefore, bears little resemblance to the stereotype of the destitute, uneducated Irish peasant emigrating for the sake of survival. Nevertheless, developments in Ireland at this time were not encouraging for a young man of ambition. County Limerick and other regions in the west of Ireland were in the throes of the Land League agitation. Furthermore, agriculture was seriously depressed because of a series of general crop failures beginning in 1877. To compound the unpromising outlook, an industrial recession had begun earlier in the 1870s and had not yet run its course. For building craftsmen, therefore, prospects were not sanguine.

On the other hand, reports from Chicago, where three of McCarthy's sisters were living, must have been good. The American economy was recovering from the depression of the 1870s, and employment conditions were improving. When Mr. McCormack learned that his apprentice was hoping to leave for the United States with some friends in early April, "He advised me that if I desired to go with my friends, it would be quite alright [sic] with him."[43] Thus, he left for New York only a few days before April 12, 1880, when his four years were up. Although he does not identify the port of embarkation, it was most likely Queenstown. The name Pat McCarthy appears on the passenger list of several ships arriving in New York from Queenstown in late April of 1880, but it is not possible to be certain which is the right one. Financing the trip was also left unexplained by McCarthy. Mrs. Margaret Twoomey of Killoughteen, McCarthy's niece, is of the opinion that it was financed through a loan from his brother William.[44] It is also reasonable to assume that help was forthcoming from his sisters in Chicago. McCarthy spent a few days in New York visiting with friends before arriving in Chicago on May 2, 1880.

Young McCarthy bore little resemblance to the typical emigrant of the famine Irish coming to America in pre-Civil War days. Unlike these earlier refugees, the bulk of whom were unskilled agricultural laborers, frequently illiterate and often Gaelic speaking, McCarthy enjoyed the advantage of a substantial education obtained in the national school system and was equipped to support himself adequately by virtue of his thorough training in a skilled craft. This skill in particular permitted him to avoid the hazard of so many Irish who were consigned to ethnic ghettos in cities of America's Atlantic coast. It afforded mobility by enabling him readily to find work as a carpenter in Chicago, Saint Louis and San Francisco. McCarthy acknowledged the value of his training in this way: "For after all is said and done, a mechanic thoroughly versed in his trade, equal to the task of dealing with any phase of it, is a mechanic who, if he has health, can always feel quite rich in the world's goods and absolutely independent."[45] Furthermore, he could count on the aid of relatives in the United States to cushion his adjustment to a new land.

EARLY ASSOCIATIONS WITH CARPENTERS' UNION

Stopping briefly in New York, McCarthy, on May 2, 1880, arrived in Chicago where, for the first time, he encountered the attitude of American employers toward unions. Moving in with a married sister and her family, young McCarthy quickly obtained work in the building industry. His first job was on a building going up on Halsted Street. It lasted exactly one day. During the lunch hour, McCarthy and his fellow tradesmen discussed the merits of the Amalgamated Society of Carpenters, an old and influential organization in Great Britain, a chapter of which had been established in Chicago by men who had been members in England before coming to America. McCarthy's memoirs relate that his favorable attitude toward trade unions was duly reported to his employer by a "confidential employee," and he was called in, paid his time ($2.25 for a ten-hour day), and told that he was a disturbing element among the men.[46] For a young man of his temperament, this experience merely strengthened his belief in the necessity of unions. After securing a new job the very next day, he interested himself in locating other carpenters who shared his concern about organizing the trade. McCarthy relates that while in Chicago he was first made aware of the difficulties associated with organizing workmen of diverse nationalities and the advantage this situation afforded to American employers in discouraging unionization. An older carpenter among a group with whom he was talking:

seemed to take umbrage at a young fellow like myself trying to talk trades unionism to men who were very much his senior; he knew quite well that trades unionism could never amount to much in a city like Chicago, the tradesmen of which had come from all parts of the world, precluding the possibility of bringing them together with any degree of confidence in each other. It had been tried before and failed and why try to bring it up again.[47]

McCarthy noted that organizing was retarded by "racial dislikes, fraternal differentialism, and in no small measure, religious bigotry. Those three smoke screens were . . . worked overtime by the opponents of the trade and labor movement of America."[48]

McCarthy remained in Chicago from the spring of 1880 until the fall of that year when he migrated to Saint Louis. The move to Saint Louis was auspicious for a young man who aspired to leadership among workingmen because it came at a period crucial to the establishment of permanent trade unions in the United States. In 1880 Saint Louis was the scene of organizing activity carried on by Peter J. McGuire, which led shortly to the founding of the Brotherhood of Carpenters which, in turn, became a cornerstone of the American Federation of Labor.

It was McCarthy's good fortune to become associated with McGuire soon after arriving in Saint Louis. He describes McGuire as having a great advantage for union work there because he could speak German fluently. McGuire was employed on a job known as Filley's Foundry. His organizing campaign was given impetus when, in the middle of the winter, carpenters on the job were notified that their pay would be reduced from $3.00 to $2.50 per day. McGuire called mass meetings at a place called Euricks Cave, located at Washington and Jefferson Avenues, and the work of convincing men to protect themselves with a union was carried forward.[49] Thus McCarthy learned the craft of organizing American workingmen from a master whose dedication and success in the cause of his own union and a number of others became a legend. He never absorbed McGuire's hatred of capitalism, although he did acquire his zeal for business unionism. Of his own efforts in this period McCarthy says:

I recall one instance where I personally visited the homes of 35 carpenters in St. Louis in two weeks. During that time I either talked with the head of the family or some member of the family, preferably his wife, if I could not talk with himself, and I have rarely failed to convince either or both of the advisability of joining the union.[50]

Illness prevented McCarthy from participating in the founding convention of the Brotherhood of Carpenters and Joiners of America in Chicago on August 12, 1881, although he had been much involved in preparations for it. Association with an accomplished organizer of the stature of P.J. McGuire undoubtedly furthered McCarthy's aspirations toward a career in labor leadership. It remained for him to apply the lessons he had learned to organizing on the Pacific Coast. But not for a few years.

McCarthy did not leave Saint Louis until 1886 and then only to take an extended tour of the West Coast lasting seven weeks in the company of two young men whom he does not identify except to explain that one was an architect and the other worked in his own father's shoe manufacturing firm in Saint Louis. McCarthy was still single and, from the character of the tour and the nature of his traveling companions, apparently in reasonably comfortable circumstances. It was in the course of this trip that McCarthy yielded to an impulse to remain in San Francisco. Bidding farewell to his two companions, he again sought a job in the carpenters trade and on August 6, 1886, joined Local 22 of the carpenters' union. Local 22 was the oldest carpenters' union in San Francisco. When Local 22 began to decline, McCarthy felt compelled to lend a hand. He was soon elected president and served six consecutive terms during which membership grew from 165 to 760.[51] Of his efforts to provide leadership for Local 22, McCarthy says: "This I did unreservedly, taking hold as tho [sic] it was my own private business in which was invested my all."[52] In revitalizing Local 22 he acknowledged being "ably assisted" by a number of "fellow carpenters;"[53] but, the operation was distinctively his own, and the almost proprietary view of the operation that he assumed was characteristic of his activities in the trade union field.

Local 22 was the oldest and strongest of three carpenters' unions then operating in San Francisco. The others (Local 304 and Local 483) were smaller, and Local 304, consisting exclusively of German carpenters, conducted its affairs in German. When, as a result of brothers failing to maintain their cards, total membership of these three locals fell to less than three hundred, a movement began to combine them into a consolidated local. McCarthy, quite conscious of the ethnic differences and possible frictions, opposed the idea, pointing out that it would not only be unfair to members, but it would not solve the problem. He proposed that initiation fees be reduced and that mass meetings be called to bring all carpenters into the fold, giving them the choice of which union to enter. His views prevailed when members of the three locals met to vote on the issue. Within three months, according to McCarthy, membership in the three unions increased over 400 percent, and a new Italian-speaking union had been formed.[54]

This incident demonstrates McCarthy's perception of the hazards for organized labor presented by ethnic differences and his methods for dealing with them.

BARONY IN SAN FRANCISCO

P.H. McCarthy is remembered chiefly for his conduct of the San Francisco Building Trades Council as its president for nearly a quarter of a century. In his memoirs, McCarthy asserts, "I decided definitely to organize the San Francisco Building Trades Council, a central body embracing all the building trades, artisans, mechanics and laborers, from the foundation to the roof" because "I became convinced that it was the only way thoro [sic] organization could be maintained."[55] He was referring to trades, such as plasterers, for whom "the organizing of unions and the disbanding of the same within a short period of time was the rule and not the exception."[56] Their behavior resembled "on again, off again, gone again, Finnegan, organized today, disorganized six months later."[57] Success in achieving the eight-hour day had, in fact, subsequently been eroded by such developments. In addition, some building crafts had never been organized. Thus,

after several months of preliminary work, the Building Trades Council of San Francisco was, on the 6th of February, 1893, founded. Its constituents at the time consisted of a few local unions then organized in San Francisco, plus the locals of the United Brotherhood of Carpenters and Joiners of America, in one of which I held membership.[58]

McCarthy credits a number of associates for their part in "the great work of building up and conducting that organization."[59]

While McCarthy undoubtedly was instrumental in the formation of the Building Trades Council, his account does not agree with those of labor historians, Frederick L. Ryan and Ira B. Cross, who date its beginning from February 6, 1896, and identify Henry Meyer of Local 22 as its first president. They also point out that three other men succeeded Meyer as president before McCarthy was elected to that office on July 31, 1898.[60] Furthermore, organization of the council was in fact the culmination of numerous efforts toward centralization in the building trades, which had been attempted as early as 1883.[61] Although the Cross-Ryan account undoubtedly is accurate, no one questions the fact that it was McCarthy who molded the organization into the dominating force it became in the building industry. The most memorable and successful of his efforts was the triumph over the Planing Mill Owners Association in 1901. The issue was the eight-hour day, which at the time was enjoyed by all but a few crafts in the construction industry. McCarthy, however, was determined to make it universal.

On February 12, 1900, the Building Trades Council notified all parties concerned that beginning on August 13, 1900, no member of a union affiliated with it would any longer work more than an eight-hour day. Little resistance developed except that of the planing mill operators, who produce finished wood products for the building industry. The Planing Mill Operators Association, led by William H. Crocker, banker and son of Charles Crocker of the Central and Southern Pacific "Big Four," was determined to fight the issue in a generalized effort to restore the open shop and destroy the power of the Building Trades Council once and for all. Accordingly, the association countered by announcing a lockout of all organized millmen to begin on August 13. The lockout was observed by the great majority of mills, and the dispute lasted for six months before the mill operators finally agreed to arbitration after haughtily rejecting it early in the conflict. The arbitration award accepted by both parties called for an eight-hour day effective in three months and an eight and one half-hour day in the meantime. The union shop was to be enforced in all mills after six months. This amounted to a thorough victory for McCarthy. It removed all doubt as to the power of the Building Trades Council and the caliber of its leadership.

An appreciation of McCarthy's leadership qualities emerges from an examination of his endeavors in this dispute. McCarthy's achievement was not secured haphazardly nor through simple good luck. Far from it. He knew it would not come without a struggle. Success was the result of a carefully thought-out strategy and painstaking preparation, both characteristic of his approach to leadership. He had been conscious of how often "brother members, entirely sincere . . . claim while on the floor of their own union that the Building Trades Council was neglecting the millmen; that something should be done for them." But extending the eight-hour day to them, he pointed out, could be accomplished only if the council were able to protect mill owners who agreed to it "from competition ushered in on them by competitors whose work day constituted more than 8 hours per day." This problem was dealt with in resolutions recommended to the council by McCarthy and his fellow officials, which said in part,

that the council give the owners of those plants six months' notice of the change requested, which time will serve to finish old contracts and prepare for the new, the council refusing to handle any material coming from other than 8 hour establishments employing union operators, that all overlapping contracts be finished on the old basis or the difference in cost paid to the employer in cash by the council, as the employer may desire, that the 8 hour day be put into full force and effect Monday, August 13, 1900.[62]

Refusal to install millwork not produced under eight-hour conditions was the key to exerting the leverage of soundly organized building craftsmen on behalf of millmen whose union was untested and weak. These resolutions were voted through the council itself and then referred to each affiliated local union where 79 percent of all members voted for them. McCarthy recalls that he attended each of these local union meetings, explained the resolutions and left prior to the vote in each instance–all in the interest of an informed and unified rank and file.[63]

An essential feature of McCarthy's strategy was to maintain good relations with the building contractors, who, if they supported the mill owners, could spell defeat for the council. Accordingly, when the Builders' Association invited leaders of both sides in the dispute to a meeting in the Builders Hall to present their positions, McCarthy gladly accepted. The meeting was held on Saturday afternoon, August 18, the first week of the lockout. When, in the course of the meeting, the Builders' Association offered to act as arbitrator for the dispute, McCarthy quickly agreed, but mill owner representatives scornfully rejected the offer. The attitude of the mill owners had been expressed by Robert Moore, manager of the Hooper Mill and Lumber Company, of whom McCarthy said, "Mr. Bob Moore, the wild-eyed 'Billy Sunday' of the millowners' admiration society, declared that he would drive me out of California."[64]

McCarthy was careful to explain clearly his willingness to accept arbitration to reporters after the meeting adjourned. He cultivated the press throughout the dispute in the interest of preserving good relations with the builders and the public at large.

Vital to a strategy of retaining the good will of the building contractors was the effort to minimize disruption of construction activity during the lockout. Maintaining a flow of millwork to building sites was essential since without it work on them would necessarily grind to a halt. It was attempted by several means, one of them being to increase production at those few mills in the city that had accepted the eight-hour day. This was done through added shifts. Another means was to rule that millwork produced by non-eight-hour establishments outside the city could come in and be installed until the eight-hour day was uniformly adopted in San Francisco. A third and most elaborate method was for the council itself to build and operate a planing mill. This tactic was not without precedent in San Francisco labor disputes—having been used in 1867 by the Carpenters' Union[65]—but never was it employed with greater effectiveness. McCarthy had thought through the project well in advance of the lockout and considered it a contingency plan to be undertaken if the mill owners proved obdurate. Success in this venture would, he felt, demonstrate to the public the feasibility of operating mills on an eight-hour day. In addition, it would employ a number of locked-out union members, and finally, by supplying needed millwork to building sites, it would avoid unemployment for many building craftsmen.

The venture was begun in mid-September with a capital of $100,000 raised from union sources. The point of McCarthy's trip to Scranton during the lockout becomes clear when it is understood that the Carpenters' Union Convention he attended there voted $40,000 to assist the planing mill project. This was done, however, only by overcoming the opposition of many delegates, who were quite aware that unionizing planing mills was unheard of outside of San Francisco and who found the idea of winning an eight-hour day for them bizarre. Such was the reasoning of P.J. McGuire, the union's national secretary, McCarthy's old associate from the days in Saint Louis, who assured the convention that it would be throwing the union's money away so small was the chance of winning. Of his response to the motion, McCarthy recalled: "No member of the Mill Owners' Association could oppose the eight hour request made by the Building Trades Council more effectively than he."[66] Nothing if not tenacious, McCarthy moved that consideration of the question be laid over until the following day and, approaching 90 percent of the delegates thereafter, won majority support for his motion requesting financial aid the next morning.[67]

Successful operation of the council's mill was decisive in persuading the Mill Owners' Association to agree to arbitration on February 12, 1901. Members selected for the arbitration panel were James Britt and Jeremiah Mahoney for the Building Trades Council, with Oscar Lewis and David Kerr representing the Mill Owners' Association. Their deliberations must have resembled negotiations more than arbitration since they did not choose an impartial umpire as planned. Nevertheless, the agreement proposed by the panel after six days was immediately signed by both organizations on February 19, 1901, and became, in the eyes of Frederick L. Ryan, the principal determinant of industrial relations in the San Francisco building industry from its inception until 1921.[68] It embodied McCarthy's conceptions, including a collusive arrangement quite attractive to mill owners, whereby none of the council's members would handle millwork unless it was produced in shops observing an eight-hour day and employing union men exclusively. This part of the settlement was construed to mean that, in order to be used in San Francisco, finished wood products must either bear the union label—proof of their processing by local mills—or come from other mills that observed wage and hour standards at least equal to those in the city. Thus San Francisco mill owners were protected from unfair competition and were able to pass higher costs on to their customers.

McCarthy's triumph unquestionably was most satisfying. He had bested the mill owners with superior strategy, outmaneuvered them at every turn, and realized every objective of his campaign. At the same time, he retained good relations with building contractors who, as a group, refused to side with the mill owners. They admired his thorough grasp of the realities of the construction industry and the businesslike manner in which he conducted himself. The victory established him as a force to be reckoned with not only in the industry but in the city at large.

BREAKING RANKS

Friction with the San Francisco Labor Council developed when that organization refused to support a boycott of Recreation Park (conducted by the Building Trades Council) and permitted its name to be displayed on "a wagon conveying the idea that the boycott was declared off by union labor," which was pulled through the streets of San Francisco, particularly Market Street. Leaders of the Labor Council also intervened in the dispute and attempted to settle it by consulting with both parties. At that time, Walter Goff and Ed Rosenberg were the chief officers of the Labor Council. McCarthy believed that actions of the Labor Council were motivated by jealousy of the Building Trades Council's victory in the eight-hour movement and resentment at the news that McCarthy planned to establish a state building trades council in December of 1901. In any case, the Building Trades Council promptly called a meeting and angrily adopted a rule that stipulated that its affiliated unions were henceforth prohibited from holding membership in the Labor Council. Those failing to comply were suspended. This measure was effective in the case of all but a few large affiliates. This division in the ranks of organized labor in the city was not healed for nine years, and even then the Building Trades Council never resumed its status as a subordinate body of the San Francisco Labor Council.

Historical accounts of the split in the labor movement in San Francisco have given great weight to McCarthy's intense ambition as the underlying cause. They point out that until that time the Building Trades Council was merely a subordinate unit of the Labor Council, and McCarthy participated in it only as a delegate from the Building Trades Council, holding no position of leadership in the larger organization.[69] Playing second fiddle was unacceptable to him and therefore, it is believed, he simply chose the opportunity afforded by the dispute over a cabinetmaking firm to make his organization independent of the San Francisco Labor Council.

This division in the ranks continued for a number of years, but it was finally healed early in 1910, when McCarthy suggested that dual affiliations for construction locals would be appropriate. To understand McCarthy's change of heart on the question, it is well to remember that he had, in 1907, embarked on a political career in which the united support of labor would be most valuable. Furthermore, in 1908, a Reverend Peter C. Yorke, an influential labor priest, friendly with both McCarthy and Michael Casey, a leading figure in the Labor Council, attempted with some success to persuade the two men to conciliate their differences for the good of all concerned.[70] Thereafter, cooperation characterized relations between the two organizations. Under McCarthy, however, the Building Trades Council never resumed its status as a subordinate unit of the Labor Council.

Late in 1901, at the time he had disengaged his organization from the local labor movement, McCarthy ventured to extend his influence to the building trades statewide. In a sense, he was countering his rivals in the San Francisco Labor Council, who had taken the initiative in founding the California State Federation of Labor in January of 1901. McCarthy and his associates established the State Building Trades Council of California on December 16, 1901. He may have dreamed of a western empire in the building trades. Anything may have appeared possible in the aftermath of his great triumph in the mill men's dispute. Some observers were convinced that he intended to eliminate all influence of national unions on locals in his domain. Ryan's account notes that: "It was said that during 1900–04, he wished to force all building trades unions to withdraw from their national and international affiliations so that they could be welded easily into a state organization."[71] The state council became an effective instrument for organizing building trades councils in all communities where there was sufficient construction activity to warrant it. By 1911, nineteen local councils were members of it.[72]

The state council operated almost like an adjunct of the San Francisco Building Trades Council and had for its president, from 1901 to 1922, P.H. McCarthy. In 1910 the state council, along with other organizations, mounted a campaign to organize Los Angeles. At that time (and until after World War II in fact), Los Angeles was the polar opposite of San Francisco with respect to organized labor. It was a thoroughly open shop town. At this point, McCarthy's right hand-man, Olaf A. Tveitmoe of the Cement Workers Union and secretary of the State Building Trades Council, as well as the one in San Francisco, became engaged in the campaign to organize Los Angeles—with disastrous results. In October of 1910, a bomb was exploded in the Los Angeles Times Building, killing twenty employees. Revelations concerning the explosion linked Tveitmoe to the McNamara brothers of the Iron Workers Union, who eventually pleaded guilty to the crime. In 1912

Tveitmoe was convicted of interstate transportation of dynamite, but this conviction was set aside on appeal, and his active career continued.

STABILIZING CONSTRUCTION

The acumen McCarthy had demonstrated in the mill men's dispute was equal to the task of dominating the San Francisco Building Trades Council until 1922. He gathered to himself a group of roughly fifteen men from the important affiliated local unions and ethnic groups in the construction work force and established what became known as the "McCarthy machine." These loyal lieutenants—Scottish, Scandinavian, German, Irish and English—managed to get themselves reelected delegates to the council with a consistency that dismayed McCarthy's opponents. Once entrenched, this oligarchy provided the almost unchallengeable control that McCarthy needed to carry out his plans for the construction industry. He was intent upon nothing less than economic health and stability for this highly competitive and cyclically volatile industry.

One key member of the machine, Olaf Tveitmoe, leader of the Cement Workers Local, was secretary-treasurer of the Building Trades Council and editor of its organ, *Organized Labor*, during nearly all of McCarthy's reign. By no means a sycophant, this Norwegian immigrant and former schoolteacher somehow blended loyalty to the organization with a philosophy of anarchism—openly espoused in issues of *Organized Labor*. His radicalism was essentially subordinated to the practical needs of building tradesmen, but it remained with him until his death in 1923. Not only McCarthy's right-hand man, he was also the vigorous president of the Asiatic Exclusion League. He served two months in Leavenworth until his appeal in the dynamite case met with success.

Another member of McCarthy's machine, also implicated in the dynamite case (at the time of the Los Angeles Times bombing) was Anton Johannsen, a German immigrant carpenter and special organizer for the California State Building Trades Council, who spread the McCarthy approach to building trades unionism in Alameda, Stockton and Los Angeles. He had also been associated with John Fitzpatrick and Edward Nockels of the Chicago Federation of Labor at one time. With Tvietmoe he shared the paradoxical combination of radical ideology with adherence to business union practice. He became a general organizer for the carpenters' union nationally.

Cleveland L. Dam was, for many years, chief counsel for the Building Trades Council. He was also Mayor McCarthy's legal advisor and campaign manager for his unsuccessful bid for reelection as mayor in 1911. Best man at McCarthy's second marriage, he died in 1916. Numerous others recognized and loyally supported McCarthy's management of the building trades. Among them were Frank MacDonald of the Tile Layers Union, who was a business agent of the Building Trades Council and succeeded McCarthy as president of the State Building Trades Council in 1922; Lawrence Flaherty of the Cement Workers Union also

was a business agent of and successor to McCarthy as president of the
San Francisco Council. Many of these loyal cohorts found their positions to be steppingstones to political office. Flaherty, for example,
became a state senator and U.S. congressman, while MacDonald served
as California state labor commissioner.[73]

What McCarthy did was to centralize control over collective bargaining in his hands through bylaws, which required that all demands
for whatever craft be made exclusively by the council and only after
approval of the council. This meant that negotiations were conducted
by McCarthy and enabled him to administer a councilwide policy for all
crafts on wages, hours and working conditions. In other cities, bargaining was the function of the local craft union and a building trades council acted only in a support role. In the construction industries of other
cities, written agreements were common, but in San Francisco they
were not used because McCarthy opposed them. In other cities, working cards for each union member were issued by the individual local,
and the requirement that each craftsman carry one was policed by the
local union. In San Francisco, working cards were issued by the Building
Trades Council, and policing construction sites was carried out by business agents of the council. Unruly craftsmen or craft locals were dealt
with severely. On occasion, an obstinate local union found itself confronted with another local union for its craft newly chartered by the
council under the stern instruction of Mr. McCarthy. Craftsmen in violation of McCarthy policy, in some cases, found their working cards lifted and were no longer permitted on construction sites in the city.

McCarthy was equally paternal in his approach to employers in the
industry, never permitting them to deal with the council as an industrywide association, but insisting on dealing only with separate associations of contractors in each department of the building industry.
Needless to say, bargaining power on the side of the council was substantially superior. But this considerable power was exerted with
admirable restraint so that contractors grudgingly came to respect
McCarthy's judgment and even to rely on his assessment of what economic conditions in the industry would permit. Excessive demands by
overly militant locals were scaled down to realistic proportions as they
passed through the council's procedures. New locals, weak and inexperienced, were enabled to do much better than they expected in
virtue of the council's—McCarthy's—handling. In times of crisis, such as
the earthquake of 1906, a statesmanlike, if not altogether successful,
effort was made to control the soaring costs of construction. In the
same period, the council struggled to prevent skinning and other shod-
dy building practices in the face of the turmoil brought on by the invasion of "earthquake mechanics."[74]

When construction of the Panama-Pacific exposition required substantial increases in the work force, McCarthy prevailed upon local
unions to open their books and admit the needed additional craftsmen.
Furthermore, the contractor's perennial nightmare of jurisdictional
stoppages was greatly diminished through techniques innovated by

McCarthy to resolve the conflicting jurisdictional claims that cause them. Thus, virtual mastery of the industry was sustained through more than two decades of this century, but not without the presence of an underground of disgruntled rank and file and socialist elements frustrated in their inability to deter the established hierarchy of the council and share in the decisionmaking of an organization more oligarchic than democratic in its operations.

POLITICAL VENTURE

McCarthy's interest in politics may be understood in terms of his strong personal ambitions. It was rumored that he wanted to be governor and would vigorously have sought that office had his campaigns for mayor met with greater success. As it turned out, his political career was distinctly secondary to his union career. Even while mayor of the city, he continued as president of the Building Trades Council (BTC) and actively conducted its affairs. On occasion he used the office of mayor to further the interests of his union organization and the construction industry. On the other hand, he tempered his separatist tendency in the local labor movement in order to widen his support in political campaigns.

Originally a Democrat, McCarthy supported the administration of reform Mayor James D. Phelan, who rewarded him with an appointment to the city's board of civil service commissioners. He had also been elected to the San Francisco Board of Freeholders, which drew up a new charter for the city in 1900. When the Union Labor party was organized in San Francisco in 1901, McCarthy opposed it, taking the traditional stand of AFL unionists that trade unions should limit themselves to nonpartisan involvement. By 1905, however, he had become a staunch advocate of the party, which by then had twice succeeded in electing its candidate for mayor. It is probable that McCarthy had begun to see the party as a vehicle to serve his ambitions for the future. Both he and his fellow BTC officials quickly adapted to the new political situation resulting from emergence of a successful working men's party.[75]

The spring of 1907 found McCarthy and his council, uncharacteristically, cooperating with the San Francisco Labor Council to support a strike outside the building industry. The contest was a bitter and violent one between the Carmen's Union and the United Railroads, which operated street railways in the city. The motive for this unusual action by McCarthy was, according to Knight, his political ambition.[76] At this time, Eugene Schmitz, elected to the office of the mayor three times on the Union Labor party ticket, was convicted and imprisoned for extortion. This presented McCarthy with an opportunity difficult to resist. Urged by his colleagues to seek the nomination of the Union Labor party in spite of his insistence that "holding of political office held no inducement" he, "not wishing to play the dog in the manger act, consented."[77] Prosecution of those alleged to be involved in graft exposed in the Schmitz case was a large issue in the campaign, and McCarthy's stand on it gave many people the impression he was not serious about pursuing the prosecutions. For this reason, a number of important labor leaders, Michael Casey and Andrew Furuseth among them, supported his opponent. McCarthy and the Union Labor party went down to defeat. The political rift also caused cooperation in support of the carmen's strike to deteriorate and contributed to its eventual failure.

Again in 1909, in the role of reluctant nominee, McCarthy vigorously campaigned for election as mayor under the banner of the Union Labor party. His campaign is remembered for its calculated effort to appeal to those tired of the graft prosecution (and the attendant bad publicity for the city) and those who preferred a reputation for San Francisco as the "Paris of America," a kind of wide-open tourist town. He also cultivated an image of himself as "friend of both capital and labor" and no narrow advocate of unionism. On this occasion, McCarthy enjoyed, except for a small socialist faction, the unanimous support of labor, including the San Francisco Labor Council and leaders who had opposed him in 1907. His victory was a stunning comeback for himself and the Union Labor party. The victory saw nine men from organized labor elected to the Board of Supervisors of the city. Several other important city offices (auditor, county clerk, coroner) were won by labor candidates.[78]

The Union Labor party, under Building Trades Council leadership, stood for more than merely winning political office. By no means socialist in its ideology, it nevertheless had a sense of the future in which the excesses of capitalism were curbed or eliminated. Furthermore, the leaders of the council distrusted the Progressives, whom they considered middle-class reformers lacking an understanding of the problems of manual workers, and often campaigning for changes, such as prohibition, that workers simply did not want. The platform of the Union Labor party embraced municipal ownership of public utilities whose present owners, it held, were enriching themselves at the expense of the people. For the Labor party, a case in point was Patrick Calhoun, operator of the United Railroads, a bitter foe of organized labor. Once in power, the Labor party initiated a plan to build the first city-owned tramway. It also undertook to build a new, larger, much-needed water system, the first to be developed by the city government. The McCarthy administration's inept handling of these two projects contributed to its defeat in 1911.[79]

McCarthy's two years as mayor were characterized by relative industrial peace, labor unity and gradual disappearance of concern over graft scandals. As a labor leader in political office, he made it his conscious policy to see that "one or more trades unionists should be a member of every commission called for within the law governing San Francisco over which I, as mayor, exercised control."[80]

In 1911 McCarthy was defeated for reelection by James Rolph, a candidate who proved to have enduring appeal. It was the last political campaign for McCarthy and the end of the Union Labor party as a formal political party. The campaign was perhaps notable for two speeches made in behalf of McCarthy by Samuel Gompers, then in California on AFL business.[81]

McCarthy's loss in the 1911 election was in considerable degree attributable to the personality of his opponent, "Sunny Jim" Rolph, an attractive man very much in the, then popular, Progressive mold. He enjoyed an uncanny ability to reassure all groups in the electorate of his interest in their behalf. The contrast with the leader of a labor administration oriented toward the interest of workers, although proclaiming evenhandedness, was rather vivid. There was also the faulty management of the water and street railway projects, which cast a doubt upon the Union Labor party's ability to govern effectively. McCarthy's appointees for police commissioners proved to be albatrosses around his neck as well. The first, John B. Martin, excessively conscious that liquor dealers and related businesses supported McCarthy, failed to police the city's tenderloin properly and outraged religious leaders and women's groups. His replacement, John Seymour, went to the opposite extreme and was also forced to resign. Finally, business community and news media skeptics of a working-class government waited expectantly for instances of fraud to appear and to be publicized, but finding none, they extravagantly advertised each mistake of the McCarthy administration, although they were errors of judgment rather than anything else.[82]

McCarthy's career as a labor leader was finally the victim of postwar turbulence which, in spite of his manifest leadership skills, he was unable to control. He resigned as president of the San Francisco Building Trades Council on January 12, 1922. What finally ended his career was the wave of open shop fever, deceptively labeled the "American Plan," which swept across the nation and carried even the enlightened business community of San Francisco in its train. It actually restored open shop conditions to the city's construction industry for the duration of the 1920s.

It was a sorry chapter in the proud career of a man who had devoted himself to labor's cause and who, for a generation, had captained an organization which, up to now, had been more than a match for its adversaries. His effectiveness in meeting the crisis had been impaired by the loss of close and loyal associates. Cleveland Dam had died in 1916. Olaf Tvietmoe had suffered a stroke in 1918 and never regained the vigor that had made him such an important member of McCarthy's team. Anton Johannsen had moved back to Chicago to help in the defense of his antiwar friends. Tight oligarchical control over the years had both denied the development of enough able young bloods to replace those who were gone and had sharpened the opposition of some elements among affiliated unions, who were ready to defy his leadership the moment he showed signs of weakness.[83] When he resigned as president of the San Francisco Building Trades Council, McCarthy commented that "ably assisted by my loyal associates, I have succeeded in building up and maintaining one of the greatest, most beneficial and respected industrial organizations to be found anywhere in the country."[84] A short time later, on March 19, 1922, he also resigned as president of the California State Building Trades Council. He explained that these steps were taken to fulfill a promise to his family to retire at the end of the world war but had been delayed by the controversy in which the council was embroiled.[85]

A more plausible version of the developments that precipitated McCarthy's resignation is offered by Ryan. Inflation during World War I and postwar recession seriously disturbed wage relationships in the building industry. Employers, united behind the Builders' Exchange, adopted the "American Plan" and campaigned to break the power of construction unions. Unable to counter these adverse forces effectively, McCarthy uncharacteristically vacillated in response to a highly unfavorable arbitration award. Confidence in his leadership ebbed, and a repudiation of his autocratic methods set in until he finally resigned.[86] Thereafter, McCarthy became a building contractor and investor in real estate. He died on July 1, 1933.

INFERENCES

P.H. McCarthy was an immensely ambitious, self-confident and able man. He was also blessed with a flair for innovation. In San Francisco he found perhaps the most receptive community in the country in which a young Irish immigrant could pursue the calling of trade union organizer. His strategy in opening a union-run planing mill and operating it successfully during the mill men's dispute bespeaks a remarkable business acumen and a thorough grasp of the economics of construction. It is apparent that he could have been a highly successful contractor had he chosen to be. These qualities enabled him to achieve a kind of paternal control of the building industry in San Francisco. Searching for power, he found it through a truly innovative use of a building trades council. Making the council the center of authority in collective bargaining, he displaced the power of local unions and, in fact, for a time, challenged the power of national unions over their locals.

McCarthy's authoritarian approach, which aroused some rank-and-file opposition, nevertheless, had enabled his machine "to push its way into civic affairs and to negotiate on roughly even terms with members of the urban elite."[87] Feeding on early successes, especially the victory over the mill owners, his ambition led him to reach for statewide influence over the industry and to embark on a political career. In both instances, his efforts met with only limited success. His ambition, combined with the separatist tendencies of building tradesmen, caused a temporary split in the San Francisco labor movement.

McCarthy's career exhibits distinctively Irish features. Even as a newly arrived immigrant, his language was an essential asset and enabled him to put his considerable powers of persuasion to work almost at once. This underlies the ease with which he cultivated the arts of organizer, developing quickly under the tutelage of the astute P.J. McGuire. From the earliest days, he perceived the implications of ethnic diversity in the labor force and adapted to them as had his fellow Irish in the arena of American politics. His capacity for forming a machine representing various nationality groups and construction crafts and the use of it to fasten a hierarchical structure on the building industry seem to be the trade union counterpart of features characteristic of the big-city Irish politician. In common with the Irish politicians, he employed the substantial power that was his to achieve stability rather than radical change. His goal was to establish predictable relationships in a notoriously unpredictable industry through the instrumentality of a building trades council. To a remarkable degree, he succeeded. Realization of this objective was aided in no small degree by his acceptability to businessmen of the city. Basically, this was a function of his pragmatic approach to economic and social issues—attributes found in most Irish politicians.

NOTES

1. Patrick H. McCarthy, unpublished memoirs, xeroxed, n.d., 36 (hereinafter referred to as simply memoirs). A copy of the memoirs was made available by P.H. McCarthy, Jr., labor attorney in San Francisco.
2. Seamus Breatnac (James P. Walsh), "The Difference Remains," in *The San Francisco Irish, 1850-1976*, James P. Walsh, ed. (San Francisco: Irish Literary and Historical Society, 1978), 148.
3. Moses Rischin, "Introduction: The Classic Ethnics," in Walsh, *The San Francisco Irish*, 4.
4. Robert A. Burchell, *The San Francisco Irish, 1848-1880*, (Berkeley: University of California Press, 1980).
5. Frederick L. Ryan, *Industrial Relations in the San Francisco Building Trades* (Norman: University of Oklahoma Press, 1935); Ira B. Cross, *History of the Labor Movement in California* (Berkeley: University of California Press, 1935); Robert E.L. Knight, *Industrial Relations in the San Francisco Bay Area, 1900-1918* (Berkeley: University of California Press, 1960); Selig Perlman and Philip Taft, *History of Labor in the United States, 1896-1932* (New York: Macmillan, 1935), 76-81.
6. Ryan, *Industrial Relations*, 33fn.
7. Ibid.
8. Ibid.
9. Ibid., 131.
10. Ray Stannard Baker, "A Corner in Labor," *McClure's Magazine*, February 1904, 373.
11. Ibid.
12. Microfilm of parish register examined in Dublin Castle with aid of Donal F. Begley of the genealogical office, and verified through correspondence with Canon Daniel G. O'Brien, parish priest of Newcastle West (letter to author dated April 4, 1975).
13. Interview with Robert V. Cussen, Sr., Newcastle West, April 3, May 26, 1975. Canon O'Brien's letter mentions two Hough's of note: "An Feah Mor," who was principal of the Ring Gaelic College, County Waterford, a pioneering center for the revival of Gaelic; and Billy Hough, still living, a famous hurler on the County Limerick team.
14. Interview with Kevin Danaher, University College, Dublin, May 12, 1975.
15. Memoirs, 3.
16. Ibid.
17. Griffiths Valuations (Dublin, 1852).

18. Michael McCarthy enjoyed some local renown as a man of scholarly interests with an extensive library and as secretary of the local Gaelic Athletic Association in which capacity he was known as a stern protector of its constitution.

19. Memoirs, 1.

20. Killoughteen School, established in 1846, is still in operation and, with the cooperation of Master Nicholas Walsh, an effort was made to obtain McCarthy's records. It was not successful. Master Walsh explained that, during World War II the government directed that all school records prior to 1890 be sent to Dublin to make paper pulp to meet the wartime shortage.

21. Memoirs, 1.

22. Ibid., 3.

23. Ibid.

24. Ibid., 5.

25. Ibid., 6.

26. Ibid., 6-7.

27. Ibid., 7.

28. Interview with Michael O'Grady, Ballingarry, County Limerick, April 4, 1975.

29. Memoirs, 7.

30. Interviews with Joseph and Patrick McCormack, Ardagh, County Limerick, April 4, 7, 1975. Joseph and Patrick McCormack, grandnephews of James McCormack, operate a joinery in Ardagh. Said to be third largest in Ireland, it employs seventy men.

31. James Archdeacon Begley, *The Diocese of Limerick From 1691 to the Present Time* (Dublin: Browne and Nolan, 1938), 558-59, 604.

32. Ibid.; Memoirs, 7-8.

33. Interview with Srs. Philomena and Eucharia, Convent of the Sisters of Mercy, Ballingarry, County Limerick, May 25, 1975.

34. Memoirs, 8.

35. Ibid.

36. Ibid.

37. Ibid., 10.

38. Ibid.

39. Ibid.

40. Ibid.

41. Ibid., 12.

42. Ibid.

43. Ibid.

44. Interview with Mrs. Margaret Twoomey, Killoughteen, County Limerick, May 26, 1975.

45. Memoirs, 6.

46. Memoirs, 15-17.

47. Ibid., 16.

48. Ibid., 61-62.

49. Ibid., 21.

50. Ibid., 25.

51. *Organized Labor* (organ of the San Francisco Building Trades Council), January 12, 1901, 4.

52. Memoirs, 39.

53. Specifically; Harry M. Saunders, John P. Horgan, James Saunders, John T. Byrnes, John J. Swanson, John Cliff and F. Maulsbury. Ibid., frontispiece, no page number.

54. Ibid., 53-57.

55. Ibid., 58.

56. Ibid., 61.

57. Ibid.

58. Ibid., 58.

59. They were Olaf Tveitmoe, William Page, John E. McDougal, E.J. Brandon, John D. Campbell, L.N. Wandell, W.E. Smith, Edward L. Nolan, Charles Nelson, William Ermie, Joseph Tuite, William Dwyer, C.C. Murphy, Joseph Ault, Thomas Doyle and George Newsome. Ibid., frontispiece, no page number.

60. Cross, *History of the Labor Movement*, 222; Ryan, *Industrial Relations*, 25-27. The others were a Mr. Collins, H.C. Hinchen of the Paperhangers' Union and F. Crawford of Carpenters Local 22.

61. Cross, *History of the Labor Movement*, 336.

62. Memoirs, 77.

63. Ibid., 79.

64. Ibid., 83.

65. Cross, *History of the Labor Movement*, 44.

66. Memoirs, 113.

67. Ibid., 115.

68. Ryan, *Industrial Relations*, 131.

69. See Ryan, *Industrial Relations*, 44; Knight, *Industrial Relation*, 1900-1918, 57.

70. Bernard C. Cronin, *Father Yorke and the Labor Movement in San Francisco* (Washington, D.C.: Catholic University Press, 1943), 208-9, 213.

71. Ryan, *Industrial Relations*, 43.

72. Cross, *History of Labor in Movement*, 234.

73. Michael Kazin, "Barons of Labor: The San Francisco Building Trades, 1896-1922" (Ph.D. diss., Stanford University, 1982), 569-71.

74. Memoirs, 153-55, 158-62.

75. Knight, *Industrial Relations, 1900-1918*, 162; Michael Kazin, *Barons of Labor: The San Francisco Building Trades in the Progressive Era* (Champaign: University of Illinois Press, 1987) 113. (This book was adapted from Kazin's previously cited dissertation.)

76. Knight, *Industrial Relations, 1900-1918*, 194.

77. Memoirs, 177.

78. Knight, *Industrial Relations, 1900-1918*, 219; Kazin, *Barons of Labor*, 184-85.

79. Kazin, *Barons of Labor*, 189-93. In his Chapter 7, entitled "The Misgoverning of San Francisco, 1908-1911," Kazin provides a thorough analysis of the McCarthy administration's time in office.

80. Memoirs, 183.

81. Knight, *Industrial Realtions, 1900-1918*, 244-45.

82. Kazin, "Barons of Labor," 395-423 (dissertation).

83. Kazin, *Barons of Labor*, 244.

84. Memoirs, 202.

85. Ibid., 200.

86. Ryan, *Industrial Relations*, 165. Thereafter, McCarthy's removal from all remaining offices in the trade unions occurred due to rumors that he had accepted a bribe from Pacific Gas and Electric Company to oppose the plan for a public power system, which the Building Trades Council voted to endorse. Hearings before the California State Senate in 1928 confirmed that a bribe of $10,000 had, indeed, been paid to him. See Kazin, *Barons of Labor*, 274-75.

87. Kazin, *Barons of Labor*, 150.

John Brophy, c. 1946. Courtesy of The George Meany Memorial Archives, Silver Spring, MD.

John Fitzpatrick, c. 1945. Courtesy of Irwin E. Klass, Former Editor of *Federation News*, Chicago Federation of Labor.

Elizabeth Gurley Flynn, 1908. Courtesy of International
Publishers, New York, NY.

William Z. Foster, 1918. Courtesy of International Publishers, New York, NY.

Mother Jones and Terence V. Powderly, c. 1920. Courtesy of John Michael Powderly, Grandnephew.

Patrick H. McCarthy, c. 1909. Courtesy of Pat McCarthy, Grandson.

Joseph Patrick McDonnell, c. 1890. Sketch by L.A. O'Donnell, based on engraving from The Paterson Labor Standard.

Peter J. McGuire, c. 1886. Courtesy of Iris Rosselle, Granddaughter.

Philip Murray, c. 1910. Courtesy of Historical and Labor Archives, Pennsylvania State University, University Park.

Mike Quill, c. 1960. Courtesy of Transport Workers Union of America, New York, NY.

Frank Roney, 1883. Reprinted from Ira Cross, *Frank Roney, Irish Revolutionary and California Labor Leader*. Copyright © 1931 The Regents of the University of California. Courtesy of University of California Press.

5

A TRIO OF RADICALS: FLYNN, FOSTER AND JONES

At an outdoor meeting in the Bronx on a warm summer evening in 1908, Elizabeth Gurley Flynn stood listening to a fiery old Irishwoman scold her audience for failing to help the western miners in their strike. The speaker was Mary Harris "Mother" Jones, and her tongue was so sharp and her depictions of the bloodshed and suffering so vivid that Elizabeth Flynn, then eighteen and pregnant, fainted. James Connolly, the Irish socialist, a family friend, caught her as she fell, and after Mother Jones interrupted her diatribe long enough to command "get the poor girl some water," he accompanied the young woman and her husband to their home.[1]

This was the first of several encounters between these two legendary female agitators in the cause of labor. Both enjoyed the gift of inflaming their audiences, and each devoted a lifetime to the cause. Both were conscious of their Irish ancestry and found inspiration in experiences in their own families though in somewhat different ways. Fortunately, each of them has left us a record in the form of an autobiography, in Miss Flynn's case, one that she wrote while a prisoner in the Federal Women's Reformatory in Alderson, West Virginia.[2] She served more than two years for a conviction under the Smith Act in 1952.

Flynn and Jones were friends and associates of William Z. Foster, third member of the trio of Irish radicals considered here. Mother Jones served as an organizer for W.Z. Foster and John Fitzpatrick in the national campaign directed by them to unionize the American steel industry in 1919. From 1921, when he joined the American Communist party after a three-month stay in Moscow (occasioned by attendance at the Red International Labor Union Congress) until his death in 1961, Foster served in positions of greater and lesser importance in the party, standing as its candidate for president of the United States in the 1924, 1928 and 1932 elections. In 1937 Elizabeth Gurley Flynn was admitted to membership in the American Communist party with sponsorship of her old friends William Z. Foster and Ella Reeve Bloor. In spite of their reputations as individualists earlier in their respective careers, Flynn and Foster observed party discipline faithfully for the remainder of their lives. Flynn's column "Life of the Party" became a regular feature of *The Daily Worker*, and in 1961 she was elected chairman of the American Communist party. In September of 1964 she died in Moscow where she had gone only a short time before for a vacation and to begin work on the second volume of her autobiography.

This chapter leans heavily on autobiographical works of the three radicals studied. It is influenced by historian Emmet Larkin's observation that "the political history of modern Ireland is largely a study of biography."[3] It does not attempt to encompass the entire careers of the trio, but emphasizes the formative experiences of earlier periods in their lives. It explores the development of their ideological and religious convictions and looks for influences stemming from their Irish ancestry. Development of their organizing methods and communication skills is essential for trade union activists and will be regarded duly.

ELIZABETH GURLEY FLYNN

Elizabeth Gurley Flynn was born in Concord, Massachusetts, in 1890. She was the daughter of Annie Gurley, who came from Galway in 1877, and Tom Flynn, whose father emigrated from County Mayo in the 1840s. The Flynn family revered heroes of nationalist movements against the English—Emmet, Davitt, Tone, Parnell, O'Donovan Rossa—and communicated the rebel spirit to its children through Irish songs and stories. Of her childhood Flynn recalled "we drew in a burning hatred of British rule with our mother's milk."[4] All this became intensely personal for her as she learned that her four great grandfathers—Flynn, Gurley, Ryan and Conneran—had been United Irishmen and fought along with the French in the rising of 1798. One of them, great-grandfather Flynn—known as "Paddy the Rebel" of County Mayo—led a column of French and Irish from Ballina through the hills in a successful attack on the English at Castlebar. A fugitive for a time after the rising failed, he nevertheless survived to a ripe old age and fathered eighteen children, among them Tom Flynn (Elizabeth Flynn's grandfather), who left Ireland at the time of the famine. As a parting gesture of defiance to the English landlord who caught him poaching fish during the famine, grandfather Flynn threw lime in the landlord's stream and ran off to America. He settled in Maine, and participated in the abortive Fenian invasion of Canada by Irish veterans of the Civil War, in 1866, led by Colonel John O'Neill.

Steeped in this tradition, embittered by discrimination shown the Irish at this time, Tom Flynn, Elizabeth's father, was determined to seek a better life. A laborer in the granite quarries of New England, he had been permanently blinded in the left eye by a flying chip while still a boy. He had, says Miss Flynn, seen all but one of his male relatives die working at quarrying. In his twenties he married Annie Gurley, who had come to Boston from Galway. Although of a Presbyterian "lace curtain" Irish family, which had owned land in Galway, she shared his sentiments about Irish freedom and a better life. This social distinction, however, was sufficiently important that both the Gurley family and the Flynns refused to attend the wedding. Annie Gurley was, in her daughter's eyes, a remarkable person—an educated woman, she held advanced ideas about the role of women. With her encouragement, Tom Flynn applied and was admitted to Dartmouth College where he studied civil engineering. He demonstrated a ready grasp of mathematics, but was unable to complete the degree for financial reasons. Thereafter, he followed the vocation of itinerant city mapmaker, painfully moving the family with him, more often than not, around New England and as far west as Cleveland. Finally, in 1900, at Annie Gurley Flynn's insistence (for reasons readily imagined), the family settled permanently—in a cold-water flat in the South Bronx.

Not satisfied that the system had yielded him a sufficiently better life, Tom Flynn's thinking evolved from sympathy for greenbackism and populism to support for Eugene Debs and the Socialist party. In the meantime, he became alienated from the Catholic Church because of its handling of Father McGlynn over his advocacy of the single-tax movement. However, Tom Flynn's attitude was somewhat more complex than this. He recognized that Catholicism was deeply embedded in the national traditions of the Irish and doubly so because of the penal laws. He therefore respected it and resented bigoted attacks on it in America or by the English, but since Annie Gurley professed no religion at all (though raised by Presbyterian grandparents), the Flynn children were reared without religion, save socialism. All the celebrated labor struggles—Molly Maguires, Haymarket, Pullman, Danbury Hatters—were the everyday currency of the Flynn household. There were meetings at the Bronx Socialist Forum and the Harlem Socialist Club where mother and father Flynn consistently brought their children. Elizabeth, oldest of the children, remembered them well and absorbed ideas she heard there, even though annoyed by her father's habit of bringing all four children, especially the younger ones who could not yet comprehend the goings on and should have been in bed. The adolescent Elizabeth Gurley Flynn began serious reading: Bellamy's *Looking Backward*, Sinclair's *The Jungle*, Kropotkin's *Appeal to the Young, The Communist Manifesto*. She was introduced to Emma Goldman by her first beau (Fred Robinson). She attended a party in honor of Alexander Berkman (Goldman's companion) on his return from the prison where he had been sent for an attempt on the life of Henry Clay Frick during the Homestead strike of 1892.

In Public School Number 9, Gurley Flynn joined the debating society, "took to it like a duck to water" and won prizes. She argued for public ownership of the mines when the issue arose during the anthracite strike of 1902 led by John Mitchell and opposed by George Baer, president of the Reading Railroad, one of the "Christian men to whom God in his infinite wisdom has given control of the property interest of the country."[5] A lifelong fascination with the Bill of Rights was awakened in her by James A. Hamilton, one of her teachers who drilled his students in the American Constitution. Before long Miss Flynn, still only sixteen, was ready to launch her career as a public advocate of her blossoming radical convictions. She did so on January 31, 1906, at the Harlem Socialist Club where her exegesis on the rights of women was well received. Invitations to speak began to arrive. Soapbox efforts on the street were undertaken. Completing high school was shelved permanently. A slender, dark-haired, attractive girl, she caught the eye of famed American producer David Belasco who became interested in her for a part in a drama about working people. To the astonishment of her mother, who accompanied her to an interview with Belasco, she rejected the opportunity adding, "I'm in the labor movement and I speak my own piece."[6] Theodore Dreiser, then an obscure editor of *Broadway Magazine*, boosted her vanity further by writing a laudatory column about her entitled, "An East Side Joan of Arc."

Miss Flynn joined the Industrial Workers of the World (IWW) only a year after it was established at Chicago in 1905 by a motley assortment of socialists, anarchists, syndicalists and others—including Mother Jones. Never having worked, it was not clear how she was admitted, since being a wage earner was a strict requisite. Nevertheless, its mission to eliminate the wage system, its fighting spirit and aura of rebellion appealed to her profoundly. Her association with the IWW endured until the demise of that organization during World War I. Satisfying her youthful sense of adventure, it took her all over the country organizing relief for strikers and their families, speaking at protest demonstrations and free speech fights. It exposed her to physical danger and caused her to be jailed frequently. It even led to immortalization of a sort in the form of a song, "The Rebel Girl," written about and dedicated to her by Wobbly troubadour Joe Hill. At one protest meeting, sponsored by the Socialist Labor party in 1907, she first met socialist (and later Irish national hero) James Connolly. Then thirty-nine, Connolly was on the second of his two visits to the United States, where he was growing more visible as a socialist pamphleteer and strategist, while at the same time eking out a living for his large family which he had brought over from Dublin. Shortly after meeting Miss Flynn, Connolly was forced to leave his job at Singer Sewing Machine Works in Elizabeth, New Jersey. Fortunately, he obtained an appointment as organizer for the IWW in New York City and moved his family to a shabby flat on Elton Avenue in the Bronx near the Flynns. The two families became good friends. Their younger children became playmates, while the adults collaborated to create the Irish Socialist Federation and made their homes gathering places for countrymen of that persuasion.

One of the countrymen who appeared at the Flynn's door in 1914 was James Larkin. He arrived haggard and exhausted from the great Dublin strike of 1913. Founder of Ireland's largest union, the Irish

Transport and General Workers Union, he was ostensibly on a fund-raising trip, but surely also here to recuperate from his heroic exertions. He announced simply, "James Connolly sent me." Thereafter, he was a frequent visitor to the Flynn household while in New York, delighting to drink tea with Mrs. Flynn whom he referred to as "His Countrywoman." The connection was County Carlow where, according to Mrs. Flynn, her great grandfather, John Gurley had come from and, also, at one time the Larkins. Larkin hated alcohol and called it the curse of the Irish, a view not shared by Tom Flynn. He was also critical of the Flynns for allowing their daughters to have such "free ways," as smoking and wearing silk stockings. Annie Gurley (Flynn) chided him and pointed out that when a young girl she "used to light my grandmother's pipe with a live coal from the hearth."[7]

Before coming to America for his second visit in 1903, James Connolly had organized the short-lived Irish Republican Socialist party (IRSP) and subsequently affiliated the Irish Socialist Federation, founded with the Flynns, to the Socialist party of Ireland, successor of the IRSP in Ireland. He did this to strengthen his ties with the movement there. This move suited his future plans admirably, since he devoutly hoped to return to Dublin.

Connolly encouraged "Lizzie Flynn," as he called her, and found her apt and receptive as a student as well as a charming, forceful exegete for someone so young. Gurley Flynn admired the quick grasp of foreign languages which Connolly used to evangelize for socialism among immigrant workers. James Connolly, an able man, was tireless, with endless patience and tenacity in the cause of socialism and Irish liberation. Nevertheless, he was not happy in America. In fact, he yearned passionately to return to Dublin. According to Samuel Levenson, one of his biographers, he confessed as much to Mother Jones with whom he apparently was acquainted at this time.[8] He found capitalist institutions deeply rooted in America and unyielding. American socialists appeared quarrelsome and ineffectual. He had a memorable confrontation with Daniel De Leon, "Socialist pope" and reigning genius of the Socialist Labor party. When Connolly organized Irish Catholic longshoremen in New York for the IWW, De Leon persuaded IWW leaders to hold a secret meeting in which he accused Connolly of being a Jesuit agent sent over to undermine the entire movement. De Leon disapproved of Connolly's appeal to the ethnic identity of immigrants, as well as his efforts to reconcile religion and socialism. Characteristically, De Leon considered Connolly, like anyone who disagreed with him, a heretic and beyond hope. Partly because of his irresponsible accusations against Connolly, De Leon was forced out of the IWW at its 1908 convention.[9]

Connolly was delighted at the opportunity to return to Ireland in 1910 to join Jim Larkin in establishing trade unions and to organize forces for independence. His martyrdom in the Easter Rising was less than six years away.

Spirited, precocious, eager for a western venture, seventeen-year-old Elizabeth Flynn, in the fall of 1907, jumped at the chance for a speaking tour of the Mesabi area of Minnesota when invited by Jack Jones, a Wobbly organizer she had met at the IWW convention in Chicago earlier that year. Jones, a miner and fifteen years her senior, was located in Duluth, and embodied the romance of the movement and of the West for Miss Flynn, if not for her parents who had serious misgivings about the trip. The trip confirmed their apprehensions. Not yet eighteen, she married Jones in January of 1908, but the marriage did not go well. When the first child arrived prematurely, the couple found themselves in a cheap room on the near North Side of Chicago. The baby lived only a few hours. Friends believed that the premature birth might have been related to the condition of the small flat in which her husband kept buckets of paint and turpentine while he experimented with wall-sized versions of the IWW's "Wheel of Fortune," originally created by Thomas J. Hagerty, a defrocked Catholic priest, who was one of the founders of the IWW.[10]

After this misfortune, Jones and his young wife were often sent on separate assignments—Elizabeth frequently on wide-ranging speaking tours in the West. In spite of the arrival of a second child (who thrived), their marriage did not survive. Their last time together was spent during the free speech fight at Missoula, Montana, where both were jailed, but Elizabeth only briefly, and with considerate treatment.

Among the first free speech fights of the IWW, Missoula was typical of many others, though involving less violence. Initially, large crowds were attracted to IWW street meetings. Next local merchants objected, and a city ordinance outlawing street meetings was hastily passed, only to be defied by Wobblies as unconstitutional. Jailings began. A national call for volunteers was sent through the IWW network. Wobblies streamed into Missoula. Jails overflowed. Taxpayers began to object to the expense. Finally, exasperated local officials dropped charges and permitted meetings. Things quieted down. Most Wobblies moved on to the next scene of agitation. In this case, it was Spokane, Washington, and Elizabeth Flynn was in the thick of it, though with child and unaccompanied by her husband.

Spokane was at the center of the market for migratory work in logging, mining and agriculture in the Northwest, and the IWW was campaigning against employment agencies that fleeced migrants outrageously. It was December of 1909, and migrants crowded the town for their winter "laying up" season. Events transpired much as they had in Missoula, but this time Gurley Flynn was accused of criminal conspiracy, jailed overnight, treated despicably by police chief Sullivan, tried, convicted and finally acquitted on appeal. Her published accounts of the experience received national publicity and exercised women's rights groups.

WILLIAM Z. FOSTER

During the Spokane fight, Flynn met William Zebulon Foster, a man destined for remarkable organizing campaigns in meatpacking and steel and leadership of the Communist mission to American labor. Flynn described him as "tall, slender, blue-eyed and soft-spoken,"[11] but he was a wiry, vigorous wanderer who at twenty-eight had sailed around the world twice and had cultivated a radical spirit almost from boyhood. He had come to Spokane to cover the action for a paper published by a left-wing faction expelled by the Socialist party in Seattle.

Almost immediately, Foster joined the fight and was jailed for two months, joining the IWW while locked up. He became a leader of the strike committee on his release and engineered a settlement in negotiations with the mayor. Foster was no stranger to jails, or life as a migratory laborer, or rebellion for that matter. There was never a doubt in his mind about the necessity for revolutionary change; he simply was preoccupied with finding an effective way of bringing it about. In the course of his career, he experimented with, theorized and wrote about numerous methods, but never discovered the right one for American society.

Foster's quest for the right revolutionary method caused his association with the IWW to be brief. Sailing to Europe in 1910, he spent six months with French syndicalists in the Confederation of Labor, who taught him some French and converted him to the method of "boring from within" existing (conservative) unions to radicalize them to the point where they became a revolutionary force. On the same trip, he stayed in Germany where experience with the leaders of the Social Democrats caused him to doubt the revolutionary commitment of their movement. While preparing for sojourns in Spain and Italy, Foster was cabled by IWW General Secretary Vincent St. John to represent the Wobbly organization at the International Trade Union Secretariat Conference scheduled for Budapest in August of 1911. Foster managed to get himself expelled from that conference by chairman Karl Legien after causing an uproar that lasted two days when he challenged the credentials of the AFL delegate, James Duncan. Returning to Chicago for the IWW convention of 1911, Foster undertook to convert comrades to his new credo. The implication of it was that the IWW would cease to be a bona fide trade union and its members would join AFL unions and infiltrate them with revolutionary spirit. Foster stirred controversy in the organization, but was unable to get his policy adopted and so left the IWW early in 1912.[12]

Subsequently, he founded the Syndicalist League of North America (SLNA), an organization never consisting of more than a handful of loyal followers, and was off hoboing through the West in the dead of winter to convert rank-and-file Wobblies to the SLNA and its "boring from within" approach.[13] He felt encouraged in this by the low ebb to which the IWW had fallen as indicated by the mere thirty-one delegates present at its 1911 convention, but Foster's timing proved inauspicious. The IWW was on the brink of a dramatic resurgence occasioned by the successful strike at Lawrence, Massachusetts, in January of 1912, and the Paterson, New Jersey, strike in 1913. Gurley Flynn, no convert to Foster's new beliefs, played a leading role in both strikes.

William Zebulon Foster was the son of James Foster, an uneducated Irish peasant and Fenian who emigrated from County Carlow in 1868 to escape capture by the British. A plot to foment revolt among Irish soldiers in the British Army failed when it was betrayed by an informer, and James Foster's involvement forced him to depart in haste. Of his father, W.Z. Foster wrote: "His main interest was in independence for Ireland and during my boyhood my political meat and drink at home was militant Irish nationalism."[14] The elder Foster worked as a livery stableman first in Taunton, Massachusetts, and then in Philadelphia where he moved his family in 1887, when William was six. They settled into an Irish ghetto at Seventeenth and Kater Street called "Skittereen" about which Foster harbored bitter memories. His description of it—poverty, gang warfare (the "Bulldogs" owned Skittereen turf), alcoholism, prostitution, gambling—reads much like that of a black ghetto today. Only the drugs were missing. Foster's parents produced no less than twenty-three children, only five of whom survived beyond infancy. The Foster's tenement on Kater Street was visited by numerous Irish patriots. Many of them had been associated with the Molly Maguires in the anthracite region of Pennsylvania during the 1870s.

As a boy, Foster responded favorably to the urgings of his father that he dedicate himself to the cause of Irish independence and to the efforts of his Scottish-English mother (Elizabeth McLaughlin) to develop in him a devotion to Roman Catholicism as deep as her own. Foster describes his father as also being a Catholic "but a negligent one." Nevertheless, at one time the idea of his becoming a priest was seriously entertained. Neither of these ambitions survived his immersion in the workaday world, which he entered at age ten after only three years of school, and the serious reading in science and history (especially of the French Revolution which fascinated him), begun as a precocious preteen, which he claimed to have been. These ideals, however, may well have influenced his lifelong quest for revolutionary change of society.

The career of William Z. Foster bears curious resemblances to that of James Larkin, the extraordinary Irish labor leader who was born only five years before him. Foster and Larkin did meet each other on at least several occasions through their associations with John Fitzpatrick of the Chicago Federation of Labor, but apparently remained merely acquaintances. Also among their mutual acquaintances were two other leading syndicalists of the day, Tom Mann and "Big Bill" Haywood.[15] Foster and Larkin owe their eminence to legendary organizing campaigns—Foster for the Chicago stockyard drive of 1917 and the great steel strike of 1919, Larkin for the Belfast strike of 1907 and the great Dublin strike of 1913. Like Foster, Larkin was raised in an English-speaking Irish ghetto outside Ireland. Liverpool, in Larkin's case, if anything, was a more depressing slum than Skittereen in Philadelphia. Larkin was said to have had ancestors from County Carlow as well, and both men were friends of Elizabeth Gurley Flynn; Larkin often dropped in for tea at the Flynn household in the Bronx during his sojourn in New York. Each enjoyed approximately three years of formal education and were apprenticed at age eleven—Foster to an old German sculptor and engraver named Kretschman—but for lack of interest and insufficient pay both abandoned their apprenticeships.

Thereafter, their working lives became absorbed in a series of uninspiring odd jobs which, in the case of each of them, were physically injurious, and along with other aspects of slum life, disillusioned them with the capitalist society in which they were growing to manhood. From work in a lead company, a type foundry and fertilizing plants, Foster contracted tuberculosis. Larkin was disabled for nearly five months when struck by a piece of machinery on the Liverpool docks. Their conversions to socialism took place while yet in their teens upon hearing about it from street evangelists for the cause. Foster embraced it on the occasion of his first exposure to socialist doctrine on the corner of Broad and South Streets in Philadelphia on a summer night in 1900—a moment he judged to be a great turning point in his life. According to Foster, "the speaker and his presentation won me immediately and completely."[16] To escape the dreary and disheartening experiences of their young lives, Larkin and Foster went to sea. Foster remained at sea for three years. He sailed all over the world in square-rigged British merchant ships and emerged an able-bodied deep water seaman with his lungs restored to health, an important consideration in his decision to ship out.

At this point, the pattern of their careers diverges somewhat. Larkin returned from the sea after one year. Resuming work on the Liverpool docks, he became an active member, leader and organizer for the dockers' union. Organizing first in English and Scottish ports, he then moved to Belfast, and finally to Dublin, where he established the Irish Transport and General Workers' Union (ITGWU). Larkin became the central figure in the climactic strike of 1913 in Dublin. Foster, on the other hand, resumed his calling as a jack of odd jobs largely in the American West where he became, at the same time, an accomplished hobo skilled at riding the rods, the trucks and all other tricks of traveling by fast freight in all seasons, before he emerged as an organizer of great ability. He was by turns a shepherd, homesteader, mule skinner, metal miner, lumberjack, harvest hand, construction man, railroader, tent show canvasman, trolley car motorman and railroad car inspector. Experiences such as these gave Foster a natural affinity for the Wobblies, which he embraced at Spokane in 1909, as we have seen, but the evolution of his convictions about Marxist doctrine and practice caused his association to be brief—much more so than Larkin's. From his arrival in America in 1914 until his imprisonment in New York City in 1919, after his conviction for criminal anarchy, James Larkin was actively engaged in the work of the IWW, especially in its efforts to oppose World War I. His Marxism and his hatred of Ireland's subjugation by the British combined to form his passionate opposition to the war.

There are other important differences between Larkin and Foster. Both became dedicated Marxists, but curiously Larkin did so while retaining his Catholic beliefs, astonishing his socialist audiences on occasion by holding up the cross he wore around his neck to proclaim, "There is no conflict between Catholic religion and Marxism."[17] Foster, however, tells us that he began to lose his faith while a teenager as his omnivorous reading proceeded through Tom Paine's *Age of Reason*, Gibbon's *Decline and Fall* and Darwin's *Origin of the Species*. His atheism was firmly anchored through a reading of Spencer's *Data of Sociology* (Volume 1 of his three-volume *Principles of Sociology*) and reinforced by exposure to Marx and Lenin's explanation of the role of religion as a weapon of the exploiting classes. While Larkin embodied the spirit of Irish nationalism throughout his life, Foster rapidly lost interest in it when he found that he "did not have to look to England for the real enemy but must meet him in the United States." It was the capitalist employer. An encounter with mounted policemen at Fifteenth and Market Streets in Philadelphia, during a trolley strike at age fourteen, was a baptism of sorts as a trade unionist, and his "interest in Ireland began to sink into a secondary position." It never again engaged his passions.[18]

One skill required of an organizer is that he communicate effectively. Both men clearly met that criterion, but in the style of it lies a sharp contrast of personalities. Bert Cochran, historian of American unions and communism, tells us that Foster "was persuasive on and off the platform. People felt they were in the presence of a bluff, straight-shooting, clear-thinking workingman."[19] Foster had an orderly, disciplined mind which, while it moved from one variation of his ideology to another, was evident in his presentation of practical solutions to immediate problems faced by working people. Contemporaries referred to him as quiet, soft-spoken, intense, rather than colorful or dramatic.[20] But he was tenacious, assertive and fearless enough to disrupt the entire Budapest Trade Union conference by himself. Regarding Larkin on the platform, people must have felt they were in the presence of an awesome, thundering, unpredictable force. He was a classic agitator, a true charismatic embodying the rage of the poor—an eloquent enemy of the establishment assaulting its conscience with a vision of social justice. His biographer says of Larkin, "He learned all the techniques and tricks of demagogy, the theatrics, the repartee, the rhetoric, and the poetry that were to make him one of the most successful mob orators of his day."[21] He was explosive, outrageous and poetic—a rouser of the first rank.

Regardless of their contrasting personalities, Larkin and Foster shared a genius for organizing workers. They excelled in uniting competing ethnic and religious groups and, in Foster's case, competing craft unions. Of Larkin's 1907 effort in Belfast it has been observed, "He had the Catholics and the Protestants, the Orangemen, Hiberians, Republicans all marching together and demonstrating through the city in defense of trade union rights."[22] A rare and wondrous feat. Foster planned and, in collaboration with Irish immigrant John Fitzpatrick, head of the Chicago Federation of Labor, successfully directed the organization of the diverse labor force of the meatpacking industry consisting of immigrant Slavic, Italian, native American, white and black workers with a committee composed of a dozen jurisdiction-conscious AFL craft unions. Two hundred thousand employees were brought into the fold, according to Foster's estimate, and were the beneficiaries of a generous strike-averting arbitration award handed down by Judge Altschuler in 1918.[23]

An even larger (365,000) and more diverse mixture of immigrants and native Americans (black and white) in the steel industry came to be unionized by Foster and Fitzpatrick acting through a committee of twelve craft unions in 1918 before the prolonged strike of 1919 was finally lost to the unrelenting steel firms led by Judge Elbert Gary.[24] To Bert Cochran, historian of unions and communism, this was "a masterly achievement . . . and required drawn out complex negotiations to maneuver a dozen squabbling, narrow-minded and egocentric AFL union heads into cooperating . . . and to keep them from undercutting each other during the bitterly fought strike, Foster displayed tact and dexterity of a high order."[25] David Brody, historian of steel industry labor relations, also attests "the high order of Foster's talents which marked him as a man of promise to AFL leaders . . . and who had already demonstrated his genius as an organizer in the stockyards."[26]

An important source of strength in the strike on which Foster and Fitzpatrick capitalized was the attitude of immigrant steelworkers. During the war they had been exhorted to demonstrate their loyalty to the United States in its effort to "make the world safe for democracy." They had been urged to efforts and hours of work to the limit of their energy. They had willingly subscribed to war bond sales by employer and government appeals to their patriotism—to save democracy. At war's end they felt they had earned their citizenship. They had made a mighty contribution to the war effort on behalf of democratic freedom and now were ready to enjoy its fruits—industrial democracy, an eight-hour day, dignity in the workplace, a voice in the decisions of their industry—all the things for which the union stood. As a result, immigrant workers were the more steadfast in support of the strike than native American steelworkers—even in the face of industry efforts to incite ethnic jealousies and frictions, to brand the union a foreign and un-American influence.

The problem of the "Babel of tongues" represented in the work force of the steel industry may be understood by pointing out that in a given complex of steel plants in Gary, Indiana, or Homestead, Pennsylvania, or Youngstown, Ohio, as many as fifty or more nationality groups and languages might be encountered. Foster and his associates discovered, however, that there were usually five or six which were predominant. He coped with the problem by making sure that level-headed, competent and respected men from those five or six predominant groups were recruited and available as organizers in each situation. Their job was to get across the message to their respective minorities. In addition, English-speaking organizers were trained to take maximum advantage of the fact that most immigrants knew at least some English. By speaking as simply and clearly as possible, avoiding technical trade union jargon, employing sign language and the simplest English words, patiently repeating them and even resorting to pidgin English where appropriate, the ideas of solidarity and cooperation could be conveyed. An education process was at work here which the immigrant workers appreciated, and to which they responded with a cohesiveness that was remarkable under the circumstances.[27]

MARY HARRIS "MOTHER" JONES

One who admired Foster's work was Mother Jones, who wrote of him and John Fitzpatrick in reference to the campaign in steel: "Never had a strike been led by more devoted, able, unselfish men. Never a thought for themselves only for the men on strike."[28] Foster had secured the services of this fabled agitator, then in her eighties, as an organizer during the steel campaign. Her statement conveys an ideal of what an organizer should be, and her own career as a labor agitator, surely one of the longest on record, exemplifies that ideal. Examining it calls to mind the ordeal of Saint Paul (2 Cor. 11:27-28), "in many labors, in prisons more frequently, in lashes above measure, often exposed to death . . . in labor and hardships, in many sleepless nights, in hunger and thirst, in fastings, often in cold and nakedness." Her entire life resembled one of Foster's long hobo journeys around the country.

Foster admired Mother Jones and estimated that "she probably participated actively in more important strikes than any other labor leader of her time." According to Foster, Mother Jones "commanded a fiery militancy and homely oratory that were highly stimulating to strikers facing terrorism and starvation. Her prestige was enormous among the miners and the many groups of workers with whom she did strike service." Nevertheless, writing as a confirmed Communist functionary, Foster expressed reservations about Mother Jones and felt that "she did not have the revolutionary understanding of Mother Bloor" (a fellow Communist). In consequence,

She made many grotesque political mistakes. In one breath she would be actively endorsing the Soviet government and snorting fire and brimstone against the Capitalist system, and in the next breath she was naively appealing to the "better side" of John D. Rockefeller, Jr. to improve his workers' conditions, or openly supporting the reactionary Harding, for President. Notwithstanding her vagaries, however, she was a proletarian rebel at heart, and every strike-bound employer dreaded her presence among his striking workers.[29]

Foster goes on to tell how, during the organizing drive in steel, the committee, which Fitzpatrick chaired and of which Foster was secretary-treasurer, had to use her skills as an agitator with great care because they wanted to avoid local strikes that would upset their national strategy. Such a local strike had an excellent possibility of occurring in a town in the aftermath of her visit. Foster described how it almost happened in Homestead, Pennsylvania, where her arrest caused a demonstration so large that local authorities were forced to free her.[30]

Mother Jones literally maintained no permanent residence or office and carried what few possessions she had along with her. She traveled by passenger train, nearly always on day coaches. In the absence of train service, she would use whatever horse-drawn conveyances were available or go on foot. While photographs consistently show her attired in long, dark, grandmotherly, Victorian style dresses and hats, Lois McLean got a more earthy picture when she interviewed an elderly woman from Mingo County, West Virginia, who had once accompanied Mother Jones to an organizing meeting held back in the hills of the area in 1919. The woman recalled, "Why, do you know what she had on from the skirt down? She was wearing a pair of men's overall pants! And a man's shirt! Yes and some funny looking boots. They were sort of wool, men's kind and they came up high like they'd protect her if she fell. She had a man's hat too, pulled down on her head." When Mother Jones and her young companion arrived at the meeting site in a horse-drawn wagon, Mother Jones "got out and reached under the wagon seat and pulled out a great big club, made like a baseball bat, but not so long."[31]

At other times, according to McLean, Jones was known to be armed for her own protection with a purse weighted with a railroad spike or stone and mounted with a sturdy purse strap. Food and shelter (when not in jail) were typically found in miner's cabins where she ate with the family and slept as well—usually on the floor. In West Virginia, however, this was not possible for fear the family that harbored her would be evicted from its company-owned cabin. Such dedication, combined with a rare ability to communicate strength and instill fighting spirit in striking workers and their families, earned for her the reputation of one of America's most effective union organizers.

The sources of this dedication are not as clear as they appear to be in the case of Flynn or Foster. Mother Jones says of her family only this: "My people were poor. For generations they had fought for Ireland's freedom. Many of my folks have died in the struggle."[32] Although she was the daughter of a man who apparently was forced to emigrate from Ireland due to agitation against the English, she offers very little evidence that her family cultivated that militant spirit in her. She makes no mention of her father's flight in her autobiography, and, unlike Flynn and Foster, the cause of Irish independence does not enter into her descriptions of her upbringing, which are extremely brief in themselves, nor does it appear elsewhere in the book. Of course, this may be due to her personality, which seems to have lacked a strong impulse toward self-dramatization at least through the medium of autobiography. The autobiography, in fact, is not very revealing of her interior life and thinking, but rather, a factual, if colorful, account of her experiences with large gaps even in that. Seemingly, it was done only reluctantly in response to the urgings of friends.

What little Mother Jones offers us about her upbringing suggests that the family enjoyed a modest prosperity by the time it moved to Toronto, and encouraged Mary to prepare for the middle-class profession of an elementary teacher (as well as the dressmaking business) since she was sent to a normal school. There is no evidence that the family was financially able to provide for her education, so that she probably worked her way through. Later, she taught in a Catholic convent school in Monroe, Michigan, and still later in schools of Memphis, Tennessee. She provides no hint that these experiences inspired her or were even satisfactory. Of the Monroe episode she says, "Later, I came to Chicago and opened a dressmaking establishment. I preferred sewing to bossing little children."[33]

The wellsprings of her inspiration to embark on a life in the cause of social justice may better be understood as a response to tragedies she endured as a young woman. While in Memphis, she met and married George E. Jones, a molder by trade and an activist in the Iron Molders' Union. By her account, the marriage had produced four children before the family encountered the catastrophe of a yellow fever epidemic in Memphis in the fall of 1867. Of the six members in her family, only Mother Jones survived, and if this were not enough to either destroy her or prove her inner strength, the Chicago fire of October 1871 must have been. It destroyed the dressmaking business she established there subsequent to leaving Memphis. Homeless and living with other refugees of the fire in the basement of old Saint Mary's Catholic Church on Wabash Avenue, she first encountered the Knights of Labor. At that time the organization, then only a few years old, was holding meetings nearby in an old "tumbled down, fire scorched building." She spent evenings there "listening to splendid speakers," and found the objectives appealing and absorbing for a mind in danger of being overwhelmed by grief over her misfortunes. In her own words, she "became more and more engrossed in the labor struggle and . . . decided to take an active part in the efforts of the working people to better the conditions under which they worked and lived. I became a member of the Knights of Labor."[34] From this, it would appear that her commitment to the cause occurred almost immediately, but later on in her autobiography she says, "From 1880 I became wholly engrossed in the movement."[35] Students of her career believe that Jones remained in Chicago for some years after the fire and resumed the dressmaking business. They also believe she traveled to San Francisco during the late 1870s and stayed long enough to become acquainted with the socialist oriented Workingmen's party, organized to promote the exclusion of immigration from China, and with Denis Kearney, an Irish immigrant and rousing "sandlot orator" who was its leader.[36] One of them is convinced as well that it was in Chicago during the 1870s that she first met Terence V. Powderly at a meeting of the Knights of Labor.[37] It is known that she became a life-long friend of this labor pioneer who headed the Knights of Labor from 1879 to 1893. In her later years, she made the home Powderly and his wife Emma maintained in Washington, D.C., her headquarters between campaigns in the labor wars.

Once involved with the cause of labor, her commitment became total. Contemporaries who knew her soon became aware of it often because of her disagreement with them. The most perceptive statement about her is to be found in Clarence Darrow's brief introduction to her autobiography. He said of her that: "She has the power of moving masses of men by her strong, living speech and action. Her deep convictions and fearless soul always drew her to seek the spot where the fight was the hottest and the danger greatest." He saw that she "was always doubtful of the good of organized institutions," that "these require compromise and she could not compromise. To her there was but one side, right and wrong were forever distinct. The type is common to all great movements." Her cause was organized labor, particularly among the miners where "the mountainous country, the deep mines, the black pit, the cheap homes, the danger, the everlasting conflict for wages and for life, appealed to her imagination and chivalry."[38] Of her own earliest contacts with the Knights of Labor, Mother Jones commented: "Those were the days of sacrifice for the cause of labor. Those were the days when we had no halls, when there were no high salaried officers, no feasting with the enemies of labor. Those were the days of martyrs and saints."[39] Referring to district leader Wilson of the United Mine Workers (UMW) in Pennsylvania, she commented: "Everything that he had he shared. He ate dry bread and drank chicory. He knew every hardship that the rank and file of the organization knew. We do not have such leaders now."[40]

These observations go a long way toward explaining conflicts she had with UMW presidents John Mitchell and John L. Lewis, socialist organizations and the Catholic Church. They also help in understanding her loss of interest in the IWW after taking part in its establishment. Mother Jones could not tolerate what she called "labor bureaucrats." What she had in mind were AFL union officials who, she perceived, were living on salaries derived from hard-earned wages of members and who were spending most of their time in offices rather than in the front lines of battles with employers where she herself insisted on being. It is an attitude akin to the battle-hardened soldier's disdain for the behind-the-lines officer who functions in safe and relatively comfortable headquarters. She was above all militant and impatient with the conciliatory and conservative approach of John Mitchell.

While Mitchell recognized her ability and effectiveness as an organizer, during the anthracite strike of 1900 he began to question the wisdom of one of her favorite tactics—the frequent marches she organized of miners and their wives into unorganized mining communities. Mitchell felt that they involved undue risks of violence, particularly with sheriff's deputies, and could cause public opinion to turn against the cause of the UMW. The 1902 anthracite strike proved to be pivotal to the union. In a letter to Mother Jones, written prior to the strike,

Mitchell anticipated as much. He said: "I am of the opinion that this will be the fiercest struggle in which we have yet engaged. It will be a fight to the end, and our organization will either achieve a great triumph or it will be completely annihilated."[41] During the 1902 anthracite strike, there was strong disagreement between the two when Mitchell accepted President Theodore Roosevelt's recommendation to submit the dispute to arbitration. Mother Jones was convinced that the strike had been won and that mine owners had no alternative but to accept UMW demands. She believed that Mitchell had felt the same, but accepted arbitration because of his vulnerability to flattery, particularly the flattery of those in high office.[42] Concern about her attitude is evident in a letter to Mother Jones from John Mitchell in which, responding to her admonitions, he said:

I deeply appreciate what you say, Mother, concerning the future. I have always felt I could count on your friendship. I know, only too well, what has come in the past to those who have been applauded by the public. You may be assured that the demonstrations which have been made have no ways turned my head.[43]

The final break came in the 1903 strike in Colorado where Mitchell decided to settle with operators in the northern fields rather than await settlement in the southern fields where prospects for success were very poor. In this case, Jones actively campaigned against the northern settlement, and when her position did not prevail, she resigned for a time as a UMW organizer. She explained her position in a letter to John Walker, a UMW organizer and longtime friend:

I resigned because I fought; some of those dirty ignoramuses that represented the national office were against me. I do not want to put John in the position where he would have to oppose them; his fight is hard enough. John Mitchell does not know everything those fellows did out there. I will fight the cause of the miners anyway, whether I am directly in their service or not. John Mitchell can always depend on me. I know whatever mistakes he has made, he is right at heart.[44]

Although this letter expressed a very conciliatory attitude and bespeaks her continuing loyalty to Mitchell, she apparently could not forgive him for joining the National Civic Federation (NCF) after leaving the presidency of the union.

In 1911, three years after he resigned as president of the union, she spoke in favor of a motion at the UMW convention requiring Mitchell to give up his UMW membership unless he resigned his salaried position with the National Civic Federation. The NCF, an organization made up of leaders of capital, labor and the public, was organized to promote conciliation between management and unions. In the eyes of Mother Jones, it was a capitalist tool to confuse the wage earner, and she could not abide partisans of labor who "dine in fashionable hotels with representatives of the top capitalists, such as the Civic Federation."[45] These included Samuel Gompers.

Her differences with John L. Lewis in the 1920s concerned his efforts, admittedly high-handed and undemocratic, to centralize control over the UMW in his own hands. His objective was to eliminate the chaos of the system of decentralized bargaining by autonomous UMW district officials in the highly competitive bituminous coal industry, which had prevented the union for many years from developing effective economic leverage. Lewis was opposed by Alexander Howat, an old friend of Mother Jones, and the numerous allies Howat could count on from Illinois. Jones strongly sided with the Howat faction in its unsuccessful struggle during the 1920s when the heroic activism of this aging native of "Rebel Cork" gradually moderated. She could never countenance Lewis's authoritarian endeavors which exemplified for her how "the rank and file have let their servants become their masters and dictators."[46] Nevertheless, Lewis's endeavors were ultimately responsible for making the UMW a most efficient economic force for obtaining benefits for members and earned for him the undying loyalty and gratitude of the rank and file.

As for the Catholic Church, from which she was estranged most of her career, she could not comprehend its caution and inability to commit itself unhesitatingly on the side of working people who in the America of her day encompassed nearly all of its communicants. Yet Mother Jones was born and raised in the Catholic Church and died in it.

An individualist by nature, Mother Jones did not get on well with a number of figures in the Socialist party. In 1911 she precipitated a party investigation of one of its editors, J. Mahlon Barnes, when she accused him of failing to repay $250 he had borrowed from her five years previously, although he claimed to have done so. In 1916 she worked for the reelection of an Indiana democrat, Senator John W. Kern, who had helped to obtain her release from detention by the military in West Virginia in 1913. Her efforts on behalf of Senator Kern were interpreted by Ohio Socialist Margaret Prevy as motivated by a desire to jeopardize the campaign of Eugene Debs, who in 1916 was running for Congress in the Fifth Indiana District on the Socialist ticket. Debs and Jones were, of course, old comrades. When Prevy wrote to Mother Jones asking her to clarify her intentions, she received a reply that expressed Mother Jones's impatience with the socialists:

I want to say here that I owe the socialists no apology, nor will I offer one to them. I have seen enough of their treachery to those who have fought the battle and want to keep the party clean; but one of these days, Margaret Prevy, we are going to clean house and we will have a real socialist movement and we will see that neither lawyers nor sky pilots are running our affairs.[47]

The socialism of Mother Jones was not much like that of Foster or even Flynn. Where Foster was clearly the activist and theorist, Jones was basically an activist and left the contemplative or theoretical aspect to others. Her socialism was of a generalized or indefinite nature. For her, it was a necessary alternative to the existing unsatisfactory system, but the specifics of it were never a concern. It is clear that she had no stomach for endless debates over what doctrine is the correct one and what method is the proper one to follow, or the innumerable factional struggles and splits which took place among American socialists over those questions. Rather, Mother Jones was as deeply conscious of the social evils of capitalism as one would be who devoted most of her life to the coal industry where the injustices in the system were more intense and more vivid than in almost any other part of the economy. Her attitude toward socialism was that it represented an alternative to the system which brought so much suffering and cruel poverty to the men and their families with whom she was in day-to-day contact and with whom she shared those same hardships. She was not concerned with distinctions between Fabianism, Bernsteinism, bolshevism, syndicalism, or other variations. A desire for action burned in her soul, and she had no time for the sentimentality or the debating club atmosphere of most socialist organizations. Debates of this kind within the IWW in its early years are the likely cause of her losing interest in that organization.

In methods she was not the careful planner that Foster was, but more of an imaginative and resourceful improviser. Her forte was, as we have seen, marches. Marches into unorganized communities, marches to the mouth of a mine shaft where men were on strike, or where she judged they should be on strike or where strikebreakers were employed. A frequently used part of her repertoire was the march of women in support of their husbands. She normally had to persuade them to ignore the charge that this was unladylike. In one instance, where women were jeering at strikebreakers in front of a mine, all of them were jailed by a judge for disturbing the peace, but Mother Jones urged them all to sing the night through each night until the judge was deluged with complaints that no one in the neighborhood could sleep and so ordered their release. Mother Jones would speak at meetings wherever she could, in a hall, in a school, in a barn, in a field or in the back woods. In one locality where posting notices of a meeting was forbidden, she directed men to circulate around the town in pairs—one pretended to be deaf, and the other shouted into his ear the whereabouts of the meeting as they walked about the town. Notice of the meeting was thus spread.[48]

Perhaps the most famous of her marches was the one held in the summer of 1903. At that time, she was bent on calling attention to the evils of child labor. The method she devised was to recruit children who worked in the textile mills of Kensington in Philadelphia and, with permission of their parents, some of whom accompanied her, conduct them on a march from Philadelphia through New Jersey to New York and finally to President Theodore Roosevelt's summer home on Oyster Bay, Long Island. Many of the children had lost fingers or had hands crushed or were stunted in their physical development because of their work in the mills. Most communities along the route were hospitable and provided the children with food and shelter, but it was a hot summer and more than a few children had to return home before their destination was reached. At Princeton, New Jersey, Mother Jones addressed a crowd consisting in considerable part of professors and students from the university there. Her message that day was:

"Here's a textbook on economics," I said pointing to a little chap, James Ashworth, who was ten years old and who stooped over like an old man from carrying bundles of yarn that weighed seventy-five pounds. "He gets three dollars a week and his sister who is fourteen gets six dollars. They work in a factory ten hours a day while children of the rich are getting their higher education."

President Roosevelt refused to grant her an audience or answer her letters, but she claimed credit for a child labor law passed in Pennsylvania shortly thereafter.[49]

As a speaker, Mother Jones was more colorful, humorous and inflammatory than Foster, something of a model for Flynn, and probably the equal of James Larkin when it came to bringing an audience to its feet in a spontaneous display of emotion. She could, in the words of Saint Paul, be all things to all men—a scourge to employers, a scold, a backbone, a challenge to the manhood of strikers as the occasion required to maintain solidarity or revive sagging morale. To wives, she was generally a force to inspire their support for their husbands' efforts to organize, or strike, or continue a strike that had begun to weaken. In this regard, she was rather old-fashioned. No feminist, she was, in fact, not even an advocate of the vote for women. To children, she was grandmotherly, protective and far more decorous in her speech. She was capable of language as rough as any heard in a barracks or a coal pit, if such was necessary to move her audience. She could also be excessive in exhorting men to "arm yourselves" when faced with Baldwin-Felts private police in West Virginia or the Coal and Iron Police in Pennsylvania.

The formation of this Queen Maeve of American labor agitators is just beginning to emerge from the mists and fogs which have surrounded it. She is partly responsible for the legends about her since she was careless about dates and the correct sequence of events. For example, her autobiography asserts that she was born in 1830, enabling her to participate in a well-publicized 100th birthday party in 1930, but a search of parish records in Cork City by biographer Lois McLean revealed that she was actually born in 1837—and was therefore ninety-three when she died in 1930.[50] Part of the confusion arises from fabrications and half-truths concocted by employer groups whose efforts to discredit her led them to accuse her of being employed in and proprietor of houses of prostitution in Denver, Omaha and other cities in the American West. Her refusal to either categorically deny or admit their truth has not helped to clear up these questions.

Richard Harris, her father, emigrated from Ireland before the rest of the family, and it is likely that anti-English agitation was responsible for his departure. As yet, this remains to be documented. However, Lois McLean has found that Mary Harris herself arrived in Boston in 1850 and that the family lived in Burlington, Vermont, for some period of time while Richard Harris worked on railroad construction crews before moving to Toronto.

EPILOGUE

William Z. Foster's mutually advantageous arrangement with the Communist party did not prove particularly fortunate for his career. Until 1929 it gave some impetus to the Trade Union Education League he established in 1920, which was dedicated to "boring from within," but little success was achieved in that endeavor. In 1929 the organization was dissolved and replaced with the Trade Union Unity League, an organization designed to compete with the AFL. Its dual union approach was not notably successful either, and in 1932, not long before the Congress of Industrial Organizations (CIO) emerged to successfully organize America's mass-production industries, Foster was overtaken by a severe heart attack which took him out of action for a number of years when his organizing skills might have given him a crucial role in the dramatic events of that period. He became a prolific author of books and pamphlets in behalf of the Communist cause, some of which were useful to those who actually succeeded in organizing the steel industry on a permanent basis.

Elizabeth Gurley Flynn escaped prosecution as a leader of the IWW at the time of World War I under circumstances which prompted one historian of the organization to comment, that: "In the end, Miss Flynn's version of events can only be understood as a belated effort to rationalize her betrayal of comrades and of principles to which she swore allegiance as late as August 25, 1917."[51] Thereafter, Miss Flynn became one of the founders of the American Civil Liberties Union in 1920 and spent much of her time until 1927 campaigning on behalf of dismissal of murder charges brought against immigrants Nicola Sacco and Bartolomeo Vanzetti whose celebrated trial and appeal ended in their execution in 1927. For Miss Flynn the shock of hearing about their execution was such that she suffered a nervous breakdown and was kept inactive by various illnesses for ten years. She had broken off a common-law relationship of thirteen years with Italian anarchist Carlo Tresca in 1925, and had no one with whom to share the burden of her hardships other than her old friend Dr. Marie Equi of Portland, Oregon, who nursed her much of the time until she returned to New York and joined the Communist party in 1937.[52]

In her last years, Mother Jones retired to the Powderly home in Washington, D.C., in the care of Emma Powderly who had been a widow since 1924. However, when her care became more than Mrs. Powderly could handle in the spring of 1929, Mother Jones moved to the home of a retired carpenter, Walter E. Burgess, and his wife on a farm near Hyattsville, Maryland. There she died on November 30, 1930. She was buried according to her wishes in the miners' cemetery in Mount Olive, Illinois. It remains for scholars to accord Mary Harris from County Cork the place she rightfully deserves in the history of worker struggles.

Sketches of these Irish radicals reveal a commitment to the cause of industrial workers around the turn of the century. Predictably, all three gravitated to the IWW—a labor body representing the most important effort to organize American workers on an industrial basis prior to the CIO in the 1930s. Although only Flynn's association was continuous (differences of ideology or impatience with excessive debates over ideology caused the departure of Foster and Jones), the careers of all three reflect a deep involvement in the cause of organizing industrial workers. The inspiration of these activists and their perceptions led them to espouse the welfare of that part of the work force that had grown most rapidly in the post–Civil War period and for whom the AFL had done very little. Conditions in mining, steel, meatpacking, textiles and clothing represented among the worst social evils of the time, and they were suffered by a relatively defenseless labor force composed largely of recent immigrants. Capitalist leaders of the growing corporations in these industries were relentless innovators in the art of preventing their employees from organizing to improve hours, wages and working conditions. They made the challenge far more dangerous and, to these three militants, more exciting.

The stereotype of volatile Irish wit and oratory seems to fit both Flynn and Jones reasonably well, but Foster not so well. Flynn and Jones earned wide reputations for their rhetorical powers and, as we have seen, were much in demand in organizing campaigns, strikes, or free speech demonstrations around the country. Foster, on the other hand, was competent in communicating with worker audiences if not inspiring. His gift was in fashioning practical methods for bringing cohesion to the ethnically diverse work forces found in American industries. Innovations such as he developed in organizing were the industrial equivalent of those of the skilled Irish-American "ethnic" politicians who built alliances and worked out compromises acceptable to the various nationality groups on the American electorate. Flair for welding together the numerous ethnic groups in the American work force was characteristic of most Irish-American labor leaders, but the radicalism of these three was not characteristic of the vast majority of them. The typical Irish-American union leader adopted rather naturally the pragmatic, conservative business unionism of the AFL, epitomized by the approach of John Mitchell and P.J. McGuire. It does stand out that this trio was incapable of compromising their ideals with such "labor bureaucrats," although surprisingly both Flynn and Foster eventually sacrificed independent thinking for the rigid discipline of Marxism-Leninism.

The impulse to activism on behalf of radical change in society has common roots as well. All three came from families who, for generations, were engaged in the fight against British rule in Ireland. A deep sense of the injustice of it was passed down from parents to children. We know that Flynn and Foster were not only regaled with songs and stories of the heroes of Irish risings, but their parents were eager to enlist them in the cause of Irish nationalism. From this background, it was not a large step to embrace the cause of social justice for the industrial worker in America.

The poverty of the families and their unwillingness or inability to communicate the Catholic faith to their young also paved the way for social radicalism to take root—indeed, it was cultivated in the Flynn household.

Mary Harris lived her formative years in the Ireland of Daniel O'Connell and the Young Ireland movement. We may speculate that her organizing tactics, especially the use of marches, reflect those she witnessed as a young girl in County Cork. It is almost as if the spirit of the early Celtic missionaries who left family, hearth and homeland to spread the gospel was reborn in the careers of these militants, but now the gospel was socialism (or syndicalism) and the watchword was solidarity. Certainly all three had an irrepressible sense of adventure and delighted to travel across the land with very little in the way of personal belongings.

NOTES

1. Elizabeth Gurley Flynn, *The Rebel Girl*, rev. ed. (New York: International Publishers, 1973), 88.
2. Ibid. All the information about the three radicals in this chapter is drawn from their autobiographical works except as otherwise noted. Only references to direct quotes from the autobiographical works appear in the notes hereafter.
3. Emmet Larkin, *James Larkin, Irish Labor Leader* (Cambridge, Mass.: MIT Press, 1965), 159.
4. Flynn, *The Rebel Girl*, 23.
5. Letter from George F. Baer to William F. Clark during the 1902 anthracite coal strike, reprinted in C.W. Bakke, Clark Kerr and Charles Anrod, *Unions Management and the Public* (New York: Harcourt, Brace and World, 1967), 213.
6. Flynn, *The Rebel Girl*, 23.
7. Ibid., 26, 30, 86. Mrs. Flynn also mentioned that James Gurley of County Carlow was George Bernard Shaw's grandfather. Her comment about the Larkins does not agree with Emmet Larkin's biography of James Larkin in which he explains that Barney Larkin, grandfather of James, operated a farm that he rented in the parish of Lower Killeavy near Armagh town. See Larkin, *James Larkin*, 3; also 197, for reference to the Flynn family.
8. Samuel Levenson, *James Connolly* (London: Quartet Books, 1977), 156.
9. Melvyn Dubofsky, *We Shall Be All* (New York: Quadrangle Books, 1969), 135-36.
10. Ibid., 84-85 for an illustration of the Wheel of Fortune. See also Flynn, *The Rebel Girl*, 87.
11. Flynn, *The Rebel Girl*, 110.
12. William Z. Foster, *Pages from a Worker's Life* (New York: International Publishers, 1939), 289-93; William Z. Foster, *From Bryan to Stalin* (New York: International Publishers, 1937), 49-50. Karl Legien was chief of the German Federation of Trade Unions and Karl Kautsky was a leading theoretician of the Social Democratic party with whom Foster had quarrelsome conversations. Both of these Germans came around to support Edward Bernstein's reformist and class collaboration policies. While in Germany, Foster lived in the home of Fritz Kater, head of the Syndicalist Union, and became acquainted with Karl Leibknect and other Social Democratic figures.
13. Elizabeth Gurley Flynn, *Labor's Own William Z. Foster* (New York: New

Century Publishers, 1949), 18; Joseph North, *William Z. Foster: An Appreciation* (New York: International Publishers, 1949), 20; Foster, *From Bryan to Stalin*, 59. The loyal followers included Jack Johnstone, Earl G. Ford, Tom Mooney, Lucy Parsons, Sam Hammersmark, Frank Little, Joe Manley, Jay Fox and Esther Abramowitz, who became Foster's wife in 1912. The organization, which lasted only two years, was succeeded by his International Trade Union Education League and Trade Union Education League, both equally small and also of relatively short duration. For a detailed account of Foster's syndicalist period, see Edward P. Johanningsmeir, "William Z. Foster and the Syndicalist League of North America," *Labor History* (Summer 1989): 329-53. Johannningsmeir's research reveals that Foster developed a dismal conception of workers' intelligence and their ability to conduct organizations. Foster's experience convinced him that only a "militant minority" was capable of leading the "ignorant mass" of workers to revolution. Once capitalist institutions had been overthrown, only technically sophisticated officials could effectively direct industry. He conceived of something akin to scientific management rather than industrial democracy. This attitude of Foster's explains why he readily embraced the economic plans of Lenin and even Stalin at a later time. Stalin's brutality never deterred Foster.

14. Foster, *From Bryan to Stalin*, 11; William Z. Foster, "How I Became a Rebel," *The Labor Herald*, July 1922, 24.

15. See Chapter 6 ("John Fitzpatrick: Humanitarian") for mention of Larkin and Foster meetings. For Haywood, see *Bill Haywood's Book* (New York: International Publishers, 1929), 235-37, 272-74; Philip S. Foner, *History of Labor in the United States*, vol. 4 (New York: International Publishers, 1965), 430; Flynn, *The Rebel Girl*, 175. Haywood met and became acquainted with Tom Mann in England and with Foster in Paris in the course of his (Haywood's) trip to the Socialist Congress of the Second International held in Copenhagen in 1910. Foster arranged Tom Mann's speaking tour of the United States in 1913 through the Syndicalist League of North America, while in the same year Haywood joined James Larkin in England for a series of speeches in Larkin's "Firery Cross" campaign and also spoke at Liberty Hall in Dublin during what had been planned as a vacation trip to recuperate from ulcers contracted during the IWW strikes at Lawrence, Massachusetts, and Paterson, New Jersey. In Dublin, Haywood also talked with James Connolly whom he had known in the United States.

16. William Z. Foster, *The Twighlight of World Capitalism* (New York: International Publishers, 1949), 159.

17. Larkin, *James Larkin*, 194-95.

18. Foster, *From Bryan to Stalin*, 14-15.

19. Bert Cochran, *Labor and Communism* (Princeton, N.J.: Princeton University Press, 1977), 93.

20. Flynn, *The Rebel Girl*, 110.

21. Larkin, *James Larkin*, 11.

22. Andrew Boyd, *The Rise of the Irish Trade Unions* (Tralee: Anvil Books, 1972), 75.

23. Foster, *Pages from a Worker's Life*, 153-56.

24. William Z. Foster, *The Great Steel Strike of 1919* (New York: Arno Press, 1969), 1, 194-200.

25. Cochran, *Labor and Communism*, 93.

26. David Brody, *Labor in Crisis: The Steel Strike of 1919* (New York: Lippincott, 1965), 62-63.

27. Foster, *The Great Steel Strike*, 200-205. According to David Saposs, who worked for the Committee of the Interchurch World Movement, which pub-

lished *Report on the Steel Strike of 1919* (New York: Harcourt, Brace and Howe, 1920), the idea for Foster's book on the strike came from notes Saposs himself had made. Foster supplied all minutes of the meetings of the union strike committee to Saposs, whom he trusted. Originally recorded chronologically, the minutes became far more revealing when Saposs rearranged them according to subject. When Foster read the reorganized minutes, he recognized their potential and subsequently wrote the book. See Oral History Interview with David Saposs by Alice M. Hoffman, January 18, 1968, Pennsylvania State University, University Park, Pennsylvania, 2.

28. Mary Harris Jones, *Autobiography of Mother Jones* (Chicago: C.H. Kerr, 1925), 214.

29. William Z. Foster, *More Pages from a Worker's Life*, Occasional Paper no. 32, Arthur Zipser ed. (New York: American Institute of Marxist Studies, 1979), 5-6.

30. Ibid., 6.

31. Lois C. McLean, "I'll Teach You Not to Be Afraid," *Golden Seal*, January–March 1980, 22.

32. Jones, *Autobiography*, 11.

33. Ibid.

34. Ibid., 14.

35. Ibid., 17.

36. Interview of Lois C. McLean by author, Philadelphia, October 4, 1980; Dale Fetherling, *Mother Jones the Miners' Angel* (Carbondale: Southern Illinois University Press, 1974), 10.

37. Fetherling, *Mother Jones*, 10.

38. Jones, *Autobiography*, 6-7.

39. Ibid., 14.

40. Ibid., 38.

41. Letter from John Mitchell to Mother Mary Jones, May 10, 1902, John Mitchell Papers, microfilm.

42. Jones, *Autobiography*, 59.

43. Letter from John Mitchell to Mother Mary Jones, March 3, 1903, John Mitchell Papers, microfilm.

44. Letter from Mother Jones to John Walker, January 4, 1904, John Mitchell Papers, microfilm.

45. Jones, *Autobiography*, 241.

46. Ibid.

47. Letter from Mother Jones to Margaret Prevy, October 13, 1916, Mother Jones Papers, Catholic University of America, Washington, D.C.

48. Jones, *Autobiography*, 41.

49. Ibid., 76-77.

50. Lois C. McLean, Interview by author, Philadelphia, October 4, 1980.

51. Dubofsky, *We Shall Be All*, 428. She called for a strategy whereby all IWW leaders got their cases scheduled for individual rather than mass trials. She then obtained, through influential friends, expensive lawyers to do just that for herself and three associates, Joseph Ettor, Carlo Tresca and Arthuro Giovannitti. Other defendants, lacking influential friends, and opposed to the strategy on principle, were convicted while charges against Flynn and her three associates were dismissed on March 15, 1919.

52. Marie Equi and Flynn had been friendly in the early IWW days. Equi was a wealthy physician and a radical, who opposed American involvement in World War I. For her opposition she paid the price of a term in San Quentin Prison in 1920–21. According to Rosalyn Baxandall, Equi was a vigorous birth

control advocate and abortionist with a reputation as a lesbian. The Flynn family feared that Elizabeth was being prevented from leaving Portland by Dr. Equi, and both of Flynn's sisters visited her to try to help her break away. See Rosalyn Fraad Baxandall, *Words on Fire: The Life and Writing of Elizabeth Gurley Flynn* (New Brunswick, N.J.: Rutgers University Press, 1987), 31–32.

6

JOHN FITZPATRICK:
HUMANITARIAN

John Fitzpatrick grew to manhood in a Chicago still recreating itself after the great fire of 1871. He came from a town on the Shannon River to the city of "Broad Shoulders" celebrated in the verse of Carl Sandburg. He saw the "Gem of the Prairie" become a metropolis of over a million people by the turn of the century—boasting of its stature as a center for grain milling, railroads, meatpacking. Chicago could point proudly to the rise of its manufacturing industry in steel, farm and rail equipment and apparel. It could hardly boast, though, of its treatment of the immigrant labor force it had attracted from diverse nations and races as evident in the policies of its Swifts and Armours, its Pullmans and Harvesters and its United States Steel corporations. Tensions and rivalries between ethnic groups were easily inflamed for the sake of per-petuating a docile, ill-paid and often sweated work force—a tactic com-mon enough among employers. As in the Haymarket case, trial by pub-lic hysteria kept the protestor, the striker, the radical at bay.

The Irish had entered the Chicago scene earlier than other immi-grants in 1836, before Chicago was incorporated, to dig the Illinois and Michigan Canal as part of a waterway linking Lake Michigan and the Mississippi River. By 1890 first-and second-generation Irish Americans comprised almost 17 percent of the city's population.[1] In addition to longer experience in Chicago and acquaintance with the problems of greenhorns, compared to later immigrants, the Irish enjoyed the advan-tage of command of the English language and institutions, especially government ones. They could, as well, identify with later immigrants on the basis of the Roman Catholic faith, which they shared with many of them. These circumstances gave Irish people the opportunity to play a role of intermediary or broker among different nationality groups in the work force—a chance to build some kind of cohesion for mutual protection. Their presence among the leadership of Chicago trade unions was unmistakable and extremely important.[2] No one better exemplified the best of Irish trade union leadership—of extending the hand of brotherhood and encouragement to other immigrant workers— than did John Fitzpatrick.

Fitzpatrick was a creature of the Progressive era whose leadership was maturing when Teddy Roosevelt was in the White House, when Jane Addams was pioneering settlement house work among immigrants in Chicago, and when Upton Sinclair was exposing conditions in the meatpacking industry there. Fitzpatrick became the highly visible, activist president of the Chicago Federation of Labor (CFL) from 1905 until his death in 1946. The nickname "Honest John" was given him out of respect for his integrity, indeed for successfully battling corruption in labor's ranks.

Fitzpatrick challenged the American Federation of Labor (AFL) to reach out to black workers and the new immigrants from Eastern and Southern Europe, with whom he worked as a young man in the Chicago stockyards, and to experiment with industrial structure for organizing the expanding mass-production industries in which many in these ethnic groups found work. Despite opposition by Samuel Gompers, Fitzpatrick lent support to formation, outside the AFL, of an industrial union in the men's clothing industry in Chicago by his friend Sidney Hillman. An optimist devoted to progressive reform, he enthusiastically undertook to found a labor party, also, in the face of Gompers's disapproval. In addition, John Fitzpatrick found energy in his life to devote to the cause of Irish independence, and attempted to enlist American unions into support of that goal.

Fitzpatrick was born in the town of Athlone, County Westmeath, on April 21, 1871. He was the youngest of seven sons born to Adelaide Mingey, a native of Suffolk, England, and John Fitzpatrick, a retired sergeant of the British Army. His father had met her while stationed in Great Britain. Only two years old when his mother died, the boy was barely ten when his father perished. However, his father had married an Irish Catholic woman after his first wife (a Protestant) had succumbed. A widow by the name of Mary Coughlan, she raised the Fitzpatrick children until the death of her second husband. It was she who reared them in the Catholic faith. His stepmother was responsible for John Fitzpatrick's memory of resentment for British rule present in his family.[3] He was brought to Chicago in 1882 to live with his uncle, Patrick Fitzpatrick, and attended public schools there until his uncle died suddenly in February of 1884.[4] As a result, the boy, not yet thirteen, was obliged to help support himself and his foster family, which he did by finding work with Swift and Company, in the killing pens of the stockyards. After three years with Swift, he left for work in a brass foundry. Two years later, he began a five-year apprenticeship in the horseshoers' trade, after which he joined Local Four of the Journeymen Horseshoers' Union.[5] He was elected to various offices in Local Four and served as its business agent for five years.[6]

Characteristically, Fitzpatrick resigned as Local Four's business agent because most of the work was necessarily transacted in taverns. A neighbor of his was becoming an alcoholic, and the spectacle persuaded young John to give up drinking.[7] It is for this reason, as well as the fact that he was a man of modest tastes who lived simply, that, although a gregarious Irishman with a good sense of humor, he rarely attended the numerous balls and other social gatherings to which he was invited. Fitzpatrick married a cousin, a schoolteacher, Katherine Fitzpatrick, in 1892. The couple lived in an unpretentious bungalow in Bridgeport, the same Irish neighborhood that produced Richard T. Daley and Finley Peter Dunne. The couple had one son, John Patrick, born in 1912, who served in the army during World War II. Educated as an engineer, he worked in the Argonne Atomic Laboratory west of Chicago. He died in 1970.[8]

Tall, physically imposing, with an engaging Norman visage, Fitzpatrick's deepest instinct was, by all accounts, humanitarianism. The ventures he undertook in a long career point to it. His personal relations reflect it. He had no desire for wealth or luxury. Mollie Levitas, a young Jewish woman born in Latvia, who was hired as the first female secretary for the CFL in 1926, described him as "a man of great courage, and he was a man who had principles and stood by them."[9] She remembered him as an affable, easygoing, pipe-smoking gentleman "who could get fired up if the occasion demanded it."[10] Such occasions did arise when he chastised visitors for their anti-Semitic remarks in the presence of Miss Levitas.

At that time, the Chicago Federation of Labor operated out of an old loft without partitions at 166 West Washington Street in Chicago's loop. Fitzpatrick and Edward Nockels, secretary of CFL and a native of Luxembourg, conducted business there at rolltop desks placed side by side. In these surroundings, Miss Levitas found great difficulty tolerating the profanity habitually used by Nockels, the far more volatile of the two.[11] The fruitful association of these two men, somewhat akin to that of McCarthy and Tvietmoe in San Francisco, was long-standing, based on shared values and mutual trust. In one instance, Nockels, a diabetic, became so ill that doctors decided to amputate his leg, but Fitzpatrick and another friend, Anton Johannsen, a carpenter union official, refused to permit it. They took Nockels to a sanitarium in Battle Creek, Michigan, where he recovered over some months.[12]

In 1919, after a mandate from delegates to CFL meetings, Fitzpatrick and Nockels began publication of the *New Majority*, a weekly newspaper designed to counteract the antiunion bias of the daily press. Edited by Robert M. Buck, a Chicago journalist whose reform ideas blended with those of Fitzpatrick and Nockels, the paper was inspired by the ideas of Edward Bellamy, reformer and author of the utopian novel *Looking Backward*, who had published a newspaper called *New Nation* in the 1890s.[13] The masthead of the *New Majority* contained a statement which exaggerated the tone of the paper: "Dedicated to the hand and brain workers of the United States . . . who will form a new majority that will sweep all opposition before it." A lively sheet, it was illustrated by Fred C. Ellis with cartoons of powerfully muscled, shirtless workers dra-

matically posed in the act of confronting some social evil. Terms such as
"plute" (presumably plutocrat), "big biz," "kept press," and "steel trust"
commonly appeared in its columns. *New Majority* included such features as the serialization of *Three Soldiers* by novelist and social critic
John Dos Passos and a lengthy treatment of the Teapot Dome scandal.
Regular reports of developments in Ireland were carried in the *New
Majority* to offset what, according to John Fitzpatrick, the daily press
reported in highly biased fashion because, he said, "English interests
bought enough United States Newspapers to control the press."[14]

New Majority reflected values to which Fitzpatrick had committed
himself. They were those of a reformer of the Progressive mold strongly opposed to grafting Irish trade union officials like Martin B. "Skinny"
Madden or "Umbrella Mike" Boyle, who owed his nickname to a habit
of accepting payoffs in a folded parasol, as well as Irish ward healers,
such as "Bathhouse John" Coughlin and Michael "Hinky Dink" Kenna.
Indicative of the CFL leader's ideals were Fitzpatrick's admiration for
Illinois Governor Peter Altgeld, who pardoned Haymarket martyrs, and
his close associations with Jane Addams of Hull House and labor attorney Frank P. Walsh, chairman of the United States Commission on
Industrial Relations—also a strong Irish nationalist.

Fitzpatrick worked for revitalization of democracy in society at large,
but especially in local government and in the labor movement. An advocate of female suffrage and unions for women workers, he had abiding
faith in restoring power to the rank and file. He proposed to ensure
equal rights to blacks, to extend industrial unions to workers in mass-
production industries and to balance the influence of "big biz," which
he distrusted, with greater involvement of government in the economy.
He was not a socialist. Wage and hour laws, protective labor legislation
for women and children, health and safety regulations for industry and
municipal ownership of utilities constituted Fitzpatrick's agenda. A
strong, liberal-minded labor movement, he thought, could become an
economic and political force capable of bringing about these changes.

Fellow trade unionists recognized Fitzpatrick's gifts as a leader
when, after his participation in the founding convention of the Chicago
Federation of Labor in 1895 as a delegate from Local Four of the
Journeymen Horseshoers, the convention elected him president of the
Labor Federation in 1899. Although he retired from that office in 1901
to accept a position of organizer for CFL, he became president again in
1905, after Martin B. "Skinny" Madden of the Plumbers' Union migrated to the CFL after his "strike insurance" and other corrupt practices
had finally fomented a revolt by employers in the building industry. In
1900 contractors conducted a lockout in Chicago which caused the
demise of the Madden-dominated Building Trades Council.[15] Madden
used strong-arm tactics and ballot-stuffing methods to carry elections,
and he applied them successfully to taking over the CFL.

Reform elements turned to John Fitzpatrick to restore integrity in
the organization. In the crucial CFL election of 1905, ballots were
counted under the watchful eyes of two women delegates from the

Chicago Teachers' Federation, a union whose formation and affiliation with CFL John Fitzpatrick encouraged. The two watchers had brought candles to illuminate the hall in order to prevent mischief by Madden agents during the brief period around midnight, when electric lights had to be turned off and gas lamps were lighted. The watchers and the candles were insisted upon by Margaret Haley, president of the Chicago Teachers' Federation, a battler for women's rights who was a close friend of John Fitzpatrick. By her account, the lighted candles signaled to Madden "that the jig was up."[16]

Fitzpatrick's election benefited substantially from the help of Anton Johannsen. An immigrant from Germany and a radical, Johannsen was a delegate in 1905 to the CFL from the Woodworkers' Union, which was later absorbed by the Brotherhood of Carpenters. At a recent AFL convention in Pittsburgh, Fitzpatrick had actively opposed Johannsen's candidacy for an office in that organization. Nevertheless, for what he understood to be the good of Chicago labor, Johannsen gave decisive support to Fitzpatrick. Johannsen himself had been rumored to be Madden's candidate for CFL president, but, when nominations were opened, he refused to stand for the office, denounced Madden's faction as corrupt and threw his support to John Fitzpatrick. This selfless act marked the beginning of an enduring friendship between the two men.[17] Except for the year 1908, Fitzpatrick was president of CFL until his death just after World War II. During that time, which extended through the Capone era in Chicago, the CFL was never again compromised.

COMMITMENT TO ORGANIZING

The Irishman's long tenure as head of the Chicago Federation of Labor was that of an activist campaigning to "organize the unorganized" rather than a bureaucratic one of defending the status quo. Each Saturday afternoon Fitzpatrick maintained office hours at the CFL for anyone needing assistance. One Saturday he was visited for the first time by Sidney Hillman and Samuel Levin, who described the poor working conditions of the mostly Jewish immigrants from Slavic countries in the clothing industry of Chicago. Fitzpatrick counseled them on how to organize.[18] In 1910 a strike broke out in the men's clothing industry in Chicago, and Sidney Hillman, a Jewish immigrant from Lithuania, emerged as one of the strike leaders. John Fitzpatrick organized distribution of food for strikers' families.[19] A lifelong friendship developed between Fitzpatrick and Hillman, and when Hillman and others established a new union in the industry in 1914 against the wishes of the American Federation of Labor, Fitzpatrick provided financial assistance and encouragement despite his own AFL ties.

Called the Amalgamated Clothing Workers of America, the new union adopted an industrial structure, but was refused a charter by the AFL. Nevertheless, the union thrived, and in 1936, Sidney Hillman became one of the founders of the Congress of Industrial Organizations

(CIO). During World War II, Hillman, whom Roosevelt had appointed a director of the War Production Board, offered Fitzpatrick a position with that agency. Fitzpatrick declined, but recommended Joseph Keenan of the Brotherhood of Electrical Workers, who was appointed.[20] Clearly, Hillman's friendship with Fitzpatrick survived the split between the AFL and the CIO. Fitzpatrick's involvement with Hillman's union typified the support he provided to numerous others, including Chicago teachers. His commitment to organizing was a passionate one.

The most dramatic of Fitzpatrick's efforts to organize new immigrants in mass-production industries occurred in meatpacking and steel, between 1914 and 1919. In both cases, organization was attempted on something approaching an industrial basis led by Fitzpatrick and William Z. Foster. It is pointless to compare the relative importance of the two men—Foster and Fitzpatrick—in these campaigns. Their roles were, in fact, highly complementary. Foster was the consummate planner and strategist, while Fitzpatrick was the forceful, decisive leader and spokesman highly regarded for his personal honesty. The essential role of Fitzpatrick is attested to by Foster's letter to him after the 1918 AFL convention in Saint Paul, which passed Foster's resolution endorsing an organizing drive in the steel industry. Regarding the necessity for choosing the right man to lead the campaign in steel, Foster wrote:

Frankly, I don't know of another man in the country qualified to do this, with any reasonable hope of success, outside yourself. . . . With whatever earnestness I may possess I would urge you to take this matter up seriously with Sam Gompers and Frank Morrisson and see that the movement takes the right course. I have done all in my power to make the thing a success. But now I have reached about the limit of my resources. I need help. When that conference convenes, if the matter is left to me to put over I feel reasonably certain that the whole thing will fail, but if you will go to bat on it as you did in the Stockyards project then I am positive that it will succeed.[21]

Neither organizing drive could seriously have been undertaken in the absence of someone of Fitzpatrick's stature. Gompers was cautious and reluctant to become involved. Most other national labor figures were dedicated almost exclusively to the interests of their own unions. Fitzpatrick, on the other hand, was that rare creature who had achieved national prominence as head of a central labor union. The force of his personality was most persuasive in face-to-face contact. His ability and reputation for integrity made him a widely respected figure who could deal with presidents of national unions on equal terms.[22]

Further confirmation comes from David Saposs, a well-known specialist in labor relations, who was an investigator during the 1919 steel strike for the Inter-Church World Movement study of that dispute. An oral history interview with him in 1966 included the following: "I used to go to Chicago occasionally, and I knew John Fitzpatrick intimately." When asked what sort of man Fitzpatrick was, Saposs replied:

Oh, he was really an extraordinary man, a great idealist, too. And a man of great intuition; I don't think he had much education. His wife was a grammar school teacher. But he had a wonderful intellect, and, of course, he was a big Progressive and he was, in those days, really regarded as the opponent that led the Progressives against Gompers. And he was the one that made it possible for Foster to organize the packinghouse workers, you know, that's what he did first. On the basis of bringing together a group of unions, realizing that you couldn't do it any other way. Then he [Fitzpatrick] was responsible for forcing through the AF of L organization of the iron and steel committee and bringing in these 21 unions and he [Fitzpatrick] backed Foster.[23]

John Fitzpatrick's first job was in a plant of Swift and Company. His concern to bring unions to its employees and those of other packing firms was evident in World War I. Historian James R. Barrett thoroughly analyzed CFL's drive to unionize stockyards in Chicago. His published volume on the subject is the basis for the following description.[24]

Undertaking to organize the meatpacking industry was a daunting challenge. Its employee force epitomized the diversity of American working people at that time, consisting of German and Irish workers from earlier immigrations (typically filling the skilled occupations). Newcomers (concentrated in common labor occupations), were from Lithuania, Bohemia, Slovakia, Russia and Mexico, but also included black workers, who migrated from America's South. Persuading this variety of ethnic groups of the need for organization and solidarity involved major difficulties. Blacks were the least receptive, since they had been cultivated by packing companies and employed as strike-breakers during an unsuccessful strike conducted by the Amalgamated Meatcutters and Butcher Workmen of North America in 1904.

This union, established in Cincinnati in 1897 and led by Michael Donnelly from Omaha (an effective organizer), gained a foothold in the Chicago yards especially among German and Irish skilled workers. Its strength grew through their enthusiasm to pass on the spirit of unionism to latecomers from Slavic countries. It also benefited from support of an Irish subculture present in neighborhoods adjacent to the Chicago yards. Shop floor committees surfaced spontaneously and challenged foremen's authority to control the pace of work and other matters—to the great consternation of packing firms—a development repeated in the 1917 organization effort.

The 1904 strike failed after almost two months when dominant packing firms, concluding that the union was gaining too much control in their plants, vowed to hire strikebreakers from the pool of unemployed which had grown substantially—thanks to the recession of that year.

Donnelly called off the work stoppage on the basis of employer assurances of fairness in rehiring strikers. In the event, however, employers did not rehire activists and blacklisted them along with Donnelly. Thereafter, the union's decline was precipitous.

Revival of organization during World War I was a collaborative effort of John Fitzpatrick and William Z. Foster. Wartime conditions brought rising profits, inflation, labor shortages and worker demands for improvements. In midsummer 1917, Foster established the Stockyards Labor Council to coordinate all organizing with full support of the CFL. It drew upon remnants of the Amalgamated Meatcutters Union and all other local (craft) unions in the packing firms. Slavic workers embraced the movement vigorously. Native skilled workers were more hesitant, but came on board; black workers were dubious. One reason being that, in the course of being Americanized, Slavic workers had become infected with racism.

As an approximation of industrial unionism, the system of federating a large variety of local unions functioned with difficulty at best. Skilled workers were in locals separate from unskilled. Women had separate local unions as did black workers. Neighborhood-based ethnic locals were also created. Most locals were affiliated with an international union as well as the Stockyards Labor Council.

Nevertheless, progress was made relatively quickly. When packer firms not only refused to negotiate on employee demands, but also dismissed union loyalists, pressure for a strike mounted. Alerted to the situation, President Wilson's wartime Mediation Commission sought a peaceful solution. Fitzpatrick and AFL leaders lobbied the commission to arrange for binding arbitration in return for a no-strike pledge. Packer management resisted the plan but finally acceded to it—reluctantly.

Judge Samuel B. Altschuler was chosen as arbitrator for all issues the parties were unable to settle bilaterally (which included most of them). Fitzpatrick brought his friend, labor lawyer Frank Walsh, and an economic consultant, W. Jett Lauck, as advocates for the union's position. Their persuasive representations were instrumental in winning a favorable award including pay raises, an eight-hour day, paid holidays, a forty-eight-hour workweek and equal pay for equal work in behalf of women. March 1918, when Judge Altschuler announced his award, marked the high point for the organization. The fact that this success had a short life does not detract from the achievement of Fitzpatrick and Foster's collaboration.

The demise of unionization in meatpacking after the war resulted from a variety of developments, not least of which was the will of packing firms to bring it about. Government-endorsed arbitration procedures ended in late 1921. In the same year, postwar recession reduced profits and raised unemployment. Postwar strikes, combined with a Red scare, undermined public acceptance of unions generally. A race riot, ignited by Irish street gangs in a section of Bridgeport bordering Chicago's Black Belt, broke out in July 1919. Cohesion of unions in the Stockyards Labor Council began to unravel as factional disputes arose. Finally, the dominant packinghouse firms adopted welfare capitalism with its full menu of paternal devices, including especially employee representation plans (company unions). By 1922 conditions in the industry had reverted almost to what they had been in the prewar period.

VENTURE IN POLITICS

Although John Fitzpatrick's most important work was organizing, he also aspired to create a more influential political voice for workers in the form of a third political party. Here, again, his actions contradicted the canons of the AFL, which called for strict avoidance of partisan politics. Only an optimist with abundant confidence and, perhaps, a lack of historical perspective could have embarked so enthusiastically on the enterprise of a labor party as John Fitzpatrick did in 1918. Inspired by the rise of the British Labour party, opposed by Samuel Gompers at every turn, the Labor party embodied many of Fitzpatrick's hopes for a better society, but proved a bitter disappointment. Impatient with Mayor "Big Bill" Thompson, and with orthodox politicians generally, Fitzpatrick chose to run against Thompson in 1919 on the Labor party ticket, but received only 8 percent of the vote. When the party attempted national scope by merging with like bodies in other states, and renamed itself the Farmer-Labor party to attract farmers, Fitzpatrick ran for senator, again with discouraging results.[25]

The climax of Fitzpatrick's efforts on behalf of independent political action came in 1923 when he arranged a convention in Chicago and invited all labor, farmer, liberal and socialist elements to join in order to achieve an effective national movement. The convention, held in July, began auspiciously. Mother Jones arrived and immediately became the most photographed person attending. *New Majority* printed a picture of her with John Fitzpatrick on its front page.[26] In an address to the convention, she adapted the Sermon on the Mount for her purposes, observing that "the producer, not the meek shall inherit the earth."[27] Another old friend, William Z. Foster, of whose conversion to communism in 1921 Fitzpatrick was unaware, arrived leading the Workers' party. In the event, Communist delegates took control of the convention, which outraged Fitzpatrick and persuaded him not only to withdraw with his own delegates, but also to abandon the notion of launching a serious political movement. He never forgave Foster for his deception and became bitter in his attitude toward Communists generally.[28] Mother Jones thought it unwise to bolt the convention and stayed on, but she remained a friend of Fitzpatrick.

New Majority chronicled the sad tale of Fitzpatrick's confident loyalty to Foster through the 1919 steel strike and after—until Foster's duplicity in the 1923 convention. In July of 1920, Foster became business manager for the *New Majority*, but left in November after organizing the Trade Union Educational League (TUEL), which became his vehicle for "boring from within" American unions.[29] After Foster's return from his trip to Moscow in 1921, where he secretly became a member of the Communist party and TUEL became its official agency to infiltrate American unions, *New Majority* reported his speeches describing the Russian Revolution most favorably. At the Chicago auditorium, Foster shared the platform with Louise Bryant, widow of American journalist John Reed, speaking in behalf of famine sufferers in Russia.[30] At this time, Fitzpatrick was quite optimistic about the Russian Revolution and, along with many other Progressives, he campaigned for official recognition of Russia by the American government.

In the spring of 1923, when Foster was on trial for his participation in the underground convention of the Communist party in Bridgeman, Michigan, Fitzpatrick hired Frank P. Walsh as Foster's defense attorney. After denying that he was a Communist and that TUEL was a Communist organization, Foster was acquitted. Fitzpatrick accepted Foster's denial at face value. He hailed the outcome as a service to "liberty's cause." The CFL organ reported Foster to be the "first person to be tried on such a trashy accusation."[31] It seems fair to say that Fitzpatrick, at this time, out of loyalty or other motives, was indeed ingenuous in his attitude toward Foster's Communist affiliations.

At the Chicago convention a few months later, their friendship ended abruptly. *New Majority* observed that Foster's "Workers' Party takes advantage of its position as guest to start a dual movement."[32] The Illinois Federation of Labor, with Fitzpatrick participating, repudiated all of Foster's resolutions at its convention in September 1923. *New Majority* referred to him as a Communist leader for the first time.[33] At the next regular meeting of CFL in October, Foster was "asked to tear up his membership card after his criticism of the Illinois Convention." Finally, Foster was reported to have "further burned his bridges by asserting that he could no longer look upon John Fitzpatrick, president, and Ed Nockels, secretary of the CFL, as his friends, but rather his enemies."[34]

These developments marked a turning point in Fitzpatrick's outlook. In May 1924, a *New Majority* story headlined CFL's vote to sever connections with the Farmer-Labor party and embrace the AFL's nonpartisan political policy at the request of John Fitzpatrick who expressed disgust with "confusion and misunderstanding brought about by self-seeking individuals in order to serve their own ends." He explained that the only legitimate farmer-labor party had been the one launched by CFL and "all others are seceding or dual organizations and no thoughtful union man or woman will have anything to do with them."[35] In July, Robert M. Buck resigned as editor of *New Majority* because of the change in political policy and, in August, its name was changed to *Federation News*. It became a more orthodox trade union paper containing little of concern for Progressive causes.[36] The experiment with independent political action was at an end. John Fitzpatrick withdrew to a far less venturesome type of leadership more in conformity with the hidebound standards of the American Federation of Labor.

To understand why Fitzpatrick's disaffection with the left wing came as belatedly as it did requires some background. John Fitzpatrick was much influenced by his reform-minded Progressive friends. Margaret Dreier, leader of the Women's Trade Union League, who also sat on the CFL executive board, was a close friend and influence upon Fitzpatrick—as was Jane Addams the founder of Hull House, one of the pathbreaking settlement houses in the nation. Raymond Robins, husband of Margaret Dreier, was, like his wife and Jane Addams, a crusading Progressive of the era. A wealthy, eccentric man and ordained minister, Robins nevertheless championed the labor movement and served as an advisor to Fitzpatrick. He and others had encouraged the Chicago leader's involvement with third party, farmer-labor movements.

Raymond Robins served in Petrograd as a Red Cross official in 1917 and had befriended John Reed, the author of *Ten Days That Shook the World*, a first-hand account of the revolution. The reports of Robins and others of Fitzpatrick's Progressive friends were quite favorable about the revolution. Their reaction resembled that of muckraking journalist Lincoln Steffens, who, on returning from Russia, observed, "I have been over into the future, and it works." Fitzpatrick responded accordingly. He, too, had shared great hopes for the new society being forged in Russia in the early days. Only after the betrayal by his old friend Bill Foster in the Farmer-Labor convention in Chicago did John Fitzpatrick come to realize how treacherous the bolsheviks and their agents had become.[37]   One of Fitzpatrick's flaws was that he was slow to suspect that he was being misled by friends.

VOICE OF LABOR

Disillusionment with the far left did not mark an end to Fitzpatrick's efforts in behalf of trade unionism, nor did it interrupt his campaigning for Irish independence. In fact, Fitzpatrick contrived to marshal support for unionism and the cause of Irish nationalism through a new medium. Chicago's central labor body was responsible for another significant innovation. At Nockels's instigation, the Chicago Federation of Labor established, in 1926, WCFL, "the Voice of Labor" in Chicago—the first radio station owned by a labor organization in the United States. WCFL programs broadcast the message of trade unionism in Lithuanian, Polish, Italian, German and other languages.[38] A unique method of getting labor's message across, WCFL broadcast "Labor Flashes" consisting of news of unions culled from daily newspapers by Mollie Levitas.[39]

A popular feature of station WCFL was the Sunday evening "Irish Hour," in which traditional Irish music as well as mawkish Irish-American tunes, such as "When Irish Eyes Are Smiling," were broadcast. The program aired speakers on the subject of Irish nationalism. Irish history and a sprinkling of trade union talk completed the union-sponsored program, which proved popular with the large Irish population in the Chicago area. Maurice Lynch, who became secretary-treasurer of the CFL when Nockels died in 1937, was a strong advocate of the "Irish Hour." Lynch hired musician Tom Ennis to play the Irish pipes, and he fostered a blend of Irish nationalism and trade union loyalty.[40]

An engineer for many years at WCFL's transmitter in Downers Grove, Illinois, was Matthew Schmidt, a native of Wisconsin. He was given the job after having been paroled to John Fitzpatrick from San Quentin Prison where he served time for involvement in the *Los Angeles Times* bombing of 1910. In his early twenties at the time of the bombing, Schmidt later made a confession. Each week he appeared at CFL offices to complete his parole forms.[41] Schmidt was one of a number of beneficiaries of Fitzpatrick's generosity.

FRIEND OF MOTHER JONES

Likewise, Fitzpatrick and Nockels had close associations with Mother Jones for many years and, in her declining days, were protectors of her interests. Mollie Levitas recalled a visit of the matriarch of trade unionism to CFL headquarters in 1926. Prohibition was the law of the land; nevertheless, a policeman delivered a paper bag containing a bottle of whiskey to Nockels who took a stiff drink and presented the bottle to Mother Jones for "medicinal purposes."[42]

As attested by numerous communications in Fitzpatrick's papers and reports in *New Majority*, Jones corresponded frequently with Nockels and Fitzpatrick—now from Mexico City; now from West Virginia's coalfields; now from Washington, D.C., where she recuperated between campaigns; now in her behalf from Terence Powderly, in whose Washington home she often resided; now about the plight of Jacob Dolla, a valuable fellow organizer during the steel campaign. Dolla, who spoke five languages, was imprisoned during the strike and not pardoned until 1924.[43] In December 1927, Mother Jones expressed irritation with Tom Mooney whose release she, Fitzpatrick and especially Nockels had been working for since his conviction for the San Francisco Preparedness Day bombing of 1916. "It is sad," she wrote, "to think you have such men to deal with and that one has to put forth their best efforts to get their freedom, and then not be appreciated any more than he appreciates it."[44] Her annoyance stemmed from the fact that Mooney had been offered a parole by the governor of California, but he held out for a full pardon.

Letters from Jones in 1927 and 1928 reported her illnesses and hospital stays; one of them addressed to "My Dear Old Friends."[45] In her last years, after Powderly died and his widow was no longer able to look after her, Mother Jones was cared for by Lillie May Burgess. After the death of Jones, Burgess corresponded with Nockels and Fitzpatrick. In one letter to Nockels, she described how she had turned away people seeking Mother Jones's effects by explaining, "I told them, Green [William Green, AFL president], had nothing to do with them, that you and Mr. F. were appointed by Mother as trustees of her effects."[46] These relationships attest to the generosity and chivalry of both Nockels and Fitzpatrick.

IRISH NATIONALIST

Fitzpatrick never forgot his brief childhood in Ireland, nor his stepmother's resentment of British rule. He made at least one trip back to County Westmeath to visit relatives and returned with two nephews, one of whom obtained employment with station WCFL.[47] Fitzpatrick joined the Friends of Irish Freedom (FOIF), founded in 1916, to rally support for the Easter Rising in Dublin. The FOIF sponsored an Irish Race Convention for all Irish organizations in 1919, which pressed for an interpretation of President Woodrow

Wilson's self-determination principle, which meant independence for Ireland. To further its proposal, the convention appointed a three-man American Commission on Irish Independence, chaired by attorney Frank P. Walsh, a good friend of Fitzpatrick, to lobby for the cause at the Paris peace talks. The commission was not successful, but it helped to defeat ratification of the Versailles Treaty in the Senate after it returned home.[48]

When Eamon de Valera arrived in the United States in June 1919 to raise funds for and seek recognition of the newly declared Irish Republic, of which he was president, he was welcomed by leaders of the FOIF, but he soon realized that they had different ideas about how to proceed than he did. As a result of this conflict, de Valera created a new organization, the American Association for Recognition of the Irish Republic (AAIR), and handpicked its leaders.[49]

John Fitzpatrick joined the new organization at the personal request of de Valera.[50] Earlier, at a Farmer-Labor party convention, Fitzpatrick declared himself to be a Sinn Feiner. Thereafter Fitzpatrick was much in demand to speak at local and national meetings of the AAIR.[51] *New Majority* carried an advertisement for bonds sold by AAIR to finance the Irish Republic.[52] AAIR later came to grief over the Anglo-Irish Treaty of December 1921, which de Valera opposed.

At the 1920 AFL convention in Montreal, a resolution was passed in support of the Republic of Ireland. To give effect to it, a Labor Bureau was established in connection with the American Commission on Irish Independence. The chairman of the bureau was John Fitzpatrick, and it operated out of CFL offices.[53] It communicated with central labor councils around the country asking them to form voluntary committees to encourage support for and recognition of the Irish Republic. Arguing that American newspapers and magazines did not provide reliable information on Ireland because of British influence, it pledged to offer accurate news of developments in Ireland for these groups.[54] Its representative in San Francisco was P.H. McCarthy, president of the Building Trades Council.

The Labor Bureau appealed to unions around the country to boycott British goods and *New Majority* published a list that identified British-made goods. An editorial in that paper explained why the American labor movement should be concerned with Irish freedom.[55] Fitzpatrick's papers are replete with correspondence concerning the boycott, including one from Leonora O'Reilly, organizer of the Irish Women's Purchasing League;[56] a telegram from attorney Frank P. Walsh urging a resolution supporting the boycott at the Denver convention of the AFL in June 1921;[57] and a letter from Mary McGuigan, written on the back of a strike notice, exhorting him to "speed up the boycott of bloody england's [sic] goods" and signed "Yours for unionism and freedom for Ireland."[58]

FRIEND OF JAMES LARKIN

Irish Labor leader and patriot James Larkin arrived in America in 1914. During his stay, he and Fitzpatrick became friends, often sharing the speakers' platform at meetings of Labor and Irish organizations. In one instance, both men addressed a gathering of the International Defense League, chaired by William Z. Foster. The aim of the meeting was to develop support for the release of Tom Mooney. Well peopled with radicals, the group threatened to call a general strike for that purpose.[59] When Larkin, himself, was imprisoned by American authorities in 1919 for criminal anarchy, Fitzpatrick and others formed a James Larkin Defense Committee in Chicago. Fitzpatrick addressed mass meetings in Chicago and New York, where an identical committee had formed, and charged that Larkin had been framed because he was a danger to British imperialism.[60] The British, he said, "bought enough U.S. newspapers to control the press. It was an easy thing to secure conviction under these circumstances."

An April 1921 convention of the American Association for Recognition of the Irish Republic in Chicago voted a resolution condemning Larkin's conviction and demanded "a new trial before a fair court under a real American spirit of justice."[61] In January 1922, the Chicago Federation of Labor cabled the Dáil (parliament of the Irish Free State), requesting it to demand that the king of England release Larkin, thus implying that American courts were doing the bidding of the British.[62] In May 1922, Larkin was released on bail pending appeal of his conviction.[63] At a dinner given by friends, Larkin told of his hope to return to Ireland, and in July he and Fitzpatrick spoke before a meeting to benefit "the Ulster Defense Fund" whose purpose was "to render assistance to all the people of Ulster who are victims of foreign influences seeking to create dissension among people."[64] Ultimately, Larkin's appeal failed, and he was returned to prison.

In the fall of 1922, Larkin's brother Peter came to New York from Australia, by way of England and Ireland, to campaign for his brother's freedom. He argued that Ireland needed Jim Larkin's leadership during her time of troubles—the civil war over the Anglo-Irish Treaty. Peter Larkin requested Fitzpatrick to ask Senator William Borah of Idaho, then in Chicago, to address a rally in New York, on October 15, 1922, to protest Jim Larkin's imprisonment. The James Larkin Defense Committee had already obtained commitments to speak from Fiorello La Guardia (campaigning for Congress at that time) and from Socialist party leader Norman Thomas and Roger Baldwin, president of the American Civil Liberties Union. A month later, Peter Larkin wrote acknowledging Fitzpatrick's friendship and practical help for his brother, but also asking for financial assistance for the campaign to free James Larkin.[65]

James Larkin was finally freed in January 1923, when newly elected Governor Alfred E. Smith pardoned him as one of his first acts after taking office.[66] Larkin then journeyed to Chicago for a well-attended farewell demonstration chaired by Fitzpatrick. He held the audience spellbound and pleaded for funds to finance a relief ship loaded with supplies for Belfast—where conflict between Unionists and Nationalists was causing great suffering—and on which he proposed to sail triumphantly to Ireland. Fitzpatrick responded to Larkin's plea by asking Roger Baldwin to arrange a loan for the venture and he recommended that Larkin, on his return to the East Coast, contact Sidney Hillman and William Z. Foster, both of whom were in New York at the time.[67] The somewhat grandiose plan fell through when Larkin's request for funds from the Transport Workers Union in Dublin was turned down. He then proceeded to Washington and, on his insistence, was deported as an undesirable alien in April 1923. In June of that year he sent greetings to "all comrades in America" from Liberty Hall, headquarters of the Irish Transport and General Workers Union in Dublin.[68] A letter from Larkin in 1939 concerning the Mooney case suggests that contacts continued between him and Fitzpatrick.[69]

DECLINING YEARS

Considerable frustration awaited Fitzpatrick after the optimism following World War I faded and the artificial prosperity of the 1920s gave way to the depression of the 1930s. By then, Fitzpatrick was in his sixties. The Labor party convention in the summer of 1923 signaled the high-water mark of Fitzpatrick's initiatives as a Progressive reformer—those undertaken without the blessings of the American Federation of Labor, or in spite of AFL opposition. He was, after all, deeply committed to the trade union movement and, while he would challenge it to rise above its narrow, encrusted, craft union rigidities, he would only go so far, never willing or wanting an actual break. After 1924, Fitzpatrick was confronted with the unimaginative William Green, successor to Samuel Gompers as AFL president. The reactionary mood of the country during the 1920s—with its Red scare, open shop campaign and pillorying of anyone with views not wholly orthodox—was hardly encouraging for him.

On the other hand, Fitzpatrick, exceedingly loyal, did not personally withdraw from all Progressive associations—only those on the far left, the Communists and their allies. Furthermore, through his leadership of the Chicago Federation of Labor he continued to encourage organization, aid and support for new unions. When new locals began to appear in Chicago during the National Industrial Recovery Act period of the New Deal, CFL came to their assistance. When later, the Congress of Industrial Organizations began organizing stockyards and steel and other manufacturing industries, CFL did not argue the craft union position against it, but discussed with it how best to accomplish the job. When the split between the AFL and CIO came to Chicago, it was imposed from above and not instigated by the CFL. Dolefully, John Fitzpatrick notified industrial unions of their expulsion from CFL on June 7, 1937. He cited official instructions from the executive board of the AFL, which directed that unions affiliated with the CIO dissociate themselves from the CFL.[70] For a former leader of organizing campaigns based on an approximation of industrial structure in steel and meatpacking, it was indeed a sad occasion.

It is also true that Fitzpatrick, having been burned in the 1923 experiment with political action, was chary of the vigorous political involvement of the CIO. Having been exposed to Communist treachery in 1923, he was adamantly opposed to John L. Lewis's temporary expedient of recruiting Communists to meet the desperate need for experienced organizers in CIO campaigns.

Still a warmhearted humanitarian, if now disabused of some illusions, and perhaps skeptical of the possibility of reforming society, Fitzpatrick was, by the 1930s, past his prime. What has been called the Fitzpatrick era in Chicago labor history[71] was almost over. He had become the grand old man of the labor movement and, at his death on September 27, 1946, the tributes came pouring in.[72] In all the years he had been with the Chicago Federation of Labor he had never received from it more than one hundred dollars a week.[73]

A fair assessment of John Fitzpatrick's career would have to credit him with developing a stronger and better organized labor movement in Chicago. Though he was not the founding father of the Chicago Federation of Labor, his leadership made the CFL a powerful instrument for assisting a variety of immigrant workers to secure better conditions of employment. His valuable counsel and the financial aid he was able to make available through CFL enabled a number of new unions to become established in the developing industrial heartland of the Midwest—where exploitation of recently arrived ethnic groups was all too common. It may be argued that Fitzpatrick's efforts would have been even more successful had he not been sidetracked into third party labor politics. Not surprisingly, as an optimist who welcomed new departures—whether industrial unions, racial equality, or women's rights—he chose to try a path which proved fruitless. A limited education and consequent weak grasp of American political traditions left Fitzpatrick receptive to entreaties of his Progressive friends and advisors that he embark on such a third-party course. Probably inevitable, the debacle was certainly helped by the duplicity of his old friend William Z. Foster, by then a Marxist. Fitzpatrick's initial enthusiasm for and later disenchantment with the Russian Revolution may be explained in the same way. His effectiveness was impaired by these disappointing episodes, but his loyalty to the causes that had inspired his career—the labor movement, independence for Ireland and social justice—never waned.

NOTES

1. Michael F. Funchion, "Irish Chicago," in *Ethnic Chicago*, Peter D'A. Jones and Melvin G. Holli, eds. (Grand Rapids, Mich.: Wm. B. Erdmans, 1981), 9–10.

2. Barbara Warne Newell, *Chicago and the Labor Movement* (Urbana: University of Illinois Press, 1961), 233.

3. John H. Keiser, "John Fitzpatrick and Progressive Unionism 1915–1925" (Ph.D. diss., Northwestern University, 1965), 2. Letters to author from Mrs. Eileen Bradely White, of Lowestoft, Suffolk, England, grandniece of John Fitzpatrick, dated September 24, 1992 and January 15, 1993.

4. Interment Records, Calvary Cemetery, Evanston, Illinois.

5. Raymond Robins, "John Fitzpatrick, a Leader of Organized Labor in the

West," *Life and Labor* (February 1911): 41.

6. Keiser, "John Fitzpatrick," 2.

7. Interview of Mollie Levitas by author, March 3, 1982. (Hereafter referred to as Levitas interview with author.)

8. Ibid. Their bungalow was located at 3421 Parnell Avenue, a name evocative of Irish nationalism; letter from Mrs. Eileen Bradley White, January 15, 1993; *The Argonne News*, November 5, 1952, 10.

9. Interview of Mollie Levitas by Elizabeth Balanoff, July 24, 1970, Transcription, 1, Archives, Roosevelt University, Chicago. (Hereafter referred to as Levitas interview with Balanoff.)

10. Levitas interview with author.

11. Keiser, "John Fitzpatrick," 11.

12. Levitas interview with Balanoff, 7.

13. Telephone conversation with Irwin Klass, former editor of *Federation News* (CFL Publication), March 5, 1982.

14. *New Majority*, October 2, 1920, 15.

15. Royal E. Montgomery, *Industrial Relations in the Chicago Building Trades* (Chicago: University of Chicago Press, 1927), 21, 28–30, 40.

16. Robert L. Reid, ed., *Battleground: The Autobiography of Margaret A. Haley* (Urbana: University of Illinois Press, 1982), 93.

17. Hutchins Hapgood, *The Spirit of Labor* (New York: Duffield, 1907), 403–5.

18. Levitas interview with Balanoff, 25.

19. Selig Perlman and Philip Taft, *History of Labor in the United States 1896–1932* (New York: Macmillan, 1935), 305.

20. Levitas interview with author.

21. Letter from William Z. Foster to John Fitzpatrick, June 22, 1918, John Fitzpatrick Papers, Chicago Historical Society. (Hereafter referred to as Fitzpatrick Papers.)

22. Keiser, "John Fitzpatrick," 70–71.

23. Oral history interview with David Saposs (transcript), May 4, 1966, Pennsylvania State University, University Park, Pennsylvania, 1.

24. James R. Barrett, *Work and Community in the Jungle* (Urbana: University of Illinois Press, 1987).

25. Keiser, "John Fitzpatrick," 128, 131.

26. *New Majority*, July 14, 1923, 1.

27. Mary Harris Jones, *Autobiography of Mother Jones* (Chicago: C.H. Kerr, 1925), 238.

28. Levitas interview with author; telephone interview with Irwin Klass.

29. *New Majority*, July 31, 1920, 5; November 27, 1920, 5.

30. Ibid., September 24, 1921, 3; October 1, 1921, 3.

31. Ibid., March 17, 1923, 3; March 24, 1923, 1; March 31, 1923, 1; April 7, 1923, 1–2; March 14, 1923, 1.

32. Ibid., July 4, 1923, 1–2.

33. Ibid., September 22, 1923, 1.

34. Ibid., October 13, 1923, 5.

35. Ibid., May 24, 1924, 1.

36. Ibid., July 9, 1925, 4; August 16, 1925, 1.

37. Robert A. Rosenstone, *Romantic Revolutionary: A Biography of John Reed* (New York: Vintage Books, 1981), 309–10; Elizabeth A. Payne, *Reform, Labor and Feminism: Margaret Dreier Robins and the Women's Trade Union League* (Urbana: University of Illinois Press, 1988), 28–32. The quotation of Lincoln Steffens is from *The Autobiography of Lincoln Steffens* (New

York: Harcourt, Brace, 1931), 799.

  38. Keiser, "John Fitzpatrick," 165.

  39. Levitas interview with Balanoff, 8.

  40. Newell, *Chicago and the Labor Movement*, 200, 233–34.

  41. Levitas interview with Balanoff, 5–6.

  42. Levitas interview with author.

  43. Letters from Mother Jones to Fitzpatrick and Nockels, May 21, 1921; Mother Jones to Fitzpatrick, September 10, 1921; letter from Terence Powderly reprinted in *New Majority*, December 2, 1922, 1–2; letters Mother Jones to Fitzpatrick (concerning Jacob Dolla), December 20, 1923, February 29, 1924, July 31, 1924, Fitzpatrick Papers.

  44. Letter from Mother Jones to Fitzpatrick, December 14, 1927, Fitzpatrick Papers.

  45. Letters from Mother Jones to Fitzpatrick and Nockels, November 14, 1927; Mother Jones to Fitzpatrick, January 11, 1928, Fitzpatrick Papers.

  46. Letters from Lillie M. Burgess to Ed Nockels, 1931 (no month or day), Fitzpatrick Papers. After the death of Mother Jones, Burgess opened what she called the Mother Jones Rest Home, and wrote to Nockels and Fitzpatrick on stationery with that letterhead. She also reported that she was writing a book about Mother Jones and had given talks over Station WOL to commemorate Mother Jones.

  47. Levitas interview with author.

  48. Michael F. Funchion, ed., *Irish American Voluntary Organizations* (Westport, Conn: Greenwood Press, 1983), 17–20.

  49. Ibid., 9–10; T. Ryle Dwyer, *Eamon de Valera* (Dublin: Gill and MacMillan, 1980), 26; *New Majority*, November 27, 1920, 5.

  50. Telegrams from de Valera to Fitzpatrick and from Fitzpatrick to de Valera (reply), November 10, 1920, Fitzpatrick Papers.

  51. Letters from various AAIR officials to Fitzpatrick, July 31, 1921, July 28, 1921, September 19, 1921, Fitzpatrick Papers; *New Majority*, February 26, 1921, 13; April 30, 1921, 5.

  52. *New Majority*, November 6, 1921, 6.

  53. *Organized Labor* (organ of the California State Building Trades Council), November 20, 1920, 1; *New Majority*, November 20, 1920, 3.

  54. Letter from Labor Bureau addressed to officers and members of organized labor, November 1, 1920, Fitzpatrick Papers.

  55. *New Majority*, December 4, 1920, 10; January 8, 1921, 2; January 15, 1921, 1–2.

  56. Letter to Fitzpatrick from Leonora O'Reilly, May 28, 1921, Fitzpatrick Papers.

  57. Telegram to Fitzpatrick at Sam Evans Hotel, Denver, from Frank P. Walsh, June 21, 1921, Fitzpatrick Papers.

  58. Letter to Fitzpatrick from Mary McGuigan, Patrick Ford Council, AAIR, September 2, 1921, Fitzpatrick Papers.

  59. Keiser "John Fitzpatrick," 96.

  60. *New Majority*, September 25, 1920, 10; October 2, 1920, 15.

  61. Ibid., April 23, 1921, 2.

  62. Ibid., January 21, 1922, 1.

  63. Ibid., May 13, 1922, 3.

  64. Ibid., May 20, 1922, 3; July 8, 1922, 3.

  65. Letters from Peter Larkin to Fitzpatrick, September 25, 1922 and October 25, 1922; *New Majority*, December 9, 1922, 5.

  66. *New Majority*, January 27, 1923, 3.

67. Telegram from Fitzpatrick to James Larkin, March 3, 1923, Fitzpatrick Papers.

68. Emmet Larkin, *James Larkin, Irish Labor Leader* (Cambridge, Mass.: MIT Press, 1965), 248–49; *New Majority*, April 28, 1923, 3; May 5, 1923, 5; June 9, 1923, 3.

69. Letter from James Larkin to Fitzpatrick, July 1, 1939, Fitzpatrick Papers.

70. Newell, *Chicago and the Labor Movement*, 184.

71. *Federation News*, September 5, 1966, 54.

72. Ibid., October 5, 1946, 1–2; *American Federationist*, November 1946, 31.

73. Levitas interview with Balanoff, 54.

7

THE CIO:
BROPHY, MURRAY AND QUILL

Industrial unionism spread to American mass-production enterprises in the 1930s under the banner of the Congress of Industrial Organizations (CIO). When this occurred, the United Mine Workers Union was, in large measure, the agency that financed and provided leadership for the campaign to organize these industries.

JOHN BROPHY AND PHILIP MURRAY

The CIO was a creation of John L. Lewis, who was president of the United Mine Workers (UMW). At his side, however, were longtime associates in the UMW, many of whom were of Irish descent. Most visible of these was Philip Murray, vice president of the UMW, chairman (by Lewis's appointment) of the Steelworkers Organizing Committee and in 1940 successor to Lewis as president of the CIO.

Another key participant was John Brophy, an old adversary of Lewis within the UMW, later reconciled to him, who held the title of director of the CIO and played an important role in a number of organizing drives. The careers of these two men are analyzed here as is that of Mike Quill, leader of the Transport Workers Union (TWU) among the heavily Irish work force in New York subways. The TWU came to Lewis requesting affiliation rather than having been established by the CIO.

Murray, Brophy and Quill were all immigrants to the United States, but only Quill emigrated directly from Ireland carrying militant feelings stemming from Irish Republicanism. Quill came in the 1920s, but the other two, somewhat older, arrived closer to the turn of the century. Murray was the grandson of refugees of an Irish rising who had settled in Scotland. Brophy's parents were from Lancashire, but his paternal grandfather was a Dublin cobbler, who moved to Liverpool during the famine. The fathers of Brophy and Murray were Gladstone liberals because Gladstone advocated self-rule for Ireland. Quill's father was a member of the Irish volunteers committed to independence and passionately opposed to partition of the island.

While the Quills were farmers in the west of Ireland, the Brophy and the Murray families came from coal-mining communities with a deep commitment to trade unionism. Brophy and Murray pursued careers along parallel lines and came from similar backgrounds; their paths crossed a number of times within the UMW and the CIO—making it feasible to analyze them jointly. A later section in the chapter describes Quill's leadership.

The mining industry has been the source of much inspiration for modern industrial labor organization. As a major source of energy for railroads, iron and steel and other manufacturing industries, it was essential to the growth of the American economy after the Civil War. Coal mining has always been characterized by a highly competitive structure. This was true of the anthracite (hard coal) fields of northeastern Pennsylvania, as well as the bituminous (soft coal) fields of central and western Pennsylvania, the Midwestern states (Ohio, Indiana and Illinois) and the Appalachian areas (West Virginia, Kentucky). As a result, the coal industry has been, and still is, cyclically sensitive in the extreme. Demand for coal and, therefore, the price of it have varied sharply in response to changes in economic activity.

The reality of boom and bust in coal translates into alternate periods of high employment and rising wages for miners—followed by periods of short weeks, widespread unemployment and drastic wage cuts. The typical mining firm, under competitive pressure to reduce costs, added significantly to the danger intrinsic to work in mines. The typically isolated location of most mines required operators to provide housing for miners and their families, adding an additional degree of dependence by the miner on his employer. In addition, local and state government were under the influence of mine operators more often than not. These circumstances combined to make the life of mining families bleak at best, and often forced them to follow a kind of nomadic existence to eke out a living.

It is not surprising, therefore, that miners have a long history of attempting to achieve stability in employment and improvement in wages and working conditions. Under competitive conditions in an industry as widely scattered geographically as this one, these goals have proved to be very elusive and have been achieved only intermittently and only under favorable, but usually temporary, economic conditions. Struggles of the United Mine Workers have been bitter, violent and prolonged. They served as a framework for natural selection of and a training ground for trade union organizers. The careers of John Brophy and Philip Murray dramatize these realities.

Both men were born in mining communities in the United Kingdom. John Brophy began life on November 6, 1883, in the town of Saint Helens in Lancashire. His grandfather Brophy was a skilled shoe-

maker in Dublin, who moved to Liverpool as a young man at the time
of the famine and opened a custom order shop employing several journeymen. In Liverpool, grandfather Brophy met and married Bessie
Carroll, whose parents had come to the industrial metropolis from
Dundalk, north of Dublin, when she was a child. Factory-made shoes
were rapidly displacing handmade shoes by this time. Sons of the shoemaker saw no future in their father's declining trade and instead found
work in the mines around Saint Helens.

John Brophy's father, Patrick, went to work in a colliery at age nine
and had learned the craft of a skilled miner by the time he was seven-
teen. But the wanderlust was on him, and he "took the king's shilling"
through enlistment in the British Army. During a six-year tour he was
posted to Ireland, South Africa, Egypt and other parts of the empire. On
his return to Saint Helens, he reentered the mines and married Mary
Dagnall, daughter of an English family which had, for generations, persevered in the Catholic faith and the coal-mining industry.

At Saint Helens Irish immigrants were welcomed into the Roman
Catholic community without discrimination. A substantial number of
them settled there after the potato famine. Sharing a common faith, they
joined the same parishes, and their children attended the same parochial
schools. There were, in fact, people from a variety of locations in the
British empire of diverse religions, living harmoniously in Saint Helens,
according to John Brophy's recollections. His first experience with religious prejudice did not come until the family moved to America.[1]

During the 1870s and 1880s (after suppression of Fenianism by
the British), when the fathers of John Brophy and Philip Murray
were in their teens and twenties, movements came alive which kin-
dled the hope for home rule in Ireland and an end to unjust imposi-
tion of British and Anglo-Irish landlords on their impoverished Irish
tenants—the hated rackrents. Declines in farm prices during the
1870s had caused a crisis in agriculture, which made it doubly difficult for a tenant to pay his rent. Failure to pay too often led to eviction from the land.

In response, Irish peasants rose against landlords and their agents.
The boycott was liberally employed as were more direct measures
against property and livestock. At this time, Michael Davitt, a Fenian
who had recently been discharged from prison, founded a land league
in his home county of Mayo to attack landlordism. Shortly, it became
the National Land League. As the organization attracted widening support in rural Ireland, Irish members of British Parliament recognized its
significance. They saw the possibility of combining the movement for
home rule with that of the Land League for the sake of accomplishing
concrete results through new parliamentary law.

Most prominent and effective among these Irish MPs was Charles
Stewart Parnell, a propertied Protestant gentleman from County Wicklow.
He assumed leadership of the so-called Irish Parliamentary party and,
also, the National Land League when Davitt, acknowledging Parnell's
superior talents, withdrew in his favor.

Parnell followed a policy of obstruction in Parliament aimed at negotiating with the Liberal government of William Gladstone for passage of
home rule and tenant rights legislation. Gladstone, plagued by rural
unrest—which only grew worse through his efforts to suppress it—was
eventually persuaded to sponsor home rule legislation for Ireland.
Thereupon, Parnell became a hero not only to people in Ireland, but
also to displaced Irishmen in America and in England.

It was in circumstances of an alliance between the Irish Parliamentary
party and Gladstone's Liberal party that William Murray and Patrick
Brophy were remembered by their sons as "Gladstone Liberals."

These developments were contemporary with Henry George's single-tax land reform movement in the United States. The single-tax idea
appealed to Patrick Brophy in much the same way as Davitt's program
did—though his son doubted that Brophy père ever really understood
it. John Brophy also recalled that much interest in Saint Helens was
occasioned by a speech delivered there by T.P. O'Connor, Irish MP
from Liverpool, and around the same period by an address of Michael
Davitt then visiting from Ireland.[2]

Patrick Brophy's life was characterized by a continual search for
greener pastures, or at least ones where survival was possible. When
his son, John, was only five, messages from relatives who had emigrated to work in the bituminous coal mines of Philipsburg in central
Pennsylvania convinced him to try it himself for a year. He did so, leaving his family in Saint Helens. Although work was slack during his trial
year, he decided that possibilities were more promising here than in
England (a mistake as it turned out).

During his year in Philipsburg, Patrick Brophy served as a volunteer
to aid in restoring Johnstown after the disastrous flood there in the
spring of 1889. It was the most exciting time of his sojourn, and he carried numerous gruesome stories away from the experience. Years later
he took his son there to show him the scene of his rescue work.[3]

After returning to Saint Helens and making preparations over several years, the family, now grown to three children, left for Pennsylvania
in December of 1890. They arrived just in time for the depression of
the mid-1890s. It was a long time before they once again enjoyed living
standards equivalent to what they left behind in Lancashire.

Philip Murray was born in Bothwell, Scotland, contrary to nearly all
other accounts of his life which name Blantyre as his birthplace. Civil
records of birth and the 1891 census of Scotland identify Bothwell as his
place of birth. Specifically, he was born on May 25, 1886, at Number 77
Baird's Rows, Bothwell Park, Lanarkshire, not far from Glasgow.[4]

Baird's Rows was the name of a development built as inexpensively
as possible by mine owner (and proprietor of an ironworks in nearby
Coatsbridge) William Baird to house employees of his mining pits. It
consisted of small row houses with no indoor plumbing. When mining
expanded in this area during the 1870s, due to the requirements of the
growing iron industry around Glasgow, insufficient native labor was
available, so that workers, most of them Irish immigrants, were

brought in to satisfy the need and housing had to be provided. Philip was the second child (the first was Mary, born in 1884) of William Murray, born in 1861, and Roseanne Layden Murray, born in 1865. The parents were married at the Roman Catholic Church in Blantyre on February 7, 1884. Marriage records identify William Murray as a bachelor, coal miner, age twenty-three, and Roseanne Layden as a spinster, cotton factory weaver, age nineteen. They also record Roseanne Layden's signature as an X, indicating that she was illiterate.[5]

Bothwell and Blantyre were both traditional Scottish Presbyterian communities of Lanarkshire. Blantyre was the home of David Livingstone, famed Presbyterian missionary and explorer of Africa. Other than agriculture, employment in Blantyre was available in a cotton textile factory, where Livingstone worked as a boy. Philip Murray's mother worked in the same factory.

Although a significant seasonal migration from Ulster to labor in the farm fields of Scotland had existed for some time, and some of these migrants settled in southern Scotland, the move of Murray's forebears to Scotland did not follow this pattern. In a 1937 interview for a Pittsburgh paper, Philip Murray revealed that his Murray ancestors were from Downpatrick, County Down (Ulster) where they had operated a tavern for over 400 years. He explained that his grandfathers Murray and Layden left Ireland to escape British authorities as a result of a rising in which the two had been involved.[6] The 1891 census entry for Bothwell, which records the family of William Murray (Philip Murray's father) living in a development for miners called Baird's Square, also records the presence in the same square of Philip Murray, age sixty-three, and his wife Margaret, both natives of Ireland.[7] There is little doubt that these are Philip Murray's grandparents.

If it is reasonable to assume that grandfathers Murray and Layden were of the same generation, then it is altogether likely that the rising referred to in the 1937 interview was that of Young Ireland, which occurred in 1848 when Grandfather Murray was twenty and Grandfather Layden would have also been a young man of similar age. While it might be argued that the two men were involved in the Fenian rising of 1865, this would not be credible in view of the fact that they would have been of middle age by then and have become fathers. Even more convincing is the fact that the 1891 census entry for Murray's father, William, shows that he was born in 1861 and not in Ireland, but in England.[8] On the basis of this information, limited as it is, the conclusion is, therefore, that Philip Murray's grandfathers participated in the Young Ireland cause and were forced to flee their homeland when it failed.

The Young Ireland movement was one of the more ineffectual attempts at a rising against the British. Led by William Smith O'Brien, John Mitchell, Charles Gavan Duffy and Thomas Meagher in the teeth of the potato famine, the result is not surprising. Not seriously impaired by the famine themselves, the leaders firmly believed that those who were would rather die attacking their British enemies than die of starvation. The leaders had defected from the movement to repeal the union of Ireland and England after opposing a resolution of its leader, Daniel O'Connell, requiring every member to foreswear all methods of physical violence in efforts to achieve Irish independence or resign from the repeal association. Their estrangement widened after O'Connell died and was succeeded by his less-than-able son John as head of the association.

Leaders of Young Ireland were inspired by ferment on the Continent in 1848 where Louis Philippe of France was overthrown, Metternich was forced to flee Vienna and various other despots were routed by their angry subjects. But men at the helm of Young Ireland, totally lacking practical sense, banked on a spontaneous rising of Irish peasants, now demoralized by years of famine. Almost anarchic in their lack of organization and authority, they collected no arsenal, disdained secrecy and announced their intentions to the world.

Nevertheless, British authorities, with one eye on events on the Continent, did not view the movement lightly. They strengthened their garrisons in Ireland, dispatched naval vessels to Irish ports and arrested leaders of Young Ireland. The climax was a comic opera siege, led by O'Brien, of a squad of police barricaded in the widow McCormack's house near Ballingarry, County Tipperary. Its failure was characteristic of the entire enterprise of Young Ireland.[9] Small wonder that adherents of the cause, like Philip Murray's grandfathers, felt the need to emigrate.

When Irish Catholic immigrants came to Lanarkshire they were received with great resentment, in part because of their "popish" religion in this Presbyterian land, and in part because they were unskilled and, therefore, scorned by experienced Scottish miners proud of their own competence in the dangerous and demanding craft of underground mining. A more severe source of antagonism lay in the fact that Irishmen had been used by mine operators as strikebreakers at various times in Lanarkshire.

Unlike Brophy's account of ethnic and religious harmony in Lancashire, Lanarkshire was the scene of bitter sectarian conflict, resembling that occurring in northern Ireland a century later. Most of the Irish came to Scotland from the province of Ulster. A minority of them were Presbyterians of Scottish descent, some of whom were militant Orangemen. The Orangemen demonstrated a keen ability to stir up hostility against Roman Catholics among native Scottish Presbyterians. Mingled with the competition for jobs in mining, this created a volatile situation in Lanarkshire.[10]

There is a rich irony in the fact that Irish immigrants were used as strikebreakers in Scotland, while in the late nineteenth-century Pennsylvania anthracite fields Slavic immigrants were recruited by operators to replace Irishmen on strike attempting to establish unions there.

Those who have written the history of mining unions in Scotland believe the presence of the Irish inhibited the development of cohesive unions. They cite the frustration of (among others) Alexander McDonald, a pioneer organizer, over the issue of sectarian conflict as an obstacle to effective unionization. Another reason given is that a large proportion of the Irish miners were young males, highly mobile, who were working to accumulate funds for a return to Ireland, or to emigrate to America with little or no interest in permanent organization of workers. They also question whether disapproval of unions by Catholic priests was a factor in this but find no evidence of such an attitude among the clergy.[11]

In their efforts to be objective, these chroniclers have found examples of Irish who were activists in the cause of organizing the miners, though not very many. One of them surely was William Murray, Philip's father. Hardly a transient in Scotland, he lived there at least twenty years and raised a family, although he moved between Blantyre and Bothwell more than once. It was his misfortune to lose his wife on October 22, 1887, when she was pregnant with their third child. At the time, they had been living in the Stonefield section of Blantyre. By then Blantyre had grown to a community of approximately ten thousand. Shortly after her death, the widower and his two small children moved to Bothwell where they lived with Philip's maternal grandfather, Alexander Layden, for a time.[12]

Two years later, on November 17, 1889, William Murray married again. At Saint Joseph's Catholic Church in Blantyre he wedded Elizabeth Buchanan, age twenty-six, widow of George Dingsdale, a coal miner. Born in Ayrshire, she was a Scottish woman, who had also worked as a cotton factory weaver. Her signature was recorded as an X, signifying that she too was illiterate. At the time she had one child, Jane Dingsdale, born in nearby Hamilton, who was the same age as Philip. The couple, however, had eight more children, the first of whom, Margaret, was born in 1890 at Blantyre. The spring of 1891 found the family living in Bothwell at 18 Baird's Square, the development of miners' row houses noted above. Living just down the street at 32 Baird's Square were Philip Murray, coal miner, age sixty-three, and his wife, Margaret, age fifty-five both born in Ireland. As already noted, the latter couple undoubtedly were the paternal grandparents of Philip Murray—William Murray, in fact, had a brother named Philip who moved to Pennsylvania before he did.[13]

Philip Murray's brief formal education began in 1892 when he entered the parish school at Saint Joseph's Catholic Church in Blantyre; there being no parish school in Bothwell. Clearly, the Catholic Church was a source of identity for the Irish who were not welcome in the community and for whom the church was a social as well as religious center—indeed, in the same sense that it was for Catholic immigrants in the United States. Philip Murray attended Saint Joseph's School until the spring of 1896 when, at age ten, he entered the mine at Bothwell to work as his father's helper earning one shilling, sixpence per day.[14] He also found time for the game of soccer, which was popular among boys in Lanarkshire. In the summer of 1894, there was a long strike originally involving 60,000 Scottish coal miners over demands for a wage reduction by owners. By late October the men had returned to the pits on employers' terms. During interviews with journalist John Chamberlain, Philip Murray recalled helping after school to collect food for the miners' soup kitchen.[15] He also remembered that he was taken to his first union meeting at age six by his father, who presided at the meeting of a Scottish miners' local union.[16] William Murray is said to have become a leader of a local union of miners, a rare achievement for an Irishman living in Lanarkshire.

From recollections of his son Philip, William Murray—though sparsely educated—was literate and thoughtful. He was a studious man, informed about politics of the day and hopeful of Gladstone's willingness to support tenants' rights and home rule for Ireland. As a trade union activist, he breathed the socialism circulating in the Scottish air— preached by James Keir Hardie, founder of the Independent Labor party. In Lanarkshire, especially, "It was Socialist enthusiasm and agitation that went hand in hand with trade union struggles to build up the new organization."[17] William Murray was a patient teacher for his oldest son, spending many an evening instructing him on the necessity for trade unions, if not the need for socialism. His personality, physically vigorous, hard-working and committed to justice for workers, furnished an admirable model for his son to follow.

The experience in Lanarkshire must have impressed William Murray and very likely his son with the necessity of overcoming differences of nationality and religion in order to achieve effective organization of workers. Philip Murray's career clearly demonstrated that he had learned that lesson. Andrew McAnulty, a Blantyre native, born the same year as William Murray, was a pioneer of the Blantyre Miners' Association, in which he became acquainted with both Murrays, father and son.[18] He lived to see the miners' organization develop from a loose federation of local and county unions into a single, unified organization of all Scottish miners.[19]

McAnulty worked in Dixon Colliery number 2, which was the site of the great Blantyre explosion of October 22, 1877. Worst disaster in the history of Scottish mining, it claimed the lives of over two hundred coal miners. Only two days before the catastrophe, McAnulty and his brother were working in the mine when fire-damp gas was ignited by Andrew McAnulty's miner's lamp and caused severe burns on himself and fatally burned his brother. The colliery had been known as a "fiery mine" locally and continued to operate in spite of the Mines (safety) Act of 1872, which Parliament had passed as a result of vigorous lobbying by Alexander McDonald.[20]

While wages for coal miners in Scotland reached a peak at the end of 1900, as demand for coal had pushed its price to a record level, 1901 saw a precipitous decline in coal prices and a corresponding downward pressure on coal wages. It was not a promising time in the coal pits of Lanarkshire. William Murray began to think of moving his family, now residing in the "Barracks Section" of Blantyre, to Pennsylvania. His brother, Philip, had already settled in a coal town of Westmoreland County and William visited there to look at the prospects.[21] In December of 1902, William and his oldest son came to America on the steamship *Cedric*.

As John Brophy's father had come to America for a trial stay in 1888, so William Murray and his oldest son tested the waters in Westmoreland County, Pennsylvania, in 1902. They spent Christmas Day getting processed through Ellis Island and proceeded to the mining town of Madison, Pennsylvania, where William Murray's brother Philip had settled—and stayed with him temporarily. Mrs. Murray and the rest of the children joined them during 1903. The family was destined to remain in Westmoreland County and nearby counties surrounding Pittsburgh; just as the Brophys remained in the counties of central Pennsylvania—both areas being important bituminous coal producers. Both families produced eleven children, but only five of the Brophy children survived to adulthood.

Life in the coal-mining communities of America represents an important feature of our industrial experience. It exhibited about the worst conditions to be found anywhere. Though these two families entered into it a decade apart and in adjoining soft coalfields, their conditions were much alike. John Brophy describes them graphically in his autobiography. Indeed, life in the coal patch was hard. Located in mountain valleys of the Alleghenys where winters were long and trying, the patches were small and isolated. Housing, normally provided by coal companies, was primitive, consisting of frame buildings accommodating two families with no indoor plumbing. Fortunately, coal for heating was either cheap or free. Schools were usually one-room affairs where all grades were taught by one teacher. John Brophy found them much inferior to the parochial school he attended in Saint Helens.

Although size varied, the typical coal patch was small and without amenities provided in larger towns. Even churches were rare. There were no libraries, and very little reading matter was available. John Brophy, a precocious reader, hungered for reading material and rejoiced at the windfall when he learned of a neighbor (a butcher in the company store) who owned an entire shelf of over thirty books, which he would willingly loan.[22] The company store, although a cruel monopoly about which miners harbored bitter feelings, was about the only gathering place in the community. There, after cleaning the coal dust from their bodies, the men would come to exchange stories, gossip and even engage in singing, when not too exhausted from work in the pits. Patrick Brophy was a gregarious Irishman with a fund of stories and Irish songs. His son often accompanied him to listen to gatherings of miners, reminiscing about mining disasters they had survived.

Population of the coal towns consisted almost exclusively of miners and their families, most of them immigrants. The nationalities represented were English, Welsh, Scottish, Irish, Polish and Slovak. English, Welsh and Scottish—the earlier immigrants—normally held the better jobs. At the lower end of the hierarchy were the immigrants from Eastern Europe, who had only begun to come in the 1880s. In most cases, these later immigrants had no previous experience in mines and were more often single or, if married, had left wives and children in the old country until such time as they could afford to pay the passage to America. Rarely did they speak more than the rudiments of English.

The Irish were rather an in-between group. Their influx was subsequent to the English and Welsh but preceded that of the Eastern Europeans. With the Eastern Europeans they shared a common religion (very few Jews gravitated to mining) and with the earlier settlers a common language. While each nationality group tended to congregate by itself, this was only partially possible in the small communities that made up the mining industry. It is true that company housing reflected the occupational hierarchy with larger and more substantial one-family homes for the foreman and superintendent, who were ordinarily English or Welsh. Yet there was sharing of experience which offered a potential for organization. Furthermore, not a few immigrants from the British Isles, like the Brophys and the Murrays, brought with them not only background in mining, but also trade union experience.

Soccer was one of the few diversions which everyone in the coal town could enjoy, either as a player or a spectator. By this time it was a popular sport in the British Isles, and was brought over by immigrants from there. With minimum requirements for facilities, it was easily accommodated even in mining camps almost bereft of public facilities. Immigrants from Eastern Europe were not familiar with the game, but quickly adapted to it and became strong competitors. Young Philip Murray had played the game in Scotland. He favored the position of right wing and was a vigorous participant in Madison. The pride he took in his game suffered from criticism of his uncle Phil, in whose opinion his nephew had feet too large to make a good soccer man.[23] Nevertheless, Murray was a very active, effective soccer player in the Pittsburgh area, who enjoyed the reputation of a star right wing. He was player-manager for teams that won western Pennsylvania and Ohio championships during his early twenties, and was sought after as a referee for soccer games thereafter. For the rest of his life, in fact, he was something of a sportsman favoring boxing, baseball and the racetrack for relaxation.

The less athletically inclined John Brophy does not record soccer as one of his boyhood games. However, he undoubtedly witnessed matches. The sport was one element that fostered cohesiveness among the different ethnic groups in mining communities.

An aspect of life in American mining is the necessity to move frequently. It is related to the competitive structure, small scale of the average enterprise and the cyclical sensitivity of the industry. Hostility to union organization is important as well. When Philip Murray was working in the Keystone Company mine near Herminie, Pennsylvania, in 1904, he complained of being short weighted for the coal he had dug. He argued the issue with the weighmaster, a man named Charles Dailey, who denied it. As a result (in the words of Murray himself):

A fight ensued. The weigh boss took a shot at me with a balance weight from the scale. I hit him with a stool over the head. I happened to get the best of the argument, but I was discharged. Some 550 men went out in support of me.

Mine guards were thrown around the place; my family was evicted from the company house. That was the beginning of these things I am interested in.[24]

In this instance, the strike failed after four weeks, but the eighteen-year-old Murray was elected president of his local union. Nevertheless, after being hidden by a saloon keeper, Tom Hickey, for a few days, he was run out of town by deputy sheriffs, who put him on a train for Pittsburgh and warned him not to return to the area. This episode reveals the injustice deeply resented by Murray, which led to his life-long dedication to the cause of unions. It also illustrates the intrepid spirit of the young Philip Murray.

Philip Murray lived and worked in a variety of mining towns, including Monongahela City, Carnegie, Castleshannon, Fayette City, Hazelkirk and Madison. Shortly after coming to Westmoreland County, Murray boarded with a family by the name of Fagan for several months before moving to a job in the Jutt mine in Fayette City. At the Fagans, he became fast friends with their son, Patrick, three years younger than himself. Their friendship lasted a lifetime with close associations in the union and in organizing the steelworkers' union. Later Murray lived in a boardinghouse called the "Red Onion" in Hazelkirk while employed in a mine there.[25]

The Brophy family lived almost like gypsies for over a decade after coming to America. In fourteen years they moved eight times to different mining camps. On two occasions the family breadwinner was blacklisted after strikes that failed, and on another an argument with the mine foreman was responsible. But more often, moves were the result of earnings too low to support the family or simply the closing of a mine. The worst year was 1896, at the bottom of the 1890s depression, when the family moved no less than five times in a desperate effort to keep body and soul together. Three of the mining towns in which the Brophys lived (Urey, Horatio, Greenwich) disappeared completely.[26]

In November of 1895, at age twelve, John Brophy entered the mines for the first time at Urey, Pennsylvania. He began as his father's helper just as Murray did a year later in Bothwell. His beginning at a later age than Philip Murray may be explained by the fact that he was small for his age and less robust than Philip Murray. In November of the following year, Brophy contracted typhoid fever and remained in bed for several months. Undoubtedly, adjusting to the strenuous routine of a miner was exhausting for him. Nevertheless, he took to unionism early on, joining a UMW local in South Fork (near Johnstown) at age fifteen.

MINING UNION CAREERS

By 1904 Brophy had become secretary of a UMW local in Greenwich, Pennsylvania, after an older man resigned, and young Brophy had filled the post as a temporary acting secretary for some time. The following year, he was elected a checkweighman at the

Greenwich mine because of his father's effective campaigning for him. The position of checkweighman carried an important responsibility: to ensure each miner was given full credit by the company for all the coal he sent up. A checkweighman's pay was provided by an assessment on each miner, and only a person who enjoyed their confidence was ordinarily selected.[27] Philip Murray was a checkweighman at Hazelkirk mine number one. The absence of a checkweighman had been responsible for the dispute in which he had been forced to leave town.[28] Becoming a checkweighman was an important step for anyone aspiring to rise in the mine workers' union.

Philip Murray rose in the UMW when he was associated with a man named Francis Feehan, who became president of District 5 of the union in 1906. In 1910 Feehan undertook to organize nonunion mines in Westmoreland County. During the campaign a strike broke out, which lasted until 1912. With support from Murray, Van Bittner and others, Feehan was reelected District 5 president over the candidate of a faction that opposed the strike. Running with Feehan, Philip Murray was elected to the national executive board of the UMW.

About the same time, Feehan began a campaign for workmen's compensation legislation in Pennsylvania because of its importance to miners' welfare. Philip Murray worked vigorously for its passage. Murray and Feehan were given considerable credit for its adoption in 1915. Murray's reputation benefited considerably.[29]

When Feehan retired as president of District 5, he was succeeded by Van Bittner, vice president of the district, who held the post until appointed an international representative of the union, whereupon Philip Murray was elected president of the district.[30]

The election took place at a special convention of District 5 in July of 1916, chaired by John L. Lewis as directed by John P. White, UMW president.[31] Lewis was then only little more than a year from being appointed vice president of the UMW, due in no small measure to his effective work on behalf of president White. This was not the first meeting between Murray and Lewis. In 1913, at a labor temple in Pittsburgh, Murray came to meet Lewis, but found him fighting two boilermakers. Lewis, having dispatched one of them, asked Murray's forbearance while he finished off the other.[32] That having been accomplished, Murray and Lewis became acquainted. Undoubtedly respect for physical courage, essential for trade unionists, fostered their friendship. A close and lasting association of the two gradually developed with Murray in the role of faithful ally and lieutenant. It endured until John L. Lewis gave up his leadership of the CIO in 1940.

The extraordinary personality of John L. Lewis had a profound impact on the lives of Philip Murray and John Brophy. John Brophy's response on first encountering Lewis was quite different from Murray's. After Brophy was elected to the presidency of District 2 in 1916, he met Lewis on several occasions. On one of them Lewis's mission was to obtain Brophy's support to unseat James Maurer as president of the Pennsylvania Federation of Labor because Maurer was a socialist. By then the nation was at war, and sentiment arose that Maurer would bring disfavor to the organization and labor generally. Brophy disagreed and pointed out that Maurer's opposition to the war ended with our entry and that he was a loyal American. Lewis's effort failed, and in his autobiography Brophy commented:

As I look back on this incident, it seems evident that Lewis was concerned sole-ly with his own political ambitions. He wanted to be king maker and to have the state president under obligations to him. Ethical and human considerations were brushed aside if they interfered with his ambitions. On many union mat-ters I agreed with him, and would willingly have worked with him, yet again and again the ruthlessness and extreme egotism of the man drove us apart.[33]

The forty-year leadership of the UMW (1920-1960) by Lewis saw harsh conflicts with Brophy. Most severe was the Brophy campaign for presidency of the UMW against Lewis in 1926. Brophy lost, charged fraud (with some basis), and was eventually drummed out of the union along with his allies. In this contest, Brophy accepted support from left-wing groups.[34] Brophy opposed Lewis on economic as well as political grounds. While Lewis and Murray backed Republican presidents in the 1920s, Brophy remained a Democrat. Particularly mindful of the intense competition in soft coal, Brophy supported miners in District 2 when they remained on strike in 1922 after Lewis negotiated a settlement in Cleveland in which operators signed only for organized mines, and none of the nonunion mines owned by these same companies (having earlier pledged not to do so). District 2 borrowed substantially to provide for the strikers, but finally it had to abandon the holdout in 1923.

While there is some degree of segmentation in the market for bitu-minous coal because of transportation costs, nevertheless, all fields are interrelated in a fairly sensitive economic way. This was the rationale for the industrywide bargaining eventually established by Lewis. It was also his excuse for eliminating district autonomy by appointing his own men to leadership in most districts, according to Saul Alinsky.[35] But in the early 1920s Brophy criticized Lewis forcefully for raising wages in the unionized coalfields of the north, while making pitifully inadequate efforts to organize the mostly nonunion ones in West Virginia, Kentucky and nearby areas. Lower costs enjoyed by the Southern mines put orga-nized mines at a disadvantage and jeopardized the union's strength.

Another source of friction was Brophy's advocacy for nationaliza-tion of the mines. Lewis was against it all along, but for political rea-sons, found it expedient to make favorable noises about it. At one point, responding to a convention resolution (which he had originat-ed), Lewis appointed a committee of three, chaired by Brophy, to study the issue. Thereafter, Lewis proceeded to undermine the committee and caused its report to die of neglect.[36]

His interest in nationalization of coal, his advocacy of a labor party, and associations with James Maurer and the Brookwood Labor College in Katonah, New York (he served on its labor cooperation committee until just prior to the school's demise) gave Brophy the reputation of something of a socialist.[37] He himself said, "However, my extensive exposure to the literature of Socialism never won me over."[38] His later enthusiasm for the Industry Council Plan recommended by Pope Pius XI in 1931[39] (an enthusiasm he shared with Philip Murray) would suggest that this reputation was exaggerated, or that he had changed his mind. In any case, it did not endear him to John L. Lewis.

According to Patrick Fagan, Murray's popularity in the union got a boost during World War I, when he fought tenaciously to secure wage increases for District 5 miners, when their real wages were falling due to the rapidly rising cost of living. At the time, wages and prices in coal were controlled by the fuel administrator of the federal government.[40]

Philip Murray became acting vice president of the UMW in January of 1920, when he was appointed by the executive board of the union with sponsorship of Lewis. Lewis himself had been appointed acting president at the same time to take the place of Frank Hayes, whose resignation has been alleged to have been part of a scheme hatched by Lewis.[41] However that may be, Murray, thereafter, was regularly elected to the vice presidency and stood faithfully by John L. Lewis until 1940. In convention battles, Lewis could always count on support from District 5, where Murray's popularity endured. He could also depend on Murray's acknowledged ability as a mediator when disputes arose between or within UMW locals.

His talent for patiently bargaining out the specific terms of a coal industry contract after the UMW president, with his usual flair, had outlined the broad objectives of the union, made Murray invaluable to Lewis's leadership. Lewis praised Philip Murray's ability thus: "He has no peer in the coal industry in his knowledge of local conditions in all districts, of marketing conditions, of problems of production and of problems of organization and finance."[42]

Murray has always been regarded as an admirable, modest individual of unquestionable integrity. He was, however, not angelic. It must be remembered that he was at the elbow of Lewis when that leader wiped out many of the democratic traditions of the UMW. He stood by as Lewis pursued the goal of unchallengeable control at almost any cost, ruthlessly expelling opponents. After becoming acquainted with Murray when they were both district presidents, Brophy offered this assessment of the man:

Murray took less interest than I did in the larger social and economic problems. He was very much the trade unionist, interested in day-to-day operation of the union. His pragmatic turn of mind helps explain his long and faithful, though unhappy association with Lewis. Murray saw Lewis as a man who got things done, and was not much interested in his social views.[43]

Indeed, Murray was a highly visible critic of John Brophy when Brophy challenged Lewis's policies for the mining industry.[44]

It is important to point out here that, during the period he was Lewis's deputy, Murray's development as a leader was incomplete. It took the challenge of commanding the CIO to fully mature Murray's capacity for leadership and his ability to articulate a social and economic program.

After losing to Lewis in the election of December 1926, and being constitutionally barred from running for reelection to his district position, John Brophy had to consider making a living elsewhere. Not officially expelled from the union until May of 1928, he, nevertheless, had little opportunity for work in the coal pits during the interim since unemployment was severe. Moving to Pittsburgh in extremely straightened circumstances, he tried his hand working as a construction laborer and real estate salesman. Finally, after the crash of 1929, he moved to Indianapolis and went on the road representing the Columbia Conserve Company, owned by the Hapgood family. This was arranged through Powers Hapgood, Harvard-educated son of the family, who, as a young idealist, had entered mining and subsequently backed Brophy in the fight with Lewis. He, too, had been expelled from the UMW.

As the depression deepened and when his trade union impulses surfaced, Brophy's relations with Columbia Conserve deteriorated. But after the election of Franklin Roosevelt in 1932, things began to open up. Section 7(a) of the National Industrial Recovery Act (of 1933), stipulating employee rights to organize, offered an opportunity for the UMW to reestablish itself in the industry, and it did so with remarkable speed under Roosevelt administration encouragement. That accomplished, John Brophy received an emissary from Lewis, sounding him out about coming back to work for the UMW. The emissary was Philip Murray, and, after talks with him and Lewis, it was decided he would work for Lewis on various assignments. His own membership would be restored, but he would be forbidden to seek office for three years.

John L. Lewis sensed that American workers were ripe for unionization, and he needed the help of capable men like John Brophy. He also needed the AFL to charter industrial rather than craft unions, which it steadfastly refused to do.

BIRTH OF THE CIO

When Lewis's agitation in the AFL for industrial charters failed, he founded the Committee for Industrial Organization, consisting of seven national unions in November of 1935. John Brophy was appointed director for administration.

On November 28, 1935, Brophy opened an office of the Committee for Industrial Organization, then essentially a paper organization, in Washington, D.C., near UMW headquarters.[45] His title was director—his staff consisted of two secretaries. It marked the genesis of a bold, and ultimately successful, venture to extend collective bargaining to workers in the great mass-production industries which dominated the American economy. The committee consisted of leaders of national unions, nearly all of which were affiliated with the AFL. It was to be a long and fruitful association for John Brophy—but not without resurrection of conflict with John Lewis. As the CIO grew, becoming an enti-

ty independent of the AFL, Brophy demonstrated great ability as a troubleshooter, providing needed experience for the enterprise. He participated in organizing drives in numerous industries as mentor and
Lewis's man on the scene. The foreword of his autobiography gives a
sense of Brophy's contributions:

It was John Brophy who helped rally striking workers in Akron after they discovered that they could "shut the machines down." It was John Brophy who
climbed a barbed-wire fence in Flint to encourage sit down strikers not to surrender. It was John Brophy who went to New Orleans and Jersey City despite
publicized threats that if he addressed scheduled labor rallies, he would never
leave either city alive. And, it was John Brophy who helped form the Steel
Workers Organizing Committee.[46]

It was the task of Brophy and Murray (by now in middle age) and
their cohorts, mainly from the UMW, to do the less dramatic, but equally important, job of preparing younger men in these new unions for the
formidable organizing, negotiating and grievance handling job that lay
ahead. Toughened by work in the mines, blooded in the hostile environment of coal mining and in internal struggles of the UMW, they
were equal to the challenge.

In 1936 the Steelworkers Organizing Committee (SWOC) was established with Philip Murray as its chairman. By March 1, 1937, Lewis had
reached agreement with Myron C. Taylor, chairman of the U.S. Steel
Corporation, for that firm to recognize SWOC as bargaining agent for
its union employees. During those negotiations, Murray was not directly involved, but was aware of what was transpiring.

In the preceding month, General Motors had settled the sit-down
strike with a contract that could not have been realized without the
leadership of John L. Lewis. With these dramatic breakthroughs, numerous others were forthcoming. After its expulsion from the AFL, the CIO
achieved permanence as the Congress of Industrial Organizations in
1938, with John Lewis as president and Philip Murray as vice president.

David Brody, historian of labor relations in steel, provides a perceptive analysis of Philip Murray as revealed in his approach to organizing
this industry.[47] Needless to say, the approach owed much to his long
experience as a UMW official. Largely free of trade unionism since the
Homestead Strike of 1892, in the early 1930s steel was honeycombed
with employee representation plans (ERPs), better described as company unions.

Though appointed SWOC chairman by Lewis, Murray was given a
relatively free hand to proceed in this industry after the agreement with
Myron C. Taylor. He had, in fact, participated in the organizing drive in
steel at the end of World War I along with his friend Pat Fagan. Murray
was, in fact, a member of "The Flying Squadron," a group of seven or
eight organizers sent out by leaders of the drive to break the barrier to
public speeches in the Pittsburgh area. Ordinances in these towns
required a permit for public meetings. Prepared to be arrested frequently, individuals deployed for this purpose included (conspicuous-

ly) Mother Jones and James Maurer, president of the Pennsylvania Federation of Labor, as well as Murray.[48] His personality was well suited to wooing back ethnic communities of the steel towns of Pennsylvania, Ohio, Indiana, and elsewhere, who had been badly bruised by failure of the strike of 1919. Unlike Lewis, his was a nonmenacing image more likely to engender affection than anything else. Murray was a devoutly religious man, gentlemanly, and reassuring.[49] But lest this convey an oversimplified picture of him, note that Harold Ruttenberg, who worked for and admired him at SWOC, pointed out that "Phil Murray was a soft-spoken man with genuine compassion for his fellow man, but he was tough as nails."

Under Murray's leadership, the CIO undertook a sophisticated, many-faceted campaign to organize steel—benefiting from both the effective methods and the mistakes of the 1918-1919 drive. Racial, ethnic and geographical differences among workers had to be recognized while at the same time molded to a viable unity. Blacks, especially, had to be made to feel welcome and involved in the enterprise—to overcome their sense of isolation due to racial prejudice and past employment as strikebreakers. This objective was pursued by appointing black officials and organizers, opening SWOC offices in black neighborhoods and reaching out to their various associations, as Murray did, by calling a (successful) national conference of Negro organizations. At this conference, held in Pittsburgh, he cited the UMW's record of racial fairness as proof of SWOC's intentions. African Americans responded favorably. These efforts were fruitful, in part, because black workers' loyalty to steel firms had been eroded by racial discrimination practiced in layoffs following onset of the Great Depression.

White ethnics remembered failure in the drive following World War I. It inhibited their joining. To overcome this response, Murray's rapport with rank-and-file workers was a distinct asset. SWOC selected staffs so as to include leaders of locally important ethnic groups. The CIO deliberately chose church and community halls for its meetings. Ethnic churches and community groups reacted positively to these entreaties. They became recruiting conduits for the union. Signs, speakers and printed literature appeared in the native languages of nationality groups who were not yet comfortable in English.

CIO buttons worn on shop floors engendered a sense of union solidarity and alienation from the paternalism of employers whose welfare capitalism (other than employee representation plans) had evaporated as the Depression wore on. Union-sponsored bowling leagues, family picnics and spaghetti dinners fostered both identity with SWOC and family engagement. SWOC communicated by mailing *Steel Labor*, its newspaper (which included a women's page), to the home, as well as by reaching workers' families through radio with speeches by Philip Murray and other leaders.

These family-oriented methods also were designed to develop unity between steelworker communities in Chicago, Pittsburgh, Youngstown, Birmingham and other locations around the country. Emphasis on the goal of uniform rates for identical jobs in steel plants in all such locations was appealing in terms of wage equity, as well as recognition of the reality of a nationwide market for steel and the common interest in a unified national union to deal effectively with the industry.[50]

Indeed, Murray assured steelworkers that the campaign could be conducted without strikes or violence. No initiation fees or dues would be required in the early stages of organizing. This became possible as a result of substantial financing made available from the UMW by Lewis. The miners' union had a large stake in success for the campaign, since that could lead to winning rights to represent employees in the "captive mines," those owned by the steel firms—heretofore not penetrated by UMW. By the same token, Murray had adequate numbers of veteran organizers in the field, borrowed from and paid by the miners' union.

Criticism has been leveled at SWOC and its subsequent form (United Steelworkers) for being established from the top down, rather than (more democratically) from the bottom up. Most national organizations have arisen from efforts of local unions to build a unified national entity, enjoying only those powers delegated by local lodges. This, however, was not the case for the Steel Committee—as well as others established by the CIO. From its earliest stages, control was centralized in Murray's hands.[51] Patterned after the UMW, there was no inclination to empower local activists who might be prone to ultimatums to employers and unwise strikes. Enthusiasts from the rank and file needed lengthy seasoning and mentoring by experienced field staff of SWOC. In the meantime, organizing and administration would be in the hands of veterans drawn from the UMW—under Philip Murray's careful direction. Internal discipline was maintained.

A geographical structure of regional districts was put in place, resembling that of the miners' union. District directors were appointed (not elected) by Murray, as were all members of the field staff—and subject to dismissal at his discretion. SWOC headquarters standardized dues and initiation fees for all local units, provided for regular audits of them and prohibited strikes without its authorization. On the other hand, Murray established a Wage Policy Committee, composed of presidents of local unions, from U.S. Steel initially, but later broadened to include those from other firms. This body deliberated on an agenda supplied by the SWOC chairman. It functioned essentially to ratify his program for negotiations. Murray also instructed that uniform grievance procedures be established in all plants, but the national office retained discretion over submitting unresolved disputes to arbitration.[52]

Operation of SWOC was, therefore, far superior to that which Foster and Fitzpatrick were able to employ in 1918 and 1919. Even so, the road beyond U.S. Steel and a few other firms was rocky indeed. Unexpected resistance arose from Little Steel—Bethlehem, Republic, Inland and Youngstown Sheet and Tube. These firms, led by Tom Girdler of Republic, refused to recognize SWOC, regardless of efforts by Murray and his staff. In the summer of 1937, strikes failed to budge them. A repertoire of traditional antiunion techniques appeared and confounded the union, in spite of the Wagner Act of 1935 which had outlawed them. The 1937-38 recession also handicapped the union, causing a very large percentage of its members to be unemployed or on short weeks, consequently reducing revenues from dues severely.

Murray persevered. Not attacked frontally, company unions (ERPs) were won over, made militant and, in many cases, ended up as locals of the steelworkers' union. The strategy was helped by a Supreme Court decision in the Jones and Laughlin case of 1937, which held that the Wagner Act was constitutional—since that legislation outlawed company-dominated labor organizations.

Meanwhile, John L. Lewis was becoming disenchanted with President Roosevelt, and by 1940 resolved to support Wendell Willkie, his Republican opponent, in the election of that year. Not only did he oppose FDR's campaign for a third term, but he pledged to resign as president of the CIO if Roosevelt were reelected.

At the CIO convention in Atlantic City in November after the Roosevelt victory, Lewis stepped down as CIO president. He draped the mantle of succession over Philip Murray and gave a valedictory in his own inimitable style. It was an agonizing period for Philip Murray. For over twenty years he had stood resolutely by Lewis, countenancing the man's great accomplishments, as well as his ignoble manipulations. Now he was to head an organization in which Lewis would be in a subordinate position. He knew the man well enough to be sure that Lewis could not really adapt to such a relationship, and feared that he was expected to be a puppet for his former chief. He looked inwardly to find strength sufficient to become a leader in his own right, substantially independent of Lewis. For moral support and a sympathetic auditor for his predicament, he asked Charles Owen Rice, Pittsburgh's labor priest, to be on hand at the 1940 convention.[53]

As the CIO evolved into permanence under the title of Congress of Industrial Organizations, a new season of friction between Brophy and Lewis opened. The first hint of it surfaced when the office of secretary of the CIO became vacant in July of 1938. Lewis nominated James Carey for the post, instead of Brophy, whose capable efforts caused him to be recommended for the position by more than a few respected figures in the organization. Next, in 1939, Lewis demoted Brophy from director of the CIO to director of CIO local unions, that is those affiliated directly to the parent body rather than a national union. Finally, after an illness of several months, which kept him bedridden, Brophy returned to work in December of 1940, to find his desk and his secretary removed from the building.

Causes of these difficulties centered on Lewis's irritation at Brophy's continuing support for President Roosevelt and his interventionist foreign policy, while Lewis became steadily more disaffected from the president. Speaking before various groups, Brophy, always independent minded, made no secret of his contrary views. Another factor may have been Lewis's impatience with anyone who was a potential rival to his own leadership. It is likely that he was mindful of Brophy's challenge in 1926.

In any case, John Brophy's association with the CIO resumed following Lewis's resignation as its president when Franklin Roosevelt was reelected in 1940. Succeeding Lewis as head of the CIO, Phillip Murray appointed Brophy to an important position in the organization shortly thereafter. He became director of the local and state councils, CIO counterparts of the city and state federations of local lodges of national unions affiliated with the AFL.

At the time of the 1940 convention, the CIO was not in a strong position. Although a number of industries had been partially organized, initial contracts were minimal and provided for no checkoff of dues from members. As a result, the new unionists were very casual about paying dues, and the financial position of their unions and of the CIO was problematical. The outlook for the new leader of the CIO, therefore, was not highly promising. It was further clouded by intimations from the Lewis camp that consideration be given to replacing James Carey, secretary of the CIO, with Kathryn Lewis, daughter of John Lewis, presumably to act as his agent on the spot and transmit directives from the master.[54] Murray rejected the suggestion.

Symbolic of Philip Murray's dilemma, in this early period, was the fact that he operated as CIO president out of an office in the United Mine Workers Building in Washington.[55] His health suffered. A pancreas attack put him in the hospital for several months in the summer of 1941.[56] Relations with Lewis, already strained, worsened as Murray, who consistently supported Roosevelt, became more closely associated with him.

They reached a climax on May 25, 1942, when—at a meeting of the UMW executive council, which Murray attended as UMW vice president, a post he still retained—Murray on Lewis's initiative was stripped of all links with the UMW. These included not only his vice presidency, but also his pension rights and his membership. It was a vivid example of how vindictive Lewis could be.[57]

The new CIO president also faced difficult challenges involving Communist elements, who had obtained footholds in a number of the new industrial unions. Communist influence originated in the halcyon days of organizing in the 1930s. Badly in need of experienced organizers, Lewis recruited them wherever they could be found. Numbers of left-wing individuals welcomed the opportunity. Under the party's "popular front" doctrine of collaboration with all anti-fascists, begun in 1935, party leader Earl Browder dropped the dual union approach (of 1929-1934) and encouraged participation in the CIO. After the Russo-German nonaggression pact of August 1939, these elements opposed Roosevelt's defense mobilization program. Opposition commenced on September 1, 1939, when Germany invaded Poland and World War II began—a conflict the party line called the "imperialist war." Lewis's isolationist stance coincided with the party line at this time. Murray, however, loyally supported Roosevelt. As CIO president, he had to contend with opposition from leaders of a number of affiliated unions, who encouraged strikes at defense plants and otherwise inhibited the defense effort.[58]

These conditions lasted only until June of 1941, when Germany invaded Russia. An immediate about-face in the party line occurred. The watchword became all-out production and no strikes. Now Communists advocated conceding hard won gains in favor of speed ups.[59] It took a strong-willed leader to moderate these excesses. Phillip Murray proved equal to the task.

The fortunes of Philip Murray and the CIO turned around as America became directly involved in the world war beginning December 7, 1941. Membership in CIO unions burgeoned. Pledging to forgo strikes for the duration, Murray cooperated with the Roosevelt administration to ensure all-out production for the war effort. He participated in the National Defense Mediation Board and several other wartime agencies. Breaking free of Lewis's influence, he criticized the man for leading the miners into several wartime strikes.

Emerging from the war in a strong position (with membership totaling six million), the CIO and its leader encountered two serious problems. One was the public reaction to the wave of strikes in 1946, which was seized upon by a Republican Congress to legislate broad restrictions on unions in the form of the Taft-Hartley Act. The other problem was the significant group of CIO unions that was dominated by Communist leadership, among them Mike Quill's Transport Workers Union. The first problem proved to be more than the CIO with its Political Action Committee (organized by Murray and Sidney Hillman in 1944) could handle. The Taft-Hartley Act became law in 1947, when President Truman's veto was overridden in Congress.

The other troubling issue, Communist influence, was eventually resolved, but only at a considerable price for the CIO. An antisocialist and notorious Red baiter in the past himself, Lewis was confident he could root out Communists, once their help was no longer wanted, but his resignation left responsibility in the hands of Philip Murray.

Murray was a devout Roman Catholic and staunchly anti-communist, but early in his presidency of the CIO he was compelled to repress his inclinations because the organization was still shaky, and he was in no position to banish any of its constituent parts. Later, as America became allied with Russia in the war, there were diplomatic repercussions of such a move, which prevented action to deal with the issue. The Roosevelt administration counseled against it.

Peace and demobilization in the United States soon gave way to the Cold War. After an Iron Curtain fell across Eastern Europe, left-wing leadership, in some of its member unions, clearly following the Communist party line, became a serious liability for the CIO. The Truman Doctrine of containing the spread of communism and the Marshall Plan for European recovery were both condemned by the party. Earl Browder and the "popular front" were out—W.Z. Foster and the hard line replaced them. The matter was finally brought to a head when these unions gathered momentum in support of Progressive candidate Henry Wallace in the election of 1948. Murray was firmly committed to Truman, the Democratic candidate, as were most of the CIO unions. He refused to tolerate this effort to undermine the political clout of the CIO.[60]

The subsequent purge of left-wing unions from the CIO in 1949 was carried out.[61] John Brophy forcefully participated in the undertaking. Membership of the banished unions became fair game for those remaining in the CIO fold, and the organization survived, weakened only moderately as a result. Those who questioned Philip Murray's toughness now had to reconsider their judgment of him.

Philip Murray's militant leadership of the CIO and the steelworkers' union continued until his fatal heart attack on November 9, 1952. He died during a stopover in San Francisco, while en route to the CIO convention in Los Angeles later that month. In the summer of 1952 he had led a nationwide strike in the steel industry, notable for President Truman's assumption of control of the industry until the action was found unconstitutional by the Supreme Court of the United States.

John Brophy continued to hold positions of importance in the CIO and, after the 1955 merger, in the AFL-CIO until his retirement in 1961. He died on February 19, 1963.

MIKE QUILL

In 1926, while the UMW was suffering factional struggles and undergoing a dramatic decline in membership, Michael Quill, age twenty, arrived in New York, following by several years his brother John, who had come as a refugee from the civil war in Ireland. He was destined to become the bumptious leader of a union among subway workers in New York and to bear the nickname of "Red Mike."[62]

As Irish immigrants will, he moved in temporarily with the sizable family of Aunt Kate O'Leary (his father's sister). Lacking a marketable skill, he was fated to soldier through a litany of menial jobs—sandhog (digging subway tunnels), roach repellant salesman, doorman, elevator operator and boiler room attendant. As an able seaman, he took a cruise to South America and also served as a trainman on the Long Island Railroad.

One of his first jobs was that of a traveling salesman for a religious goods house. With his brother John, he canvassed the coal and steel towns of western Pennsylvania, taking orders for framed religious prints. One of them depicted the crucifixion. When the prints arrived with heart on the right side of Jesus, the Quills felt obliged to abandon that line of work.

Another job was that of handyman at a country club on Long Island during Prohibition. It proved to be a bootlegging operation, and Quill again sought a new situation. Finally, he landed in a job as ticket agent in a New York subway, and eventually organized (with Austin Hogan and others) the Transport Workers Union there during the Depression.

Mike Quill's rebellious nature is traceable to his childhood in Kilgarvan, County Kerry, where he was born on September 18, 1905.

Gortloughera, the Quill family farm, was a hotbed of IRA activity. He absorbed the lore of the Land Leagues and the Fenians from his father, John Quill, the village historian. Second youngest of eight children, Michael was just in his teens when his father joined the South Kerry volunteers of the IRA and its political arm, Sinn Fein. This was done in the aftermath of the Easter Rising of 1916, whereafter the leaders were systematically shot by the British.

One of these leaders was James Connolly, head of the Irish Citizens Army, who had been wounded in the rising. His death before a British firing squad instantly made a national hero of him. It (and this series of executions) also turned public opinion in Ireland strongly against the British. As a young boy, Michael Quill was inspired by this martyrdom for freedom, but learned of Connolly's working-class ideology and his conception of industrial unions only later on—in America.

Because of its involvement in the Republican movement, the Quill family was harassed by the "Black and Tans" after the end of World War I. Black and Tans was a name given to British ex-servicemen, recruited as auxiliaries to regular British troops, to counteract the guerilla campaign of the IRA in Ireland. Their dark caps and khaki pants inspired the name, but the tactics they employed made them a symbol of British terrorism.

When finally the British had tired of the endless upheavals, they agreed to negotiate for peace. The treaty with Britain, consummated by Michael Collins, which, among other things, called for an oath of allegiance to the Crown, gave Dominion status to Ireland and partitioned the island and touched off a civil war between those who accepted it and those who opposed it. The Quill family joined the antitreaty cause in the conflict and sent several of its sons to fight. Mike Quill, then only a teenager, was involved in what appears to have been a limited extent. When it was resolved in favor of the protreaty, or Free State Forces, in 1923, the demobilized sons decided that leaving for America was their only course.

Mike Quills's brother John left in 1924, and he himself sailed from Cobh in March of 1926. When, at length, he became a ticket agent for the Interboro Rapid Transit Company, the Great Depression had descended upon the nation. Conditions of work were unacceptable. Alternate employment was almost nonexistent. Something had to be done. Experience with Irish republicanism suggested a way to do it.

THE TWU CAMPAIGN

Organizing the Transport Workers Union is almost a metaphor for a rising in Ireland. Its details contain most of the ingredients of an Irish story. For oppressive denial of human rights, there are oppressive transit companies exploiting transplanted Irish peasants with low wages, long hours and abysmal working conditions; providing the illusion of self-rule without the substance, there is a company union. Bona fide attempts of workers to secure a voice in affairs of their own shops are defeated through infiltrators in the form of labor spies and company-bribed informers. Failure to accept the tyranny of absentee owners is not met with eviction from the land, but by discharge and blacklisting.

The enemy is the target of a conspiracy of young Irishmen sworn to secrecy. Its style is that of the Fenians with their circles and centres. A nucleus of leaders consists of veterans of the Irish Republican Army, toughened in campaigns against British forces and by terms in British prisons. Members confound their opponents by communicating in Gaelic. Many are from the west of Ireland and speak it fluently.

Their leader rises from the ranks; a man of limited education, but blossoming talents for mockery of authority, using wit and humor as well as bombast. He has the heavy brogue of the Kerryman, usually found engaging by his audience. He has suffered the greenhorn's agony of adjustment to America. He has worked in the subway. He is Mike Quill.

The conspirators must counteract opposition from much of the Roman Catholic clergy with its apocalyptic dread of secret organizations. The movement has an anticlerical caste; however, some less orthodox priests—Fr. Charles Owen Rice of Pittsburgh, for example—support it, even champion it. An important element of the Irish community consists of later generations of earlier arrivals, by now middle class and establishment oriented, disdainful of unions. Some are even executives of the transit companies themselves and fill the ears of their clerical friends with the dangers of workers' associations. *The Brooklyn Tablet*, a conservative Catholic paper, blasts the TWU from the union's inception.

The movement seeks allies wherever they can be had, regardless of their ulterior motives, as did the United Irishmen with the French in 1798. It finds Marxists to be helpful accomplices and effective in converting members to Leninism. The public image of the TWU shows itself to have a pinkish complexion.

New York has been the major port of entry for immigrants since early in the nineteenth century—for those from Ireland in particular. Substantial numbers of Irish settled in the city and constituted an Irish community, which was regularly augmented by newer immigrants. During the 1920s Irish immigration to the United States continued to average twenty thousand a year.[63] One important source of employment for these newcomers was the transit industry in the city.

Because they spoke English and were willing to work for a relatively low wage, it was customary for New York transit companies to hire Irish immigrants for semiskilled jobs involving contact with passengers. They were represented in lesser numbers in nonoperating jobs in car barns, repair shops, maintenance of the way divisions and powerhouses—in all of which skill requirements varied widely. It was common for the Irish to work for transit companies temporarily until better alternatives opened up. They left because it was a low paying, undesirable line of work in which one was compelled to join company unions and pay dues for the membership. In addition, hours were excessively long, working conditions were poor and, for operating crews especially, fraught with safety hazards. Conditions worsened significantly in the Depression when the labor market was flooded with hungry competitors. Turnover fell sharply.

Beginning in 1923 refugees from the civil war in Ireland, a number of them veterans of the IRA, began to appear in New York. Men such as Austin Hogan, from Cork City, and Tom O'Shea, a chemist of sorts, who had manufactured explosives for the Republican Army, arrived. Gerald O'Reilly, a conductor for Interboro Rapid Transit, earning forty cents an hour, met Mike Quill at a gathering of the Clan na Gael Club in New York. Other members of Clan na Gael were also transit workers.

Clan na Gael was the closest thing to a successor of the Fenian Brotherhood in America. Founded in 1867, it was originally dedicated to financial support for the Fenians. A secret society pledged to republicanism, its dominant personality was John Devoy.[64] In any case, by the 1920s it still retained its militant republican flavor and welcomed former IRA men. Quill had become prominent in New York's immigrant Irish community as a nattily dressed, witty and gregarious figure who was master of ceremonies for numerous dances sponsored by Clan na Gael. Such associations in Irish neighborhoods subsequently offered an excellent base for organizing.

Quill, Hogan, O'Reilly, O'Shea and perhaps eight or nine other IRA veterans played an essential role in the incubation of the TWU. Quill himself acknowledged the "dedication of volunteers who had built the TWU—the hardcore Irish revolutionaries, whose devotion to the nationalist cause had been tested in guerrilla warfare. The men who became such excellent trade unionists had endured the brutalities of British jails and prison camps."[65]

The Communist party also figured importantly in the history of the TWU. William Z. Foster's handiwork is evident in the party's earliest efforts to unionize the transit workers. The party had established Irish workers' clubs in the city for that purpose, and it was in one of them that Austin Hogan, who had earned a degree as a civil engineer in night school, first embraced the organizing campaign and the party. Mike Quill and Gerald O'Reilly were members of an Irish workers' club as well.[66]

Hogan was tutored by two apprentice party functionaries, Maurice Forge from Russia, who had Americanized his name, and John Santo, a Hungarian with an incongruous brogue acquired through working with Irish subway men. Both became officials in the TWU. Quill also looked to the party for help. It was only after the Ancient Order of Hibernians, Friendly Sons of Saint Patrick's and Knights of Columbus, with their middle-class respectability, had turned him down flat, that he did so. He confessed to Fr. Rice of having become a party member, but his accusers were never able to prove it because he arranged to have his records stolen from party files before his public break with the Communists in 1948.[67]

Successfully organizing a union in the face of hostile employers calls for certain qualities of discipline: ability to plan secretly, courage to take grave risks and refusal to be intimidated by threats. Alumni of guerrilla campaigns in Ireland possessed these talents. Single men in their late twenties to early thirties, they were adept at maintaining secrecy so necessary in the early stages of organizing. Their contacts with other employees were clandestine. Potential informers were excluded, and they succeeded in confusing company spies, or "beakies" (a label derived from H.L. Beakie, head of security for Interboro Rapid Transit Lines).[68] Roadblocks set up by transit firms had defeated a number of earlier attempts to organize bona fide unions on the subways. They were, however, unequal to the task of preventing the TWU from establishing a foothold even before section 7(a) of the National Industrial Recovery Act afforded employees some protection to organize.

Those who founded the TWU were not lacking in inspiration for strategy and structure. They found it in the example and writings of James Connolly. Men who knew of him only as a martyr in the rising of 1916 were apprised, if not by their fellow Irishmen, then by their Communist allies, of his role as cofounder with James Larkin of the Irish Transport and General Workers Union in Dublin, and his vigorous espousal of industrial unionism and of his disparagement of the craft approach of the AFL when he was an organizer for the Industrial Workers of the World (IWW) in New York. Mike Quill became acquainted with his ideas when one of his colleagues in the Irish Workers' Club (probably James Gralton) supplied him with a pamphlet Connolly wrote, entitled "Axe to the Root."[69] Connolly's socialist ideology and advocacy of an Irish Peoples Republic—to be achieved by thorough economic organizing followed by political action—had a powerful appeal. The choice of the name transport workers (rarely used in the United States for a union), rather than transit workers, is said to reflect the influence of Larkin and Connolly and their Dublin union.[70]

Quill met Elizabeth Gurley Flynn on one occasion, and she regaled him with accounts of her friendship with James Connolly—of their campaigning together for the Wobblies, of Joe Hill, Bill Haywood and the rest. By now a leader of the Communist party, she could speak of personal associations with nearly all the leftwing radicals, active since the turn of the century. He was excited by the tales of hearing Mother Jones speak, of visits by James Larkin and her battles to free Tom Mooney and save Sacco and Vanzetti. He admired her wit, charm and rebellious nature. The encounter was a challenge to the impatience he was beginning to feel with the party.[71] By 1947 Quill found William Z. Foster, who succeeded Earl Browder as head of the American Communist party, increasingly rigid and arrogant, making it difficult to deal with him.[72]

The Communist connection cut both ways. While it was a help in the beginning, where very little help was forthcoming from other sources, it tended to disturb rank-and-file employees and further alienate the older, more conservative Irish-Catholic community. To counteract this effect, Mike Quill and some of his friends appeared frequently at Sunday Mass in Irish neighborhoods. In the early 1930s these considerations also prompted the decision not to affiliate the TWU officially with W.Z. Foster's Trade Union Unity League, designed as a leftwing rival for the AFL.[73]

The TWU cause was also aided by the Association of Catholic Trade Unionists (ACTU), which propagated papal encyclicals (Rerum Novarum and Quadrogesimo Anno) endorsing workers' rights to organize. ACTU also challenged red-baiting and insisted on proof of party membership before criticizing TWU officials. It was equally concerned with corruption in old-line AFL unions, like the International Longshoremen's Association (ILA) led by Joe Ryan. One inspiration for the ACTU was Fr. John Monaghan, a professor at Cathedral College in New York City, who was known as a scourge of the corrupt leadership of the ILA. Monaghan was the original chaplain of ACTU.

The ACTU grew out of the Catholic Worker Movement in New York, established by former left-wing journalist and recent convert Dorothy Day and peasant philosopher Peter Maurin. That organization opposed both communism and American capitalism with a program sometimes calling itself Catholic anarchism. It denounced middle-class Catholics buying into the individualistic ethos of American society as a distortion of their religious values. Its "green revolution" or "back to the land" program did not contemplate labor unions, but it spoke out against detractors of labor leaders, in general, and Quill, in particular, in its penny-per-issue paper *The Catholic Worker*, which it handed out on the picket line in competition with *The Daily Worker*. Thus liberal elements of the Catholic community were, on balance, a source of strength for the TWU.[74]

The first president of TWU was Tom O'Shea of County Cork, who worked as a turnstile maintenance man. He soon proved to be a liability when he advocated the use of dynamite as an organizing device and expressed an extreme anticlericalism, which earned him the title of "pope roaster." He was not popular in the transit work force, especially with those who were practicing Catholics. Late in 1935, Mike Quill became his successor in a makeshift election. By 1938 O'Shea had turned against the Communist party. He subsequently became a regular witness before the House Committee on Un-American Activities, chaired by Martin Dies of Texas. In testimony he accused Quill, Hogan and others in the TWU leadership of being members of the party.[75]

Those who analyzed Quill's leadership have found it a paradox. He was capable of outlandish mockery of authority. For example, he was accustomed to refer to New York Mayor John Lindsay (whom he thoroughly disliked) as "Mayor Lindsley." At the same time, he was motivated by a sincere idealism to improve the working lives of rank-and-file members. He hewed to the party line consistently until 1948, but spurned the discipline of long sessions in party gatherings, listening to the perorations of its leaders. His theatricality had a definite purpose— to advance the interest of his organization and the membership. In the words of Charles Owen Rice, who celebrated his funeral mass at Saint Patrick's Cathedral (something of a paradox in itself), "He was a sincere champion of the people, particularly the distressed and disinherited. He loved the labor movement and wanted it strong, honest and efficient. He ran a good union with complete honesty and had no care for personal wealth or luxury."[76]

Quill led the TWU into the CIO in 1937 and received a charter signed by John L. Lewis, whom he admired. He became a member of the executive board of that federation and an important spokesman at its conventions. When Lewis was making his valedictory before the CIO, Quill was visible among the left-wing faction calling for the convention to reject Lewis's resignation and restore him to the presidency.[77] It was a tribute to Philip Murray's restraint and Quill's pragmatism that they were able to get along after the departure of John L. Lewis.

Mike Quill, at the head of the Transport Workers Union, had been a reliable follower of the party line, thus earning the nickname of "Red Mike." He, however, saw the handwriting on the wall in the spring of 1948, and began to free himself from his left-wing moorings. By the time it became clear that the "Dump Truman" movement was going nowhere and that Murray was solidly committed to Truman, Quill leaped on the bandwagon. With a preemptive blast at former admirers at *The Daily Worker*, he not only joined the Democratic camp, but also spared his union from expulsion from the CIO. His road ahead was a rocky one, however, because there was an abundance of entrenched left-wing officials in the TWU, who did not concur with his ideological about-face.

Another bone of contention between Quill and the Communist party was the question of a ten-cent subway fare. For many years the fare had been held at five cents, and the now city-owned system was proposing to double it. Quill believed that was essential if he were to accomplish the wage and benefit increases he had in mind. Party wheelhorses, particularly William Z. Foster, then general secretary of the party, made this the issue on which they would make their stand— five cents and no more! They argued that working people should not be burdened with a higher fare for transportation. Now denunciations rained down on the former darling of the party. No invective was too extreme for "Mike Judas Quill."

The skirmish in the TWU was played out in the TWU convention in Chicago in December of 1948. Quill assured support for himself through attendance of delegates from New York (Local 100), San Francisco and other locals on whose loyalty he could rely. Their expenses were financed by loans from the CIO and the steelworkers union, arranged with the help of Philip Murray, and through a loan from the bank of the Amalgamated Clothing Workers Union. He also accommodated delegates from the Philadelphia local, second largest in the TWU, in this way and bargained for their votes by pledging to endorse their president for an office in the international union.[78] The convention was marked by a parade of victories for the opponents of communism. First, the convention abolished the jobs in the International held by party liners Austin Hogan and John Santo. Second, all Communist party members were voted off the executive board. Quill defeated Hogan, who ran against him for the office of international president. Hogan was also faced with a recall petition signed by 15,000 members of Local 100 of which he was still president. Gustav Faber, who had rallied to support Quill, defeated a party-lining candidate, Hugh O'Donnell, for the office of secretary-treasurer of the union. Finally, an amendment was passed that restricted Communists or their "consistent supporters" from holding any office or position in the union. Significantly, the convention was addressed by Reverend Daniel Cantwell, chaplain of the Catholic Labor Alliance in Chicago.[79]

With this development, the problem of communism in the TWU seems to have been resolved. Of the purgation in the TWU, *The Labor Leader* (organ of the ACTU), spoke thus;

Something that the ACTU has worked and fought and prayed for since its founding almost twelve years ago happened this month in Chicago when the convention of the Transport Workers, CIO, threw out its communist leaders and became an American trade union.[80]

The ACTU did not claim primary credit for the ultimate evaporation of Communist strength in the TWU. It could only point to the previous attempt, which it had advised and supported. The final push, according to a journalist who studied the postwar phase of pro- and anticommunist strife in the TWU, was to a significant extent due to the work of two local union officials, Ray Wescott and John Brooks of Section 505 of Local 100, who had been trained by Reverend Phillip Carey, S.J., of the Xavier Labor School in New York City.[81]

DEDUCTIONS

John Brophy and Philip Murray exemplify important contributions of the Irish to American unions. Apprenticed in the hard school of the mining industry—in Great Britain and the United States—they had an intimate knowledge of how difficult the lives of working people could be. As a result of family and personal experiences very early in life, they became convinced that trade unions were the major hope of improvement. Exposure to socialist ideology was a factor in their outlook as well. It is evident in the youthful experience of Murray while in Scotland. It prompted Harold Ruttenberg to declare that Philip Murray was a socialist.[82] Brophy's association with the Brookwood School for Workers and his advocacy of nationalizing the mining industry (at one time) testify to this fact, as does his acceptance of support from left-wing groups in his electoral challenge to John L. Lewis in the UMW.

Nevertheless, in their mature years, neither of these men became a socialist, ideologically or otherwise. They were thoroughly committed trade unionists who also favored government assistance for workers and their organizations—evident in their support for the Roosevelt and Truman administrations—in contrast to John L. Lewis, who moved to a posture of independence from, if not hostility, toward government.

It is accurate to describe Murray and Brophy as pragmatists who sampled various ideologies, rejected some, tolerated some and finally (being devoutly religious) embraced a theory of industrial democracy, borrowed heavily from ideas of the Roman Catholic Church. It involved cooperative labor-management relations, national planning and a significant degree of government participation. The Industrial Council Plan, suggested by Pope Pius XI in 1931, was a major source of inspiration.[83] Murray proposed a program of industry councils to President Roosevelt in December of 1940, as a means to advance the defense effort and assure full employment and production in the postwar years. A year later, he outlined the plan at the CIO convention in Detroit on November 17, 1941—only weeks before Japan attacked Pearl Harbor.[84] He continued to promote the plan at each annual convention of the CIO until he died. Brophy was equally keen and persistent in evangelizing for the Industry Council Plan.

Murray and Brophy remained enthusiastic in their support of New Deal and Fair Deal administrations after John L. Lewis opted out. As such, they represented important elements in the coalition of labor, farming and black and white ethnics, which was the backbone of Democratic successes in those years. Furthermore, they bought into, indeed, promoted the idea of an American welfare state. Their pragmatism, their concept of social justice influenced by Catholic social teaching, enabled them to view activist government favorably.

These two men displayed thorough understanding of the need for ethnic and racial cohesion in the trade union movement. It was essential to their effectiveness as district leaders in the UMW. It was conspicuously evident in Murray's sensitivity to and understanding of the feelings of ethnic groups in his handling of the SWOC campaign—a remarkably successful one.

Note also that, although late-coming immigrants, these two men had little difficulty in rising to leadership positions in the union movement. Their contemporaries arriving from Eastern and Southern Europe were a generation or more behind in coming to comparable positions of leadership in labor organizations. This may, in part, be explained by the fluency in English enjoyed by Brophy and Murray, while those from Italian and Slavic areas of Europe lacked this important advantage. Another aspect which handicapped such immigrants was their lack of exposure to trade unionism, an institution both Murray and Brophy were intimately acquainted with from childhood.

Mike Quill was a generation younger than Murray and Brophy. He came directly from a rural background in the west of Ireland as a refugee from the civil war there in 1921-1922. He is, therefore, unlike them in having personal experience in revolutionary activity. Another difference lies in the fact that he came with no familiarity of trade unionism. But he, like nearly all Irish immigrants, found conditions of work in America oppressive and badly in need of reform.

Quill's story dramatizes how revolution in Ireland led to infusion of new spirit into American unions. His career demonstrates how militance in the cause of Irish liberation was transformed into dedication for the cause of organized labor. The men with whom he built the TWU were also revolutionaries—hardened in British prisons and courts.

They, like Quill, were willing to risk everything for the sake of alleviating intolerable working conditions. Skills learned in Irish risings served them well for secretly organizing a new association of workers, where earlier attempts had all failed. They were alert to the hazards of spies and informers. They made effective use of their command of Gaelic to confound these stumbling blocks.

Originally from a land politically aroused almost continually in its history, Quill and his cohorts had little difficulty in entering the political arena in the United States. Political activism was viewed as a necessary means of protecting the transport workers' organization. Quill's somewhat outlandish rhetoric was effective in his career as a member of the New York City Council (under the aegis of the American Labor party) as well as in his dealings with transit employers. It was useful early on, when these firms were privately owned, and even more advantageous later when they were municipally owned. His orotund personality made him equally visible in the councils of the CIO as one of its national vice presidents.

Coming from radical movements in Ireland, these men were receptive to involvement with radical organizations in America, which could help their cause. On the other hand, Quill and others were sufficiently pragmatic to abandon Communist associations when they became liabilities to the Transport Workers Union in the period after World War II. When forced to choose between loyalty to the CIO and loyalty to the Communist party, Quill successfully detached the TWU from its Marxist connections. In doing so, all of his political skills were severely tested. Thereby, belief that he was a mere figurehead of TWU was dispelled for good.

Quill's break with the left was marked by the characteristic bombast and humor for which he developed a special flair—well suited to street-corner or convention oratory and television appearances. Almost the last television image of Mike Quill was that of him tearing up a court injunction against a strike by TWU in 1966 while intoning, "That judge can drop dead in his black robes." For this impudence he was jailed, hospitalized, and shortly, released. In the interim, he had approved a settlement of the dispute with modish Mayor Lindsay (for whom he held only contempt) on terms favorable to the TWU. He died soon thereafter.[85]

In spite of Quill's disenchantment with much of the Catholic clergy and the doubtfulness of his own religious faith, he was accorded a funeral mass from the Roman Catholic Church (in New York's Saint Patrick's Cathedral) according to his own wishes.

NOTES

1. John Brophy, *A Miner's Life* (Madison: University of Wisconsin Press, 1964), 9–10. Information about Brophy is drawn from his autobiography except as otherwise noted.

2. Ibid., 10; Lawrence J. McCaffrey, *Ireland from Colony to Nation State* (Englewood Cliffs, N.J.: Prentice Hall, 1979), 106-8. The word boycott was coined in 1880 as a term meaning to shun agents of a landlord—famously in the case of an estate managed by Charles Cunningham Boycott.

3. Brophy, *A Miner's Life*, 13, 78.

4. Civil Records of Births, Bothwell, 1886; Census of 1891, Civil Parish of Bothwell, Enumeration District No. 2, p. 50. (Both in General Register Office, Edinburgh.) The distinction is not of major significance since both towns were mining communities located across the River Clyde from each other. The Murray family, in fact, lived in both communities at various times. But, in the interest of accuracy, it should be pointed out.

5. Civil Records of Births, Auchinstarry, 1884; Civil Records of Marriage, Blantyre, 1884. (Both in General Register Office, Edinburgh.)

6. *Pittsburgh Sun Telegraph*, March 10, 1937, 8.

7. Census of 1891, Civil Parish of Bothwell, Enumeration District No. 2, p. 50. (General Register Office, Edinburgh.)

8. Ibid.

9. Cecil Woodham-Smith, *The Great Hunger* (New York: Harper and Row, 1962), Chap. 16; McCaffrey, *Ireland from Colony to Nation State*, 64-69.

10. Alan B. Campbell, *The Lanarkshire Miners* (Edinburgh: J. Donald Publishers, 1979), Chap. 7, "The Irish"; R. Page Arnot, *A History of Scottish Miners* (London: Allen and Unwin, 1955), 193.

11. Campbell, *The Lanarkshire Miners*, 197; Arnot, *A History of Scottish Miners*, 193.

12. Civil Records of Deaths, Blantyre, 1887. (General Register Office, Edinburgh.) John Chamberlain, "Philip Murray," *Life*, February 11, 1946, 86.

13. Census of 1891, Civil Parish of Bothwell, Enumeration District No. 2, p. 50. (General Register Office, Edinburgh.) Chamberlain, "Philip Murray," 86.

14. Obituary of Philip Murray, *Blantyre Gazette*, November 15, 1952, 3; obituary of Philip Murray, *Hamilton Advertiser*, November 15, 1952, 13.

15. Arnot, *A History of Scottish Miners*, 76-88; Chamberlain, "Philip Murray," 86.

16. *Blantyre Gazette*, November 15, 1952, 3.

17. Arnot, *A History of Scottish Miners, 92; Current Biography*, 1941, 601; Chamberlain, "Philip Murray," 86.

18. Letter to Philip Murray from his cousin Peter Finney of Blantyre, dated August 27, 1943, in which he writes, "Your old friend Andrew McNulty [*sic*] is still going strong and going well. I often have a conversation with him but he has retired from political affairs owing to his age." Philip Murray Papers, Labor Archives, Pattee Library, Pennsylvania State University, University Park, Pennsylvania.

19. Arnot, *A History of Scottish Miners*, 91.

20. Ibid., 53, 60-61.

21. *Blantyre Gazette*, November 15, 1952, 3; Arnot, *A History of Scottish Miners*, see chart of coal wages and prices facing p. 110; Chamberlain, "Philip Murray," 86.

22. Brophy, *A Miner's Life*, 63.

23. Chamberlain, "Philip Murray," 86.

24. *Current Biography*, 1941, 601.

25. Oral history interview no. 1 with Pat Fagan, September 24, 1968, Pennsylvania State University, University Park, Pennsylvania, 9 (hereinafter referred to as Fagan no. 1); Chamberlain, "Philip Murray," 79. (71, 76 on reprint.)

26. Brophy, *A Miner's Life*, Chaps. 2, 3, 5–8. These chapters describe the numerous moves of the Brophy family and the hardships that brought them about.

27. Ibid., 73–81.

28. Fagan no. 1, 9; Chamberlain, "Philip Murray," 86–89.

29. Fagan no. 1, 14.

30. Brophy, *A Miner's Life*, 134–5.

31. Melvin Dubofsky and Warren Van Tine, *John L. Lewis* (New York: Quadrangle Books, 1977), 32.

32. Fagan no. 1, 16–17.

33. Brophy, *A Miner's Life*, 133.

34. Dubofsky and Van Tine, *John L. Lewis*, 127. According to these authors, Brophy welcomed support from Communists under W. Z. Foster's leadership in the election contest with Lewis. See also Selig Perlman and Philip Taft, *History of Labor in United States, 1896–1932* (New York: Macmillan, 1935), Chap. 61, "The Eclipse of Coal Unionism," espec. 564–68 on the Save the Union Committee led by John Brophy. In 1928 a dual union, The National Miner's Union, was established by W.Z. Foster's Trade Union Unity League without participation of Brophy or other Progressives. See Perlman and Taft, *History of Labor*, 568.

35. Saul Alinsky, *John L. Lewis* (New York: Vintage Books, 1970), 37–38.

36. See letter from Lewis to Brophy, C. J. Golden and William Smith, dated October 7, 1921, which created the committee, Brophy Papers, Archives, Mullen Library, Catholic University of America, Washington, D.C. Brophy, *A Miner's Life*, Chaps. 12 and 13. Lewis made a show of interest in nationalization at this time because he was preparing to contest Samuel Gompers for the presidency of the AFL and hoped to attract support of Progressives in the AFL.

37. Brophy, *A Miner's Life*, 211–12; Dubofsky and Van Tine, *John L. Lewis*, 92–93.

38. Brophy, *A Miner's Life*, 96.

39. See Pius XI, Quadrogesimo Anno, encyclical letter 1931, New York, America Press, no date, paragraphs 81–96.

40. Fagan no. 1, 10; Fagan no. 2, October 1, 1968, 7.

41. Dubofsky and Van Tine, *John L. Lewis*, 39; Fagan no. 2, 7.

42. Statement of John L. Lewis, quoted in R.E.S. Thompson, "Murray of the Miners Tackles a New Contract," *New York Times Magazine*, February 14, 1937, 8.

43. Brophy, *A Miner's Life*, 137.

44. For an example of Murray's opposition, see *United Mine Workers Journal*, December 1, 1926, 3–4.

45. Dubofsky and Van Tine, *John L. Lewis*, 222.

46. Brophy, *A Miner's Life*, v–vi.

47. David Brody, "The Origins of Modern Steel Unionism: The SWOC Era," in *Forging a Union in Steel*, Paul F. Clark, Peter Gottlieb and Donald Kennedy eds. (Ithaca, N.Y.: ILR Press, Cornell University, 1987), 13–29.

48. Fagan no. 1, 19; David Brody, *Labor in Crisis: The Steel Strike of 1919* (New York: Lippincott, 1965), 90–93.

49. Brody, "Origins of Modern Steel Unionism," 26, 29; quote of Harold Ruttenberg testifying to Murray's toughness, is from Clark, Gottlieb and Kennedy, *Forging a Union in Steel*, 129–30.

50. Description of the organizing campaign is based on "The CIO's Culture of Unity," a section of Chapter 6 of Lisabeth Cohen, *Making a New Deal: Industrial Workers in Chicago, 1919–1939* (Cambridge, England: Cambridge University Press, 1990), 333–49.

196 Irish Voice and Organized Labor

51. Brody, "Origins of Modern Steel Unionism," 27. Originally, SWOC operated on the basis of a memorandum of agreement with the moribund Amalgamated Association of Iron, Steel and Tin Workers, which held an AFL charter granting it jurisdiction over skilled workers in this industry. The union had been strong until it was defeated in the Homestead strike of 1892, after which it steadily declined. See David Brody, *Steelworkers in America: The Nonunion Era* (New York: Harper and Row, 1969); Brody, "Origins of Modern Steel Unionism," 20.

52. Brody, "Origins of Modern Steel Unionism," 27–28. Labor scholars of the New Left, who emerged in the 1960s and 1970s, are critical of Murray for curbing rank-and-file militancy in the 1930s and during World War II, when unions adopted a no-strike pledge. Reminiscent of the ideology of C. Wright Mills (in *The Power Elite*, etc.), they argue that the War Labor Board, with CIO cooperation, fostered a bureaucratic system of industrial relations that operated contrary to shop floor interests of workers. In their eyes, the system, relying heavily on the labor contract and its administration by the grievance-arbitration process, foreclosed the opportunity for a more fundamental change toward workplace democracy. They believe the system is manipulative, serves to maintain discipline in the work force, preserves power for corporate employers and stifles voices of the rank and file.

In addition, they argue that Murray erred in associating too closely with the Democratic party, specifically the Roosevelt and Truman administrations. Murray's strong support for both administrations contrasts with the position of John L. Lewis, whose alienation and independence from Roosevelt (beginning in the late 1930s) and continuing through Truman's presidency in the postwar period, was, in their view, the correct policy and in the best interests of workers. It is their belief that to become dependent on government is a seriously unwise policy with damaging effects on working people. Needless to say, they do not share Murray's attitude toward dealing with the issue of communism in unions.

For a sampling of the work of the New Left see Harry Braverman, *Labor and Monopoly Capitalism* (New York: Monthly Review Press, 1974); Nelson Lichtenstein, *Labor's War at Home: the CIO and World War II* (Cambridge, England: Cambridge University Press, 1982); Ronald Radosh, *American Labor and United States Foreign Policy* (New York: Random House, 1970); Ronald W. Schatz, "Philip Murray and the Subordination of the Industrial Unions to the United States Government," in *Labor Leaders in America*, Melvyn Dubofsky and Warren Van Tine eds. (Urbana: University of Illinois Press, 1987), 234–57.

For an analysis of New Left ideas by a respected scholar who does not subscribe to their views see David Brody, *In Labor's Cause* (New York: Oxford University Press, 1993), Chap. 6.

53. Matthew Josephson, *Sidney Hillman Labor Statesman* (New York: Doubleday, 1952), 492–93, 497, 502; Oral history interview no. 1 with Msgr. Charles Owen Rice, October 17, 1967, Pennsylvania State University, University Park, Pennsylvania, 13; Dubofsky and Van Tine, *John L. Lewis*, 369; Saul Alinsky, *John L. Lewis: An Unauthorized Biography* (New York: Putnam, 1949) 220–25.

54. Interview with Msgr. Charles O. Rice by author, Castleshannon, Pennsylvania, November 23, 1983. This assertion is discounted by Dubofsky

and Van Tine in their biography, *John L. Lewis*, 308. Their basis is deduction, not evidence.

55. Dubofsky and Van Tine, *John L. Lewis*, 408.

56. Other sources label it a heart attack, but Joseph Murray, the son of Philip Murray, says it was a pancreas attack. Interview with Joseph Murray by author, Pittsburgh, November 22, 1983.

57. Ibid.

58. Bert Cochran, *Labor and Communism* (Princeton, N.J.: Princeton University Press, 1977), Chap. 7, "Political Strikes in Defense Period."

59. Ibid., 206–20.

60. Ibid., 266–71, 297–301.

61. Daily Proceedings of Twelfth Constitutional Convention of the CIO, Chicago, Monday, November 20, 1950, 18-19 (report on expulsion of Communist-dominated unions):

We have made much headway in the course of the past twelve months. I am proud to report that despite the fact that you authorized your officers and your Executive Board one year ago this month to kick some ugly elements, some traitors out of your movement, we accepted your mandate. The Board, through its special committees conducted hearings of the officers of many of these International unions formerly affiliated with CIO, and through the democratic process of trial provided these people an opportunity to present their point of view and their testimony to our committees. Your CIO Executive Board and its committees found Mine-Mill, Food-Tobacco, United Office and Professional Workers, United Public Workers, American Communications, International Fur and Leather Workers, International Longshoreman and Warehousemen's Union, the Marine Cooks and Stewards, International Fisherman and Allied Workers guilty—found them guilty of operating communistically controlled unions, and we expelled them. We want no truck with them. We want nothing to do with them. We provided a way for other segments of our national population to do likewise, and while the Tafts and others decry and condemn and castigate the CIO, when it suits the wishes of Taft he votes Communist in the Congress of the United States. We don't—we expel them. That's the difference.

In addition to the unions that I have enumerated here two other unions also left us, because they were going to be removed—the old UE and the Farm Equipment Organizations. So here we have a total of eleven national and international unions formerly affiliated with CIO who are no longer with us, and the reason that they are no longer with us is because you don't want them. Naturally one would assume and expect that where such a large number of unions were expelled and removed from our councils that the CIO and its affiliates would experience considerable difficulty in rehabilitating and reorganizing those organizations, bringing their membership back into our fold. The action of Cleveland Convention in November, 1949 resulted in the removal from membership in our various international unions a total of about 850,000 to 900,000 members. During the past year we have brought back into our organizations approximately 70 per cent of all the members of these organizations there were expelled from our union. So that as of today, despite the expulsion of this crowd, your organization is numerically stronger that it was twelve months ago, and despite the use of large sums of money to reorganize the workers employed in these industries, we find that our organization as of today is not only financially solvent, but more strongly entrenched financially than it was twelve months ago.

62. The section on Mike Quill and the Transport Workers Union relies heavily upon the following sources: Joshua Freeman, *In Transit* (New York: Oxford University Press, 1989); Joshua Freeman, "Irish Workers in the Twentieth Century United States: The Case of the Transport Workers Union," *Saothar: Journal of the Irish Labor History Society* 8 (1982): 24–45; Shirley Uzin Quill, *Mike Quill—Himself* (New York: Devin-Adair, 1984), a biography of Quill writ-

ten by his second wife.

63. Freeman, "Irish Workers," 25.

64. See reference in Chapter 3 above ("A Pair of Fenian Rebels").

65. Quill, *Mike Quill—Himself*, 269.

66. Gerald O'Reilly, *The Birth and Growth of the Transport Workers Union*, pamphlet, no date or publisher, 3.

67. Oral history interview no. 2 with Msgr. Charles Owen Rice, Pennsylvania State University, University Park, Pennsylvania, 17.

68. Gerald O'Reilly, "The Story of the TWU," *An Gael Magazine* (Fall 1986): 22.

69. Quill, *Mike Quill—Himself*, 57; O'Reilly, *Birth and Growth of the TWU*, 4.

70. Freeman, "Irish Workers," 29.

71. Quill, *Mike Quill—Himself*, 71; Freeman, *In Transit*, 285.

72. Freeman, *In Transit*, 51.

73. Ibid.

74. See *The Labor Leader* (organ of ACTU), page-one stories: September 18, October 2, November 1, 1939; September 9, 1940; May 18, 1942; November 20, 1947; April 12 and 26, May 30, June 28, November 16, December 28, 1948. While it supported the TWU initially, ACTU eventually became concerned about Communist influence and forcefully criticized its leadership. It was, in turn, attacked by Mike Quill. Eventually the ACTU welcomed Quill's break with Communists, but disapproved of undemocratic practices it attributed to him in opposing them within the TWU.

75. Quill, *Mike Quill—Himself*, 64, 122; Freeman, "Irish Workers," 36.

76. Charles O. Rice, "In Memoriam Quill," *Pittsburgh Catholic*, February 3, 1966, 4.

77. Dubofsky and Van Tine, *John L. Lewis*, 344, 364.

78. Freeman, *In Transit*, 315.

79. *The Labor Leader*, December 27, 1948, 1.

80. Ibid.

81. Jules Weinberg, "Priests, Workers, and Communists," *Harpers*, November 1948, 50-51.

82. Clark, Gottlieb and Kennedy, *Forging a Union in Steel*, 127-30. This is clearly an exaggeration as indicated below. Ruttenberg argues that it caused Murray to be unable to trust business executives. It runs counter to all evidence that Murray was deeply influenced by encyclicals emanating from the Vatican which, to put it mildly, were unalterably opposed to socialism. Ruttenberg's statement may have something to do with his personal decision to leave the CIO to become vice president of Portsmouth Steel Company (owned by Cyrus Eaton). See *Forging a Union in Steel*, 124 (comment by John Hoerr).

83. Pius XI, Quadrogesimo Anno, encyclical letter 1931, paragraphs 81-97.

84. Clinton Golden and Harold J. Ruttenberg, *The Dynamics of Industrial Democracy* (New York: Harper and Brothers, 1942), 323-24, 343-47.

85. The injunction-destroying episode, recorded on television December 30, 1965, remains vivid in the author's memory. See report in the *New York Times*, December 31, 1965, 1, 3. For the story told from his widow's point of view, see Quill, *Mike Quill—Himself*, 3-5.

8

A RISING IN THE WORK FORCE

This exploratory study began with a survey of Irish origins, emigration and encounters with American work life. It provided a context for understanding the twelve trade union leaders examined herein. They were products both of their Irish ancestry and their experience as Irish Americans. The study has discovered traits which, to some degree, all twelve share in common. In presenting conclusions, it will be useful to briefly review both the environment Irish people found in America and their response to it. The Irish legacy for American trade unions will conclude the study.

THE ENVIRONMENT

Irish people entering the United States early in the nineteenth century found no utopia. Their Ulster Presbyterian brothers gravitated to the frontier. There opportunity existed for those willing to deal with Indians, problems of clearing the land and willing to provide their own necessities with rifle, axe and plough. Protestant conceptions of individualism were more in harmony with frontier life. But Catholic Irish, usually more penurious, were not, for the most part, attracted to the wilds or to American agriculture. They tended toward an urban locale partly out of necessity, more importantly, out of preference for a more gregarious life.

In the cities, they found a rapidly commercializing society in the process of linking its various regions with canals, riverboats, coastal and lake vessels and, beginning in the 1830s, railroads. The rapidly expanding market system was subject to wide swings in the level of business activity, which caused difficulty for all economic agents, but particularly for unskilled laborers engaged in work on canals, docks, railroads and construction in the growing cities. Young Irish women

employed in textile mills were equally vulnerable to business recessions. Paid far less than their poorly paid brothers, they still earned
more than their sisters who provided domestic service for American
families of the middle class and above. Admittedly, domestic service
was more genteel, less hazardous than factory work and often involved
in-kind payments in the form of room and board. It could, however, be
arduous, involve very long hours and be most demeaning—depending
on the employing family.

This was a society evolving from its mercantilist origins toward
growing freedom of enterprise—economic individualism was becoming
the order of the day. An inconsistent laissez faire was emerging in
which economic regulation waned, but generous government aid to
business waxed. This aid took the form of land grants, loans, protective
tariffs and the like. Rising American firms required labor, and the gates
were open to immigrants. Recruitment of contract labor was common.

But the Irish navvy was a resource of production to be used only
when needed, but otherwise discarded—certainly not to be accepted as
a citizen on an equal footing. Seen as barely civilized rustics, adhering
to a despised Roman faith, they were regarded as insufficiently grateful
for a sunrise-to-sunset work regimen. Beyond that, they absented themselves to celebrate religious and Irish national holidays—with intemperate use of alcoholic spirits.

Welcomed when hard physical work was to be done (for which earlier arrivals or native Americans were not available), the Irish found no
hospitality extended by the community beyond the work site. American
workers were preferred, and where they were available the "NO IRISH
NEED APPLY" posters went up. Indeed, immigrant labor from Ireland
was viewed as an expedient, useful in keeping wages low and for filling
jobs no one else would perform. Their status differed little from that
Americans accord migrant labor from Mexico and other Latin American
countries today—especially in regard to housing, medical care and so
forth. When overtaken by malaria or typhus while digging a canal
through some marshy backwater, or when broken by a cave-in in a
mine, or a drainage ditch, or a building site, they enjoyed no claim for
care from their employer or society generally. The fifty-seven victims of
cholera buried in a mass grave adjacent to tracks whose roadbed they
had been excavating in 1832 (cited in Chapter 1) offer a vivid example.

As outsiders without social acceptance, Irish immigrants could
expect no more from the commonwealth than their meager earnings
might command. In the balance, their value weighed less than that of
black slaves, who represented a substantial investment by their owners
and required outlays to maintain them in health and vigor for work on
the plantation. An Irishman, should he become debilitated by accident
or illness, could easily be replaced by another hungry immigrant. He
was on his own in the modern world of economic individualism.

Although religious freedom was guaranteed in the young American
republic, Irish Catholic newcomers soon learned that religious intoler-
ance was the rule. It was responsible for a number of painful episodes

of physical violence against Roman Catholic institutions and organizations. Developments in Philadelphia are illustrative of what happened
in a number of other cities. The City of Brotherly Love pioneered establishment of public schools for the benefit of all. The King James version
of the Bible was used in the curriculum. When Catholic Bishop Francis
Patrick Kenrick attempted to maintain religious identity of his flock by
a request that Catholic editions of the (DOUAI) Bible be used for their
children, what followed was an outbreak of anti-Catholic furor.
Subsequent efforts to build a separate Catholic school system were the
result. A defensive posture seemed inevitable.

As the economy grew, corporations became more common, larger in
scale and with greater freedom—less encumbered with mercantilist regulations. Demand for workers expanded and immigration largely satisfied the need. Under the circumstances, employers developed and
refined techniques for exploiting ethnic rivalries in order to maintain
discipline in the labor force. The method was evident as early as 1828
in the C&O Canal project where workers rebelled at missed paydays and
contractors attempted to bring in replacements for the Irish. The ploy
was used at Amesbury and Salisbury, Massachusetts, in 1851, when
native Americans struck and employers recruited newly arrived Irish
immigrants to take their places. Use of outsiders as strikebreakers was
employed in the 1870s at Troy, New York, as well. Racial antagonism
was visible when Irishmen displaced black workers on the New York
docks. It was painfully evident in the draft riots of 1863, where white
workers (mostly Irish) feared freed slaves would compete for their jobs.

The method of using rival, and usually newer, immigrant workers as
strikebreakers was in full flower by the 1880s and threatened all efforts
to establish effective labor organizations. Overcoming this obstacle was
probably the number one challenge for trade unions in the United
States where the work force was an assembly of immigrants from an
increasingly wide variety of nations, cultures and languages. Solidarity
was a near impossibility in such an atmosphere and under the fostering
American spirit of individualism.

Unions in the United States were a creation of skilled craft workers.
Their origins rarely involved any Irish Catholics, nearly all of whom came
from rural areas with experience only in agriculture. The early unions thus
reflected what had been the predominant ethnic composition of the population—Anglo-Saxon Protestant with additional Welsh, Scottish and Ulster
Protestant elements. The character of these unions, therefore, made them
unreceptive to inroads of unskilled Irish Catholic newcomers. Craft unionists displayed nativist tendencies found in the rest of the society and,
according to David Montgomery, prized temperance among their members and leaders. Their reluctance to accept the Irish who were, after all,
unskilled, papist and bibulous for the most part—is understandable.

Until the advent of the Knights of Labor, craftsmen demonstrated little
or no concern for their unskilled brethren. In fact, their impatience with
an organization that included substantial numbers of day laborers was a
major reason for the downfall of the Knights of Labor. These circumstances

also explain why Irish names appeared in significant numbers among American labor leaders only late in the nineteenth century—it explains why their acceptance as members and leaders was slow in coming.

As the nineteenth century wore on, capitalist institutions became more deeply rooted in America. Institutions dedicated to the interest of workers, however, suffered deep-seated antagonism at the Bar of Justice. Corporations came to be viewed as legal persons with all the rights and freedoms of persons. The judiciary interpreted the 14th Amendment guarantees of life, liberty and property in a manner that found social reform legislation for protection of employees to be unconstitutional. The conspiracy doctrine (which held that when workers combined to improve wages and hours, they were guilty of a criminal conspiracy) did not disappear after 1842, when the Massachusetts Supreme Court overturned it. Though weakened, the doctrine survived in the form of laws in some states and occasional court decisions in others. The path of the trade union organizer was strewn with injunctions against strikes, boycotts, picketing and the like issued by a judiciary influenced by a philosophy of Social Darwinism. Workers' rights of association were not really defined and constitutionally endorsed until the 1930s. The legal environment prior to that time was a hostile one for organized labor.

THE RESPONSE

The Irish wave of new entrants came from a politically aroused atmosphere. The efforts of nationalist leaders, such as Wolf Tone of the United Irishmen in 1798 and "The Great Liberator" of the 1820s, Daniel O'Connell, had guaranteed that emigrants from Ireland would not only be politically aware, but, also, come with a degree of sophistication in political engagement. Howard Harris's research into the community of Paterson, New Jersey, of the 1820s (cited in Chapter 1) demonstrates the validity of this observation.

While the Irish, by and large, chose not to enter farming, the dominant occupation in nineteenth-century America, they also chose not to resign themselves for long to the oppressive working conditions and insecurity offered by alternatives to the agricultural sector. Admittedly, their early adaptation was torturous—their presence in prisons, insane asylums and poorhouses provides ample evidence of this observation. But as early as the 1820s, we find them combining to force employers on the C&O Canal to be forthcoming with pay those employers had failed to deliver when due. Their informal combinations were evident throughout the canal building era in all parts of the nation where it took place—and in Canada. In the 1830s, along the Schuylkill River in Philadelphia, an informal association of dock workers struck for a ten-hour day; and, keeping replacements at bay, achieved it.

Irishmen came together to secure and control work on the waterfront in Manhattan. In the anthracite region of Pennsylvania, they rebelled at injustices in the mining camps and alternated between violent tactics and collective bargaining in collaboration with miners of other nationalities until negotiating failed, at which point, more drastic methods were revived. In each case, successes were temporary, but they do illustrate the Irish proclivity for combining for economic protection. Their organizations, usually limited to Irishmen at this stage, were based upon neighborhood, parish, fire company—any convenient gathering place in proximity to a work site. The resemblance to rural bodies of men formed to resist oppression in the old country are too strong to ignore.

The picture that emerges from these stories is not one of a docile or resigned displaced peasantry. It is one rather of a combative people neither illiterate nor without political comprehension—ready to challenge conditions believed to be responsible for their low estate. More accurately, it is a picture of those immigrants who survived, mentally and physically intact, the initial shock of facing the realities of the new world they entered. They adapted. But a supine acceptance does not correctly describe their response.

They came with resources of determination, political will and an ability to combine for mutual protection. Their learning curve was a sharply rising one. In time, they were able to surmount their original isolation and join with those of other nationalities and religions to forge effective union organizations in the face of unrelenting opposition of American business.

As Irish immigrants or their children became more visible in skilled or semiskilled work, these attempts to gain a foothold in employment and protect it by means of groups of their own countrymen gradually became less parochial. By the 1870s, collaboration with other ethnic groups had evolved in places like Troy and Cohoes, New York, Paterson, New Jersey, and the textile towns of New England where Irish immigrants had come to find employment. Reservations about their "papist" religion had not disappeared, but their Hibernian nationalist associations and connections with Democratic politics proved advantageous for support of organizing efforts and strikes.

The revival of unions during the Civil War period (after setbacks in the recessions of 1857 and 1860) saw the appearance of modest numbers of Irish in roles as union activists. They were visible in the National Labor Union of that period—a kind of countrywide association of labor organizations. Some of these individuals were immigrants, but more of them were children of immigrants. Their activism seemed almost equally suited for political organizations as for trade unions. Movement from one sphere to the other was not unusual.

The progression from initially protecting their foothold in employment through informal combinations advanced to substantial involvement with formal trade unions in the 1860s. This was followed by emergence of pioneer Irish labor leaders in the 1870s and from there to national prominence in labor movements in the 1880s and thereafter. This pattern, observed by David Montgomery, seems to fit the facts reasonably well.[1]

A unique case, which illustrates Irish unionists gathering support through a network of Irish social and nationalist organizations, including the Ancient Order of Hibernians, Clan na Gael, the Robert Emmet Literary Association, local (Irish) politicians and members of Catholic parishes, is found in a recent study of Butte, Montana, by David Emmons.[2] Taking place in the copper-mining industry there in the late nineteenth and early twentieth century, it is unique in that the Irish were the dominant ethnic group in the community. Even ownership and management of the main employer (Anaconda Copper Mining Company) was held by Irishmen led by Marcus Daly late of County Cavan.

Emmons refers to it as "one of most overwhelmingly Irish cities in the United States."[3] Rather than outsiders, their usual status, the Irish in Butte were insiders. They constituted the largest single ethnic group in the population. After good wages, safer working conditions and steady work, Irish nationalism was uppermost among the concerns of Butte citizens. But labor management cooperation rather than class conscious radicalism was the result. Experienced miners exercised job control in their own behalf exclusively. Working in the mines with inexperienced transients of whatever ethnicity (including Irishmen) was viewed as an unacceptable risk, so hazardous was the business of copper mining. The tight little island of the Butte Miners' Union came to grief over conflicting loyalties aroused by America's entry into World War I and the shift of control over mining operations into the hands of Rockefeller interests.

In addition to political awareness, there are several other reasons for the ascent of the Irish to importance in organized labor. An obvious one is the sheer numbers they contributed to the work force. By an accident of history (the potato famine of the 1840s), they became the first mass immigration to the United States, adding over a million souls to the U.S. population, who were destined almost exclusively to become manual workers.

The timing of their arrival was most significant, as it coincided with the beginning of almost a century-long period of vigorous growth—though one with wide cyclical variations—requiring manual workers to fill innumerable unskilled jobs. The Irish, therefore, were destined to play a key role in the backbreaking work of building what would become a giant among the world's economies. By the same token, they were destined to suffer the widespread exploitation that was part and parcel of it. They were guinea pigs, in a sense, for experimental methods of manipulating immigrant workers—methods made evermore effective as corporations grew in number, size and economic power.

This large segment of laborers could not forever be ignored as potential members by a struggling union movement. While they could be a threat to existing gains of organized workers and were at first manipulated by employers with that objective, once reservations about their popish affiliation and other cultural aspects perceived as unattractive were overcome, they were available to be recruited for support in a multiethnic movement just as they had been in the case of Democratic machines in large American cities.

Irish people, as "classic immigrants," the earliest mass immigrants, were also the ones who remained longest in lower levels of the work force. For at least a century, they were concentrated in occupations below the professional and managerial ranks. One exception was Irish women, usually of the second generation, who had managed to penetrate the teaching and nursing professions in substantial numbers by the turn of the century. But their male counterparts only rarely occupied legal, medical, academic, managerial and similar professions by that time. They had reached levels of skilled craftsmen, foremen, police and fire officers, trainmen, civil service jobs in local government and comparable occupations, but not much beyond that. Only after World War II, as a consequence of the Servicemen's Readjustment Act of 1944, did large numbers of them arrive in the professions and managerial occupations.[4] This being the case, it is not strange that, in many urban communities, unionism became an important part of Irish-American culture.

Although they came saddled with a number of handicaps, one important advantage the Irish had was fluency in the English language. The lack of it was a serious impediment for other immigrants. By the middle of the nineteenth century, approximately 75 percent of all Irish people arriving in America could read and write in English. By 1910 the proportion had risen to 97 percent.[5] This provided a key to understanding many institutions of a modern society—particularly political ones—which was not available to peasants from other nations. Furthermore, these newcomers arose from an oral tradition traceable to the pre-Christian Gaelic age when bards (poets) were accorded highly privileged status for their gifts as storytellers and bearers of the ancient legends of the Celtic race. It persisted in penal times when Catholic Irish were forced to rely on the words of hedge schoolmasters to preserve their heritage. When penal laws were lifted, the British spread their mother tongue through the national schools conducted in English.

In spite of what has been called linguistic imperialism perpetrated by England, the Irish identity was maintained and, if anything, strengthened. Paradoxically, as English came to be more commonly spoken so also did the embrace of Irish nationalism deepen. In America, Hibernians used the English language to inspire allegiance, not only to Irish nationalism, but also to Democratic parties and workers' organizations.

Affinity with the spoken word is essential for leadership in almost any sphere, certainly it is true in that of organized labor. It is fair to say that seven of the twelve figures in this study consistently demonstrated excellence in their ability to communicate with large gatherings. The others were merely effective in that regard. An associate in the labor movement wrote of Peter J. McGuire, "He spoke three languages fluently: English, German and French, and we have never produced an orator to compare with him."[6] McGuire family tradition holds that he tutored his friend Samuel Gompers in the art.[7] In any case, McGuire drew crowds to audit his exhortations for socialism as well as trade unionism all over the country. Mother Jones was an extraordinary agitator, capable of rousing the miners to greater militance to an extent that she was feared by authorities around the nation, and was jailed for her efforts on innumerable occasions whether in West Virginia, Colorado, Pennsylvania or elsewhere. Indeed, she inspired a youthful Gurley Flynn to follow in her footsteps, and this the rebel girl did with comparable success.

The oratorical skills of Terence Powderly, which he carefully cultivated as a young man, were the hinges on which his success in both
politics and the Knights of Labor rested. J.P. McDonnell began igniting
his vocal fireworks as a boy and incensed British authorities in Ireland
and England before stirring workers to action in New York and
Paterson, New Jersey. Like Powderly, one secret of the success of P.H.
McCarthy in San Francisco and Mike Quill in New York was their spellbinding delivery in political and labor forums.

This research makes it clear that those examined appreciated problems arising from ethnic and religious divisions in the work force and
made significant progress in dealing with them.

In order to become leaders, Irish people were obliged to come to
grips with the reality of ethnic, religious and cultural diversity in
American society. Their response was, in general, pragmatic and effective. As pointed out above, it was not unusual for Irish greenhorns to
be deployed as strikebreakers on arrival, and, in turn, to have immigrants of other nationalities used to undermine their own fledgling
organizations. The experience was enlightening and led eventually to
wise handling of ethnic diversity.

Powderly recognized the hazards of ethnic and religious rivalry early
in his career. He constantly exhorted members to tolerate their religious and ethnic differences. These considerations were behind his
successful efforts to remove the impediment of secrecy and sectarian
rituals for Catholics. At the same time, he realized how necessary it was
to reassure others in the organization that he was not under the thumb
of the Roman hierarchy. His defense of the rights of black members of
the Knights of Labor took place when such a thing was rare indeed.[8]

McGuire's fluency in several languages was consciously developed
to deal with the various nationality groups he was attempting to organize. He spoke fluent German, a distinct asset in an occupation where
German speakers were common. *The Carpenter* contained whole sections written in German by his collaborators. He had sufficient French
to communicate easily with French Canadians in New England. Walter
Galenson documents the variety in the carpenters union in 1886:

Some idea of the heterogeneity of the Brotherhood's membership can be
gained from the fact that thirty locals transacted their business in German, six
in French, four in Scandinavian, three in Czech, and one in Polish. There were
eighteen locals in Canada, and of the sixty-eight in the South, eleven were composed exclusively of blacks.[9]

Note that blacks were not excluded from membership in the
Brotherhood of Carpenters, although the national union chartered sep-
arate locals for them in the South.[10] It is reasonable to attribute this to
McGuire's leadership.

In Chicago, Fitzpatrick extended a helping hand to blacks in the
meatpacking industry and to Jewish immigrants in the clothing industry. He hired the first female secretary in the Chicago Federation of
Labor, a Latvian-born Jewish girl. His longtime associate, Edward

Nockels, was a native of Luxembourg. Fitzpatrick and Foster collaborated successfully on bringing unity—temporarily at least—to the wide variety of ethnic and racial groups, first, in the packinghouse industry and later in the steel industry. They were masterful in these endeavors, even keeping the peace among a number of jealous craft unions during the campaign in steel.

Philip Murray, then a miners' union official, not only took an active part in the steel drive of 1918–1919, but also in 1937, as chairman of the Steel Workers Organizing Committee, won the allegiance of these same ethnic groups, who, having been burned in the disastrous outcome of the 1918–1919 strike were reluctant to try unionism again. His understanding and sensitivity to their feelings were decisive in restoring the solidarity that had been undermined two decades earlier.[11]

It is worth noting again that the leadership of several in this study benefited from trade unionism in England and Scotland, primarily through the experience of their fathers there. This is true of both John Brophy and Philip Murray. Both their fathers were loyal unionists, Brophy in Lancashire and Murray in Lanarkshire where he was a local chairman and recruited his son, Philip, as his apprentice. Sectarian prejudice was a problem for unions in Lanarkshire and must have made Murray better prepared to deal with religious differences in the United States. J.P. McDonnell learned of workingmen's organizations at the feet of Karl Marx and might have been expected to be a lifelong doctrinaire radical, but as we know, he displayed a far more pragmatic spirit as he became acquainted with the American scene. Mining union pioneer John Siney also cut his eyeteeth in trade unionism in Lancashire, and, as a result, had the background needed for his organizing efforts in anthracite.

The secret of McCarthy's effectiveness in San Francisco was to utilize the talents of English, Scottish, German, Scandinavian and Irish members to weld his "machine" in the building trades. His objective was stability for a highly unstable industry. As such, he successfully undertook to adjust the inevitable jurisdictional disputes between craft unions affiliated with the Building Trades Council—a task he handled personally. His editor and longtime associate was Norwegian immigrant Olaf Tveitmoe. Tveitmoe perhaps symbolizes the limits of ethnic tolerance on the West Coast since he was the leader of the Asiatic Exclusion League. Apparently, the boundary of tolerance extended to persons from the Occident, but did not include those from the Orient.

Further evidence of their talent for bringing cohesion to disparate groups is found in the Pennsylvania anthracite region where John Siney, in the 1870s, achieved unity among Welsh, English, Scottish, Irish and native American miners temporarily, and later, at the turn of the century, when John Mitchell succeeded with these groups as well as the large influx of immigrants from Slavic countries.

While conflicts between Irish and black workers were common enough, most violently in the New York draft riots of 1863, there were, as already indicated, examples of collaboration. A case of particular interest that occurred in New Orleans has been described by Daniel

Rosenberg.[12] It was begun in earnest in 1872, when large numbers of
black men entered work on the docks. Subsequently, Irish unionists
organized these newcomers.[13] Thereafter, longshore strikes conducted
jointly by black and white workers took place in 1880, 1883, 1887,
1904 and 1907.[14] In 1907, a Dock and Cotton Council, headed by Irish
and black officers, defended half-and-half (black and white) work sharing against opposition from stevedore employers and most white citizens.[15] Port union leaders, such as James Hughes, Chris Scully, Thomas
Gannon and Harry Keegan, were visible throughout this period.[16]
Evident in this story is recognition of and adaptation to growing diversity in the longshore work force which Irish leaders proved capable of.

Irish nationalism was an important factor in the rise of a majority of
those in this study. The careers of Frank Roney and J.P. McDonnell illustrate a direct infusion of new blood into organized labor by refugees
from a nationalist rising in Ireland. Both of them had first-hand experience in organizing a clandestine movement involving great personal
risks and sacrifices. Their seasoning in British courts and prisons
equipped them well to satisfy the needs of struggling American unionism. Their impact as organizational innovators and, in McDonnell's
case, as labor journalist, was significant.

The failed Fenian rebellion produced a number of recruits for the
trade unions, as did other nationalist risings in Ireland, directly as in
McDonnell and Roney's experience, but indirectly in others. W.Z.
Foster was attracted to rebellion by his father, a Fenian exile. Mother
Jones wrote that her family fought for Ireland's freedom for generations, and many of them had died in the struggle. Her own father was
forced to flee the island because of his agitation against the British.
Elizabeth Gurley Flynn was raised in a family that revered Irish nationalist heroes and passed on tales of her four great grandfathers who
fought in the rebellion of Wolf Tone's United Irishmen. Her grandfather Flynn participated, she noted, in the Fenian invasion of Canada in
1866. Philip Murray took pride in telling that both his grandfathers
were thrown out of Ireland for anti-British activity.

A more recent dramatic connection between Irish nationalism and
American labor is represented by establishment of the Transport
Workers Union in New York City by men trained in the Irish
Republican Army whose use of secrecy and Gaelic language in communication enabled their organization to enlist enough support to
overcome bitter employer resistance. It was a distinct advantage that
much of the work force of the transit companies was Irish and had
been recruited as a cheap source of English-speaking labor.

A carryover of Irish nationalist fervor would be expected in immigrants from Erin or their offspring, but, clearly, this was typically the
case with those in our study. Frank Roney was an exception. He rea-
soned that by embracing citizenship in his adopted country he was
obliged to drop all activity on behalf of his native land. John Fitzpatrick
reacted in exactly the opposite way, combining his zeal for organized
labor with an equally zealous involvement with organizations dedicat-

ed to Irish independence and association with ardent nationalist attorney Frank Walsh, as well as Irish patriot and labor leader James Larkin. Fitzpatrick was the moving spirit behind a resolution at the 1920 AFL convention endorsing recognition after Ireland declared itself a republic. He headed a labor bureau to gather support for that goal from central labor councils around the country. The San Francisco representative of this Labor Bureau was Patrick H. McCarthy.

Terence Powderly found organizing unions and Land Leagues quite compatible especially in northeastern Pennsylvania. Land reform emphasis in the program of the Knights of Labor owed something to Powderly's close acquaintance with Michael Davitt. His nationalist passion led him to participate in Clan na Gael. These initiatives also opened valuable channels of alliance with New England labor reformers of native American origins.

There is no evidence of Mother Jones's connection with movements for Irish independence, but her longtime and close friendship with Powderly suggests that investigation might reveal that there was. As a boy, W.Z. Foster's "meat and drink" was his father's Irish nationalism, but he turned away from it in favor, he said, of the "class struggle." Nevertheless, he was behind establishment of Irish Workers' Clubs in New York, which the Communist party used as a stepping-stone toward organizing the work force employed in the subways there. The party under Foster held up James Connolly as an inspiration for those like Mike Quill who eventually did create the Transport Workers Union.

Elizabeth Gurley Flynn's parents were good friends of both Connolly and James Larkin, and the young woman learned much from them, especially from Connolly. Her activities, in addition to the IWW, seem, however, to have been devoted to building the American Civil Liberties Union and freeing Sacco and Vanzetti rather than Irish nationalism. Nothing that our exploration has come across links John Brophy or Philip Murray to the cause of Irish nationalism other than Murray's membership in the Ancient Order of Hibernians. Murray, as mentioned, did speak proudly of both his grandfathers' being driven from Ireland owing to their participation in a nationalist movement.

Involvement in, or exposure to, Irish nationalism was a fact for most of the individuals in this study. The question then arises: Did it lead, therefore, to continuing attachments to radical movements in America?

The issue of Irish labor leaders as radical or conservative may usefully be approached by defining terms. As employed here, radicalism means campaigning for basic change in the social and economic system; specifically, abolishing private ownership of land and capital, freedom of contract and reliance on markets for economic decision making. The term denotes communism, socialism and syndicalism in their various forms, Marxian and otherwise. It encompasses, as well, "eliminating the wage system" espoused by the Knights of Labor and other organizations. Conservatism, on the other hand, is defined as accepting the basic institutions of the existing social and economic system—a willingness to work within the framework of capitalist institutions.

Evidence arising from the careers of the twelve individuals in this study is mixed and complex, but on the basis of it, the tendency toward conservatism is stronger.

Considering the evidence, it is obvious that two of the twelve, William Z. Foster and Elizabeth Gurley Flynn, were confirmed radicals from their teenage years until death. Their careers, however, appear to be atypical. At the other extreme, P.H. McCarthy never exhibited a serious interest in radical ideas, except as notions to be opposed, his involvement in Union Labor party politics notwithstanding.

Attraction to radicalism is most intense in times of economic crisis. Thus, in the depression of the 1870s, P.J. McGuire began evangelizing for the Social Democratic party of North America and its successors. That decade saw Terence Powderly turn to labor reform and embrace "elimination of the wage system" congruent with the goal of a cooperative commonwealth. Arriving in 1873, Fenian J.P. McDonnell pursued his efforts on behalf of the International Workingmen's Association. In Omaha, Frank Roney campaigned for National Labor Reform party objectives and in San Francisco for Workingmen's party goals. In the 1920s, coal-mining distress led John Brophy to advocate government ownership of the industry and to accept Communist support for his election contest with John L. Lewis. During the Great Depression of the 1930s, Mike Quill welcomed Communist help (and became a party member) while building the Transport Workers Union. In each one of these cases, however, radicalism was eventually either rejected outright or subordinated to more orthodox approaches to trade unionism.

McGuire, Roney and McDonnell gravitated toward AFL style unionism—McGuire most vividly in building the carpenters' union, a classic bread-and-butter craft union, although for him socialism remained a dream, however remote. Powderly's departure from the Knights of Labor led to his transformation into a Republican and public servant. Brophy disavowed his earlier enthusiasm for government ownership and, with Philip Murray, another devout Catholic, endorsed the tripartite approach advanced by the Vatican. Both men and Mike Quill, as well, became vigorous anticommunists as the Cold War emerged.

Mother Jones was a longtime adherent of socialism in theory but, like McGuire, in practice she was dedicated to building union strength of an orthodox type, primarily in mining and usually at critical times of conflict. John Fitzpatrick was a Progressive, hardly a radical, but with considerable tolerance for radicals (and the Russian Revolution) until recognizing that he had been deceived.

In this study, nine of the twelve unionists of Irish descent adopted some form of radical ideology in their youth. Two of them remained radicals permanently. The others, as they matured through experience on the American scene, gradually lost enthusiasm for radical ideology or repudiated it altogether. In the American ethos, doctrinaire approaches proved ineffective. It testifies to their underlying pragmatism in a context where capitalist institutions are deeply rooted and resist change aggressively.

Religious faith undoubtedly played a role in this result, especially when devoutly held as in the case of Brophy and Murray. The absence or rejection of it was also a factor for some, as illustrated by the stories of Flynn and Foster. Even more important, perhaps, was the religious faith of rank-and-file unionists, whose support for radical ideology was minimal even in the worst of economic times and who vigorously opposed it otherwise.

The Roman Catholic faith of a majority of the Irish in the work force was both a help and a hindrance to their achieving leadership roles. It was first of all an object of prejudice as emphasized herein. As such, it was a stumbling block to acceptance by Protestant workers who dominated early unions in the United States. At the same time, it was a source of spiritual strength and social identity. It provided gathering places for social relationships and offered help for the struggling immigrant of that faith.

Nevertheless, the Church was, for a variety of reasons, slow to comprehend the plight of the wage earner in the modern world. Traditionally, it held a jaundiced view of workers' organizations, especially secret societies, whether made up of peasants in Europe or workers in the United States. On the continent of Europe, Catholicism was seen to be allied with wealth, thus, alienation of the worker became the reality. Use of violence was at all times condemned. As such the Church offered little encouragement. Yet secrecy was an essential condition in successful organizing. This was true whether the cause was Irish freedom or justice in the workplace. This was vividly the case in America where business leaders ruthlessly opposed organizing employees. The reality that employers did not scruple to use yellow dog contracts, strikebreakers, blacklists and various other means to intimidate would-be unionists, while their Church denounced secrecy and violence and usually counseled obedience to the boss, created severe conflicts for workers who were faithful Roman Catholics.

These considerations lend significance to the breakthrough instigated by Terence Powderly and Cardinal Gibbons, which eliminated risk of the Church's condemnation of labor organizations in the United States. It was the first episode in a sequence which led, through the good offices of Cardinal Gibbons, to an endorsement by Rome of the right of workers to organize in the famous encyclical of 1891, Rerum Novarum. That development greatly enhanced the respectability of unions. Also, it removed an important impediment to their growth. Unfortunately, however, this statement was slow to be disseminated by the parish clergy and elements of the hierarchy.

Irish Catholics had risen to leadership in a considerable number of national unions by the last two decades of the nineteenth century. This was a formative period for the AFL, a time when it was evolving a philosophy of conservative or pure and simple unionism. Its major architects were Samuel Gompers, P.J. McGuire and Adolph Strasser. Their personal acquaintance with Marxian and other radical ideologies was a good deal more than superficial and had convinced them of the total unsuitability of these ideologies in the American environment. AFL president Gompers's ability to prevail over opposition of a minority of socialists in the federation owed something to the presence of Irish Catholics holding national office in affiliated labor organizations. Their presence was one of the factors enabling him to defeat a program proposed to the 1893 convention, which, among other things, called for collective ownership of all means of production and distribution, as well as establishment of a labor party. The crucial vote against adoption occurred in the 1894 convention where, ironically, John McBride was elected president.[17] This proved to be the sole exception to Gompers's annual elections to the presidency until his death in 1924.

Left-leaning historians, such as Marc Karson and David Saposs, emphasize Catholic influence in forming the conservative nature of mainstream American trade unionism. On the other hand, Selig Perlman (converted by John R. Commons from the Marxism of his youth) saw it as a situation where, given the ethnic, religious and cultural diversity in the work force, adopting a collectivist ideology officially would result in forcing Catholics out of the organization in which they were a majority—clearly an unwise move for any organization—but especially for one trying to thrive in a hostile environment.

The issue of Irish Catholic impact is complicated by at least two considerations. One is the extent to which they apprehended the teachings of their Church in these matters. While the Church vigorously denounced socialism at the same time it endorsed workers' right of association in Rerum Novarum, its position was not widely understood by Catholics, Irish or otherwise. John Brophy, for example, a serious, well-read communicant, noted that he had never heard of Rerum Novarum until a generation after its promulgation in 1891. If this thoughtful, devout individual was unaware, what of the legions of less well-informed communicants?[18]

A second observation worth considering is the timing of the Catholic attempt to "invade the AFL" with its antisocialist dictum. The campaign of Peter Dietz, priest-founder of the Militia of Christ for Social Service, whose evangelizing of John Mitchell and other Catholic officials of the federation (the subject of much scrutiny by Karson and some Catholic authors), took place in the decade prior to World War I. Aside from the fact that the militia seems to have been a one-man operation existing mainly on paper, it functioned at a time when the policy of the AFL was well established and the possibility of its embracing socialism was remote. As Professor Perlman pointed out in his foreword to Karson's book, its author "has spread his nets too late."[19]

Irish Catholics were indeed involved in the AFL's avoidance of collectivist politics, but to an extent that is easy to exaggerate.

The Emmons study of Butte, Montana, is a stronger testament of the tendency for Irish efforts to result in conservative unionism rather than radicalism. What should have been a hotbed of Western-style radicalism, according to historian Melvyn Dubofsky, turns out to have been an oasis of moderation. Admittedly, a peculiarly Irish culture pervaded the community on both sides of the bargaining table; nevertheless, when satisfactory conditions could be achieved through control of the work force, the "Wild Irishmen" proved to be quite conservative. Although it arose out of a strike in 1878 (and paradoxically became Local Number One, largest affiliate of the ultraradical Western Federation of Miners), the Butte Miners' Union never again struck in its thirty-six-year history. Class-conscious radicalism, exhorted by visitors such as James Larkin and James Connolly, failed to light the fire of collectivist upheaval.[20] Strong evidence of pragmatism indeed.

The Irish were receptive to the admonitions of their Church on labor organizations when these were communicated effectively, which was rare. The endorsement of trade unions, however, was almost drowned out by harsh denunciations of socialism. Exiled from Cincinnati by his bishop, Peter Dietz was no longer heard, but a more modulated voice emerged in the person of John A. Ryan, priest, economist and professor of industrial ethics at Catholic University in Washington, D.C. One of ten children, his parents had fled famine-plagued Ireland in the 1850s. He complained of never having encountered a course on economics or social science in the seminary (then typical of Catholic seminaries), but in youth had regularly read the *Irish World and Industrial Liberator* and been fascinated by the oratory of populist politician Ignatius Donnelly. Ryan later authored volumes titled *The Living Wage, Distributive Justice and Social Doctrine in Action*. He prepared the Bishops' Program of Social Reconstruction in 1919, which foreshadowed most reforms of the New Deal. In particular, it called for legal enforcement of the right of labor to organize—as well as minimum wage legislation.[21] His ideas commanded very limited attention during the 1920s, when the dream of endless prosperity under welfare capitalism stifled reform and caused union membership to wane.

In the 1930s, as the Depression deepened, the Catholic Church became a highly visible witness to workers' rights to associate and bargain collectively. An emerging generation of "labor priests" amplified the substance of Ryan's ideas. Numerous labor schools, sponsored by Catholic institutions, sprang up around the country. The Association of Catholic Trade Unions appeared in New York and Detroit. The Catholic Labor Alliance surfaced in Chicago. *The Catholic Worker* competed with *The Daily Worker* on picket lines. These developments undoubtedly favored the success of CIO organizing drives with their plentiful representation of Irish-American activists, described in Chapter 7.

THE LEGACY

What is the legacy of the numerous leaders (and rank and filers) of Irish descent in the labor movement? Without idealizing the individuals here studied, it seems to be a consistent militance, a combativeness cultivated by their ancestors in the struggle for Irish freedom—a stubborn unwillingness to surrender their Celtic identity to that of a conquering power. Surfacing in American society, this spirit manifested itself in unwillingness to accept existing conditions in the workplace. This conclusion is based on the assumption that the twelve figures in this study are a reasonable representation of Irish-American labor leaders. It was epitomized in the always forceful and sometimes pugnacious demeanor of George Meany (president of the AFL-CIO for twenty-five years), spokesman for the entire labor movement.

As our inventory of leaders attests, the Irish became adept at bringing together diverse nationalities in labor organizations. Learned from their own experience as greenhorns, scorned, manipulated as economic rivals for other immigrants, they gradually recognized the necessity for cohesion among the variety of nationalities in the workplace. They proved to be well-suited to this leadership task. Earliest of the mass immigrants, they came with a heritage of rebellion against oppression, yet most of them spoke the dominant tongue in America. The task required that their own distaste for immigrants from other cultures be held in abeyance—a difficult challenge. But the Irish, with their traditional appreciation of rhetoric, were very good at the language of protest. It stands as an important contribution to the success of American unionism.

It is fair to say that Irish-American leadership typically exhibited a pragmatic approach in finding solutions to the economic distress of their followers.

What explains this practical bent of Irish leaders? It may partly be explained by the intense will to survive which brought them or their parents here originally. Survival required an adaptation to American realities where doctrinaire movements have consistently been rejected. But it must be added that adaptation is not identical to acceptance of the status quo. The goal of these leaders was change in conditions of work which would improve the lives of wage earners. In a word, economic justice. Their method, however, was, in the main, practical and effective, evolutionary rather than revolutionary. If their efforts sometimes involved violence, violence was often used to oppose them. It was an aspect of American reality.

From the vantage of the last decade of the twentieth century one may ask what has happened to this tradition of militance in the cause of justice in the workplace? Although it was subdued in the reactionary decade of the 1920s, it revived vigorously in the 1930s with a substantial Irish-American presence in its vanguard. The 1980s seemed to reproduce conditions of the 1920s with perhaps even more discouraging results for the vitality of organized labor.

Indeed, things have changed. As America turns the corner into a new millennium, it appears that the heyday of the Irish voice in labor affairs is over. Their dominant presence among those in the manual work force is a thing of the past. At long last, they have advanced to the middle class, even, in some cases, into its upper precincts. By the 1980s their occupational status had risen well beyond what it had been a generation or so ago. On the basis of a National Opinion Research Center Survey, Andrew Greeley revealed that, by 1981, just above 70 percent of the

Irish in Chicago and Minneapolis enjoyed white-collar positions. In both cities, almost two-fifths of them had reached the professional and managerial ranks. Half of those in Chicago earned in excess of $25,000 per year. Their educational achievement is equally impressive. They are outdistanced only by the Jews in education and occupational status. They are seen in growing numbers in graduate schools and in academic professions.[22] Irish Catholic migration to suburbia is concomitant with the above developments. It is as evident in the numerous new parish churches built there since World War II as is the regularly announced closing of their churches in the inner cities for lack of parishioners. The phenomenon of Irish names moving from Democratic to Republican on voting registers is part and parcel of this change.

In short, the Catholic Irish have "made it." They have gained respectability, but at a price—loss of their ethnic identity. Acculturation, Americanization, homogenization have melted them into the middle class—where, to put it mildly, unionism finds little favor.[23]

It is no accident that the mythical embodiment of labor's foot soldier in the battles for better wages, hours and working conditions was called "Jimmy Higgins." It signifies the importance of Irish participation. But what has become of the Jimmy Higginses? Irish America, the "urban pioneers," has abandoned the cities. It has forsaken its allegiance to the Democratic party and to the labor movement. George Meany is dead. The voice of labor has a more gentle tone. The cause of social justice in America has lost its Gaelic accent.[24]

NOTES

1. David Montgomery, "The Irish and the American Labor Movement," in *America and Ireland, 1776–1976*, David N. Doyle and Owen D. Edwards eds. (Westport, Conn.: Greenwood Press, 1980), 205–6.

2. David M. Emmons, *The Butte Irish* (Urbana: University of Illinois Press, 1989), Chap. 4, "Church, Party and Fraternity: The Irish and Their Associations."

3. Ibid., 13.

4. Lawrence J. McCaffrey, *Textures of Irish America* (Syracuse, N.Y.: Syracuse University Press, 1992), 172–73; Lawrence J. McCaffrey et al., *The Irish in Chicago* (Urbana: University of Illinois Press, 1987), 16.

5. Patrick J. Blessing, "The Irish," in *Harvard Encyclopedia of American Ethnic Groups*, Stephen Thernstrom ed. (Cambridge, Mass.: Belknap Press, 1980), 529.

6. *Newark Labor Herald*, October 1946 (letter from Arthur A. Quinn).

7. Interview with Mrs. Iris Rossell, Collingswood, New Jersey, June 15, 1989.

8. The Knights of Labor had 60,000 black members in 1886, according to David Montgomery, "Labor in the Industrial Era," in *Bicentennial History of the American Worker*, Richard B. Morris ed. (Washington, D.C.: U.S. Government Printing Office, 1976), 128. See also a description of how participation of black members in the 1886 general assembly of the Knights of Labor in Richmond, Virginia, upset the code of segregation in that city, in Leon Fink, *Workingmen's Democracy* (Urbana: University of Illinois Press, 1983), 162–64, 175–76 (notes 38–44).

9. Walter Galenson, *The United Brotherhood of Carpenters* (Cambridge, Mass.: Harvard University Press, 1983), 56.

10. Ibid., 39.

11. David Brody, "The Origins of Modern Steel Unionism: The SWOC Era," in *Forging a Union in Steel*, P.F. Clark, P. Gottlieb and D. Kennedy eds. (Ithaca, N.Y.: ILR Press, 1987), 20-21, 25-26.

12. Daniel Rosenberg, *New Orleans Dockworkers: Race and Labor Unionism, 1892-1923* (Albany: State University of New York, 1988). See also Eric Arnesen, "To Rule or Ruin: New Orleans Dock Workers' Struggle for Control, 1902-1903," *Labor History* (Spring 1987): 139-67.

13. Rosenberg, *New Orleans Dockworkers*, 56.

14. Ibid., 32.

15. Ibid., 74.

16. Ibid., 51.

17. Philip Taft, *The AFL in the Time of Gompers* (New York: Harpers, 1957), 71-73.

18. David J. Saposs, "The Catholic Church and the Labor Movement," *Modern Monthly* (May-June 1933): 225-30; Marc Karson, "The Catholic Church and the Political Development of American Trade Unionism," *Industrial and Labor Relations Review* (July 1951): 527-42; Selig Perlman, *A Theory of the Labor Movement* (New York: Macmillan, 1928), 168-69 (Perlman describes his conversion in the preface of the book); John Brophy, *A Miner's Life* (Madison: University of Wisconsin Press, 1964), 100.

19. Marc Karson, *American Labor Unions and Politics, 1900-1918* (Carbondale: Southern Illinois University Press, 1958), foreword by Selig Perlman, vii. This book lists the names of sixty-two Catholics who held the presidency of international unions in the AFL in the period from 1906 to 1918. Karson obtained the names from Frank Morrison, AFL secretary, 1896-1929, who knew them personally. Admittedly incomplete, at least fifty of the names are identifiably Irish; others may also be Irish. See 221-24.

20. Emmons, *The Butte Irish*, Chap. 6, "Irishmen and Workers: The Origins of Working-Class Conservativism, 1878-1907." Larkin visited Butte three times, see pp. 351, 357, 359; Connolly's visit is mentioned on p. 86. Melvyn Dubofsky, "The Origins of Western Working Class Radicalism, 1890-1905," *Labor History* (Spring 1966): 131-54; Butte is mentioned on pp. 134, 138, 139.

21. His autobiographical account is found in John A. Ryan, *Social Doctrine in Action: A Personal History* (New York: Harper, 1941), 1, 3, 8, 12-16, 45. He prepared *Bishops' Program of Social Reconstruction: A General Review of the Problems and Survey of Remedies* 20th Century Edition (Washington, D.C.: National Catholic Welfare Conference, 1939). Other Ryan publications referred to are *A Living Wage: Its Ethical and Economic Aspects* (New York: Macmillan, 1906) and *Distributive Justice: The Right and Wrong of our Distribution of Wealth* (New York: Macmillan, 1916).

22. Andrew Greeley, *The Irish Americans: The Rise to Money and Power* (New York: Harper and Row, 1981), 111-18.

23. See Andrew Greeley, *That Most Distressful Nation* (Chicago: Quadrangle Books, 1972), Chap. 17, "An Epitaph for the Irish"; McCaffrey, *Textures of Irish America*, Chap. 6, "Someplace or No Place."

24. In October of 1995, as the manuscript for this book was undergoing editorial review, an election for the presidency of the AFL-CIO pitted John J. Sweeney against Thomas R. Donahue. The winner, Sweeney, has promised to revitalize the labor movement. Perhaps the idea that labor has lost its Celtic voice is slightly premature.

SELECTED BIBLIOGRAPHY

MANUSCRIPT SOURCES

Brophy, John. Papers. Catholic University of America, Washington, D.C.
Edmondston, Gabriel. Papers. Reel 1 of American Federation of Labor Records, microfilm, Pennsylvania State University, University Park, Pennsylvania.
Fitzpatrick, John. Papers. Chicago Historical Society.
Jones, Mother. Papers. Catholic University of America, Washington, D.C.
McCarthy, Patrick H. Memoirs, unpublished. P.H. McCarthy, Jr., executor.
McDonnell, Joseph P. Papers. Wisconsin State Historical Society, Madison, Wisconsin.
McGuire, Peter J. Diary and letters. Iris Rossell, Collingswood, New Jersey, executor.
Mitchell, John. Papers, microfilm. Catholic University of America, Washington, D.C.
Murray, Philip. Collection. Pennsylvania State University, University Park.
Murray, Philip. Papers. Catholic University of America, Washington, D.C.
Powderly, Terence. Papers. Catholic University of America, Washington, D.C.

ORAL HISTORY TRANSCRIPTS

Curran, Philip M. Interview by Jack Severson. Pennsylvania State University, University Park, August 5, 1968.
Fagan, Pat. Interviews by Alice M. Hoffman. Pennsylvania State University, University Park, September 24, October 1, 1968; August 8, 1972.
Levitas, Mollie. Interview by Elizabeth Balanoff, Roosevelt University, Chicago, Illinois, July 24, 1970.
Rice, Reverend Charles Owen. Interviews by Ronald Filipelli, Pennsylvania State University, University Park, October 17, 1967; April 5, 1968.
Saposs, David. Interview by Alice M. Hoffman, Pennsylvania State University, College Park, January 18, 1968.

LABOR PUBLICATIONS

Association of Catholic Trade Unionists. *The Labor Leader*, 1939-1948.
Chicago Federation of Labor. *New Majority*, 1915-1924.
_____. *Federation News*, 1924-1925, 1946, 1966.
McDonnell, Joseph P., editor and publisher. *Paterson Labor Standard*, 1878-1906.
United Brotherhood of Carpenters and Joiners. *The Carpenter*, 1881-1899.

BOOKS AND DISSERTATIONS

Akenson, Donald H. *Being Had: Historians, Evidence and the Irish in North America*. Port Credit, Ont.: P.D. Meany, 1985.
_____. *Small Differences: Irish Catholics and Irish Protestants, 1815-1922*. Kingston, Ont.: McGill-Queens University Press, 1988.
Arnot, R. Page. *A History of Scottish Miners*. London: Allen and Unwin, 1955.
Barrett, James R. *Work and Community in the Jungle*. Urbana: University of Illinois Press, 1987.
Baxandall, Rosalyn F. *Words on Fire: The Life and Writing of Elizabeth Gurley Flynn*. New Brunswick, N.J.: Rutgers University Press, 1987.
Begley, James Archdeacon. *The Diocese of Limerick from 1691 to the Present Time*. Dublin: Brown and Nolan, 1938.
Bernstein, Iver. *The New York Draft Riots*. New York: Oxford University Press, 1990.
Boyd, Andrew. *The Rise of the Irish Trade Unions*. Tralee: Anvil Books, 1972.
Brody, David. *Labor in Crisis: The Steel Strike of 1919*. New York: Lippincott, 1965.
_____. *Steelworkers in America: The Nonunion Era*. New York: Harper and Row, 1969.
_____. *In Labor's Cause*. New York: Oxford University Press, 1990.
Broel, Wayne G., Jr. *The Molly Maguires*. Cambridge, Mass.: Harvard University Press, 1964 .
Brooks, George W., Milton Derber, David McCabe and Philip Taft, eds. *Interpreting the Labor Movement*. Madison, Wis.: Industrial Relations Research Association, 1952.
Brophy, John. *A Miner's Life*. Madison: University of Wisconsin Press, 1964.
Browne, Henry J. *The Catholic Church and the Knights of Labor*. Washington, D.C.: Catholic University of America Press, 1949.
Burchell, Robert A. *The San Francisco Irish, 1848-1880*. Berkeley: University of California Press, 1980.
Campbell, Alan B. *The Lanarkshire Miners*. Edinburgh: J. Donald Publishers, 1979.
Clark, Dennis. *The Irish in Philadelphia*. Philadelphia: Temple University Press, 1973.
_____. *Hibernia America*. Westport, Conn.: Greenwood Press, 1986.
Cochran, Bert. *Labor and Communism*. Princeton, N.J.: Princeton University Press, 1977.
Cogley, John. *Catholic America*. Garden City, N.Y.: Doubleday, 1973.
Cohen, Lisabeth. *Making a New Deal: Industrial Workers in Chicago 1919-1939*. Cambridge, England: Cambridge University Press, 1990.
Commons, John R. and Associates. *History of Labour in the United States*. Vols. 1 and 2.: Macmillan, 1918.

Cronin, Bernard C. *Father Yorke and the Labor Movement in San Francisco.* Washington, D.C.: Catholic University of America Press, 1943.

Cross, Ira B. *History of the Labor Movement in California.* Berkeley: University of California Press, 1935.

Devoy, John. *Recollections of an Irish Rebel.* New York: Charles D. Young, 1929.

Diner, Hasia R. *Erin's Daughters in America.* Baltimore: Johns Hopkins University Press, 1983.

Dolan, Jay P. *The Immigrant Church.* Baltimore: Johns Hopkins University Press, 1975.

Doyle, David N., and O.D. Edwards, eds. *America and Ireland, 1776-1976.* Westport, Conn.: Greenwood Press, 1980.

Drudy, P.J., ed. *The Irish in America.* Cambridge, England: Cambridge University Press, 1985.

Dubofsky, Melvyn. *We Shall Be All.* New York: Quadrangle Books, 1969.

Dubofsky, Melvyn and Warren Van Tine. *John L. Lewis.* New York: Quadrangle Books, 1977.

_____, eds. *Labor Leaders in America.* Urbana: University of Illinois Press, 1987.

Dwyer, T. Ryle. *Eamon de Valera.* Dublin: Gill and Macmillan, 1980.

Emmons, David M. *The Butte Irish.* Urbana: University of Illinois Press, 1989.

Falzone, Vincent J. *Terence Powderly: Middle Class Reformer.* Washington, D.C.: University Press of America, 1978.

Fink, Gary M. *Biographical Dictionary of American Labor Leaders.* Westport, Conn.: Greenwood Press, 1984.

_____. *Workingmen's Democracy.* Urbana: University of Illinois Press, 1983.

Fitzpatrick, David. *Irish Emigration, 1801-1921.* Dundalgan Press, 1984.

Flynn, Elizabeth Gurley. *The Rebel Girl.* New York: International Publishers, 1973.

Foster, William Z. *From Bryan to Stalin.* New York: International Publishers, 1937.

_____. *Pages from a Worker's Life.* New York: International Publishers, 1939.

_____. *The Great Steel Strike of 1919.* New York: Arno Press, 1969.

Freeman, Joshua. *In Transit.* New York: Oxford University Press, 1989.

Galenson, Walter. *The United Brotherhood of Carpenters.* Cambridge, Mass.: Harvard University Press, 1983.

Gompers, Samuel. *Seventy Years of Life and Labor.* Vol. 1. New York: Dutton, 1925.

Greeley, Andrew. *That Most Distressful Nation.* Chicago: Quadrangle Books, 1972.

_____. *The Irish Americans: The Rise to Money and Power.* New York: Harper and Row, 1981.

Gutman, Herbert. *Work, Culture, and Society in Industrializing America.* New York: Knopf, 1976.

Hapgood, Hutchins. *The Spirit of Labor.* New York: Duffield, 1907.

Jones, Mary Harris. *Autobiography of Mother Jones.* Chicago: C.H. Kerr, 1925.

Karson, Marc. *American Unions and Politics, 1900-1918.* Carbondale: Southern Illinois University Press, 1958.

Kazin, Michael. *Barons of Labor: The San Francisco Building Trades in the Progressive Era.* Urbana: University of Illinois Press, 1987.

Keiser, John H. "John Fitzpatrick and Progressive Unionism 1915-1925:" Ph.D. diss., Northwestern University, 1965.

Knight, Robert E.L. *Industrial Relations in the San Francisco Bay Area, 1900-1918.* Berkeley: University of California Press, 1960.

Larkin, Emmet. *James Larkin, Irish Labor Leader*. Cambridge, Mass.: MIT Press, 1965.

Lebergott, Stanley. *The Americans: An Economic Record*. New York: Norton, 1984.

Lyon, David. "The World of P.J. McGuire." Ph.D. diss., University of Minnesota, 1972.

Marx, Karl. *Karl Marx and Frederick Engels on Ireland*. London: Lawrence and Wishart, 1971.

McCaffrey, Lawrence J. *Ireland from Colony to Nation State*. Englewood Cliffs, N.J.: Prentice Hall, 1979.

_____. *Textures of Irish America*. Syracuse, N.Y.: Syracuse University Press, 1992.

McCaffrey, Lawrence J., Ellen Skerrett, Michael Funchion and Charles Fanning. *The Irish in Chicago*. Urbana: University of Illinois Press, 1987.

McNeil, George, ed. *The Labor Movement: The Problem of Today*. Boston: A.M. Bridgeman, 1887.

Miller, Kerby. *Emigrants and Exiles*. New York: Oxford University Press, 1985.

Montgomery, David. *Beyond Equality*. New York: Knopf, 1967.

Newell, Barbara W. *Chicago and the Labor Movement*. Urbana: University of Illinois Press, 1961.

O'Brien, William, and Desmond Ryan, eds. *Devoy's Post Bag*. Vol. 1. Dublin: J. Fallon Ltd. 1953.

Palladino, Grace. *Another Civil War*. Urbana: University of Illinois Press, 1990.

Payne, Elizabeth A. *Reform, Labor and Feminism: Margaret Dreier Robins and the Women's Trade Union League*. Urbana: University of Illinois Press, 1988.

Perlman, Selig. *A Theory of the Labor Movement*. New York: Macmillan, 1928.

Perlman, Selig, and Philip Taft. *History of Labor in the United States, 1896-1932*. New York: Macmillan, 1935.

Pius XI. Quadrogesimo Anno. Encyclical letter (Reconstructing the Social Order), 1931. New York: America Press, no date.

Powderly, Terence C. *The Path I Trod*. New York: Columbia University Press, 1949.

Quill, Shirley U. *Mike Quill—Himself*. New York: Devin-Adair, 1984.

Reid, Robert L. *Battleground: The Autobiography of Margaret Haley*. Urbana: University of Illinois Press, 1982.

Roney, Frank. *Frank Roney, Irish Rebel and California Labor Leader, An Autobiography*. edited by Ira B. Cross. Berkeley: University of California Press, 1931.

Ryan, Frederick L. *Industrial Relations in the San Francisco Building Trades*. Norman: University of Oklahoma Press, 1935.

Ryan, John A. *Social Doctrine in Action: A Personal History*. New York: Harper, 1941.

Saxton, Alexander. *The Indispensable Enemy*. Berkeley: University of California Press, 1971.

Steel, Edward M., ed. *The Correspondence of Mother Jones*. Pittsburgh: University of Pittsburgh Press, 1985.

Steffens, Lincoln. *The Autobiography of Lincoln Steffens*. New York: Harcourt Brace, 1931.

Thernstrom, Stephen, ed. *Harvard Encyclopedia of American Ethnic Groups*. Cambridge, Mass.: Belknap Press, 1980.

Walkowitz, Daniel J. *Worker City, Company Town*. Urbana: University of Illinois Press, 1981.

Wallace, Anthony F.C. *St. Clair*. New York: Knopf, 1987.

Walsh, James P., ed. *The San Francisco Irish 1850-1976*. San Francisco: Irish

Literary and Historical Society, 1978.

Way, Peter. *Common Labour*. Cambridge, England: Cambridge University Press, 1993.

Wilentz, Sean. *Chants Democratic*. New York: Oxford University Press, 1984.

Wittke, Carl. *The Irish in America*. Baton Rouge: Louisiana State University Press, 1956.

Woodham-Smith, Cecil. *The Great Hunger*. New York: Harper and Row, 1962.

ARTICLES

Arnesen, Eric. "To Rule or Ruin: New Orleans Dock Workers' Struggle for Control, 1902–1903." *Labor History* (Spring 1987): 139–67.

Baker, Ray Stannard. "A Corner on Labor." *McClure's Magazine* (February 1904): 366–78.

Boyle, John W. "Ireland and the First International." *Journal of British Studies* (May 1972): 44–62.

Chamberlain, John. "Philip Murray." *Life* (February 11, 1946): 79–90.

Doyle, David N. "The Irish as Urban Pioneers in the United States, 1850–1870." *Journal of American Ethnic Studies* (Fall 1990–Winter 1991): 36–59.

Dubofsky, Melvyn. "The Origins of Western Working Class Radicalism, 1890–1905." *Labor History* (Spring 1983): 165–97.

Erlich, Mark. "Peter J. McGuire's Trades Unionism: Socialism of a Trades Union Kind?" *Labor History* (Spring 1983): 165–97.

Falzone, Vincent J. "Terence Powderly: Politician and Progressive Mayor of Scranton, 1878–1884." *Pennsylvania History* 71 (1974): 288–309.

Foner, Eric. "Class, Ethnicity, and Radicalism in the Gilded Age: The Land League and Irish America." *Marxist Perspectives* (Summer 1978): 6–47.

Gutman, Herbert. "The Tompkins Square Riot." *Labor History* (Winter 1965): 44–70.

Harris, Howard. "The Eagle to Watch and the Harp to Tune: Irish Immigrants, Politics and Early Industrialization in Paterson, New Jersey, 1824–1836." *Journal of Social History* (Spring 1990): 119–27.

Johanningsmeir, Edward P. "William Z. Foster and the Syndicalist League of North America." *Labor History* (Summer 1989): 329–53.

Karson, Marc. "The Catholic Church and the Political Development of American Trade Unionism." *Industrial and Labor Relations Review* (July 1951): 527–42.

O'Grada, Cormac. "Fenianism and Socialism: The Career of J.P. McDonnell." *Saothar: Journal of the Irish Labour History Society* (May 1975): 31–41.

Robins, Raymond, "John Fitzpatrick: A Leader of Organized Labor in the West." *Life and Labor* (February 1911): 41–43.

Saposs, David. "The Catholic Church and the Labor Movement." *Modern Monthly* (May-June 1933): 225–30.

Shumsky, Neil. "Frank Roney's San Francisco—His Diary: April 1875 March 1876." *Labor History* (Spring 1976): 244–64.

Vedder, Richard K., and Lowell E. Gallaway. "The Geographical Distribution of British and Irish Emigrants to the United States after 1800." *Scottish Journal of Political Economy* 19 (1972): 19–35.

Walker, Samuel. "Terence Powderly Machinist: 1866–1877." *Labor History* (Spring 1978): 165–84.

Walsh, Victor A. "The Great Famine and Its Consequences." *Eire-Ireland* (Winter 1988): 3–31.

Way, Peter. "Shovel and Shamrock: Irish Workers and Labor Violence in Digging of the Chesapeake and Ohio Canal." *Labor History* (Winter 1989): 489–519.

Weinberg, Jules. "Priests, Workers, and Communists." *Harpers* (November 1948): 49–56.

Wilentz, Sean. "Industrializing America and the Irish: Toward a New Departure." *Labor History* (Fall 1979): 579–95.

INDEX

About the Author

L.A. O'DONNELL recently retired from the Economics Department at Villanova University. O'Donnell is the author of a number of articles on labor and economic history emphasizing the contribution of the Irish immigrants.

ISBN 0-313-29944-7

EAN

9 780313 299445

90000>

HARDCOVER BAR CODE